TUDOR PARISH DOCUMENTS
OF THE
DIOCESE OF YORK

Tudor Parish Documents of The Diocese of York

A SELECTION
WITH INTRODUCTION & NOTES
BY

J. S. PURVIS
M.A., D.D. (Cantab.), F.S.A., F.R.Hist.S.

WITH A FOREWORD BY
HIS GRACE
THE ARCHBISHOP OF YORK

CAMBRIDGE
AT THE UNIVERSITY PRESS
1948

Printed in Great Britain at the University Press, Cambridge
(Brooke Crutchley, University Printer)
and published by the Cambridge University Press
(Cambridge, and Bentley House, London)

Agents for U.S.A., Canada, and India: Macmillan

DEDICATED BY PERMISSION
TO
HIS GRACE
THE ARCHBISHOP OF YORK

FOREWORD

BY HIS GRACE THE ARCHBISHOP OF YORK

There are many histories of the Church of England but few of them give any detailed description of the life and work in the ordinary parish. But the living history of the Church should be found in the outlook, worship, opinions and habits of the parson and his parishioners. In this book Dr Purvis, the archivist of the Diocese of York, gives a mass of material which can be used to build up a picture of parochial life in the anxious days of Queen Elizabeth. The sources from which he draws his material have been until now almost entirely unexplored and unpublished, namely, a magnificent collection of the earlier Act Books of the Ecclesiastical Commission of York (for the rediscovery of which he was himself responsible), Visitation Books, the proceedings of the Archbishops' Courts and Papers of the Consistory Court. In using this material, however, it must be borne in mind that the most interesting of the documents of this nature refer to a minority, namely to those persons and parishes charged with some offence. If they alone are taken into account, an unduly pessimistic impression of Church-life at that time might be formed.

As we read these texts, we gain a picture of a rough and unruly age in which there is much brawling, drunkenness and disorder. Many of the churches are in bad repair, the people often walking and talking in them, even during the sermon; a football is kicked about in the Minster itself; brawls within the church and in the churchyard seem to be fairly frequent. The clergy, also, are often disorderly, some rarely preaching, some reading the services inaudibly, others refusing to wear the surplice, and yet others attempting to maintain old customs which had been prohibited. Their parishioners are ignorant and superstitious, believing in witchcraft, resorting to soothsayers and using charms.

The ecclesiastical authorities, in dealing with this position, had a twofold aim: first, to wipe out some of the old ceremonies connected with pre-Reformation worship which they still found in various parishes and which they regarded as superstitious: roods, images and holy water-stoups were destroyed or defaced; vestments confiscated or sold; and customs, such as the ringing of bells on All Souls' Eve, were forbidden. There is no doubt that this policy, which was carried out very thoroughly, led to the destruction of much of value and beauty. But the second aim of the authorities was more important—it was 'to produce an instructed people who knew the Bible intimately and were thoroughly grounded in the essentials of their faith, and the whole intellectual life of the Church of England was organised to serve this end'. One of the methods adopted to further this policy was for the Archbishop to send his domestic chaplains on circuit to test the beneficed clergy. Dr Purvis gives in full a small group of papers recently discovered in the York Registry showing the results of these examinations. Great importance was also attached to the examination of schoolmasters, and to the teaching of the Catechism. Communion was refused to those who were imperfectly instructed. There is no doubt that a very remarkable attempt was made to raise the whole standard of education, both of the clergy and of the laity.

This book is a treasure-house on which future historians will draw, and it is full of interest to all who wish to know more of parish life during the reign of Queen Elizabeth. The plentiful extracts from the original authorities have been carefully chosen and arranged. They deal with a variety of subjects, from the character of the Parson, the Services of the Church, and the duties of Church-wardens, to disputes over the occupancy of pews and the playing of bowls during the hours of Church Service. Dr Purvis has given us a most interesting and valuable book. We owe a debt of gratitude to the Pilgrim Trust for making a generous grant which enables him to continue his work as archivist amongst the mass of un-published documents in the Registry at York.

CYRIL EBOR:

April 1946

CONTENTS

III. THE FIGHT AGAINST IGNORANCE

CONTENTS

IV. THE FIGHT AGAINST SUPERSTITION

CONTENTS

INTRODUCTION

The texts given in the following pages are transcribed from documents in the Diocesan Registry of York. They are selected from three classes of archives there: from the Visitation material, from the books and papers of the Ecclesiastical Commission of York, and from the files of the Ecclesiastical Courts of York, the Cause Papers. They fall mainly, but not entirely, within the dates A.D. 1559–1600.

The Visitation material refers not only to the Diocese of York in Elizabethan times, which was more extensive than the present Diocese, but also some of it embraces the whole province of York. Thus in the archiepiscopal books are found returns from the Archdeaconry of Nottingham and also from Richmondshire with the rest of the Diocese of Chester, with which Richmondshire was then included. Few records of any but Archbishops' Visitations have survived at York, or are likely to be discovered there, lost until now. For it must be explained that there is yet no systematic index of the great accumulation of archives in the Diocesan Registry, and it is possible that some papers from archidiaconal or prebendal, or even from archiepiscopal, Visitations of this date are yet hidden amongst the Cause Papers, although, as exploration of these papers proceeds steadily in the formation of an index, the likelihood of such discoveries decreases steadily also.

The Visitation system was intended to supply the means by which the highest diocesan authority could define ecclesiastical policy, could supervise conditions in the parishes, could discover whether the instructions issued from time to time were or were not being observed, and could collect information about offenders, both clergy and laity, and correct irregularities, offences or defects. The documents resulting from this system fall into two groups. Of these, one is the 'Comperta', the 'things discovered', the actual charges or 'presentments'[1] in the Visitation made by incumbents, by church-

---

[1] The answers sent in by churchwardens to the 'articles' or questions issued by Archbishop, Archdeacon or Prebendary at the outset of a Visitation, in which they 'presented' the names and offences of those who had broken Canon Law or ecclesiastical regulations. The Queen's Injunctions of 1559 were commonly taken as the standard of reference, and were issued with that intention.

wardens, or even by parishioners; the other is found in the 'Act Books', which record what was done to such offenders in the Archbishop's Ecclesiastical Courts, especially in the Archbishop's Visitation Court known as the 'Court of Audience', and in his Consistory Court. No attempt is made here to decide, or even to discuss, what cases or presentments were selected for trial in these Courts, or why a selection was made. The evidence is still too imperfect and uncertain to allow any verdict on this point. Nor is it proposed to discuss the value, the completeness, or the reliability of Visitation records. Such discussion is outside the intended scope of the present work, and in any case has been handled elsewhere by more competent writers. The selection of texts has been made with a desire to present the situation as fully yet as impartially as possible in a reasonable space, remembering always that by their very nature Visitation documents, with their preoccupation with delinquency, may be so read as to give an unduly dark view of the general condition of the parishes and of the parochial clergy.

There are in the Diocesan Registry records of six archiepiscopal Visitations, and one archidiaconal, during the reign of Elizabeth; for only two of the former have both books survived, that is, both the 'Comperta' volume and the Act Book of the Court. Generally, it is the 'Comperta' Book which has been lost. These are supplemented by a certain number of papers from the files of the Courts, where the papers of the various Courts have now become confused without distinction. The Visitation material is amplified by that from the Ecclesiastical Commission, which forms the second great group from which these texts are drawn. It was the good fortune of the present writer to recover in the Registry the Act Books of the York Commission which corresponded to the 'High' Commission in London, in an almost unbroken but quite complete series from 1561 to 1641; these are probably unequalled elsewhere in England, both in completeness and in historical importance of their kind. They had become, in course of time, so entirely neglected, as not required in the way of office business, that their very existence was unknown to the Registrar and his staff. Moreover, in the course of current archive work, many papers were recognised which had survived from proceedings before the Ecclesiastical Commissioners or on behalf of them and had become detached from their proper associations. All these form a useful addition to the Visitation material, since many offenders in Visitations were referred directly to the Commission, and since the Commission acted regularly as a kind of Supreme Court. The Commission tended always to become something of a reinforced and superior Court of the Archbishop, because he was permanent President of the Commission and could avail himself for his own purposes of its wide powers and authority based on the Royal Commission, and because so many of the Commissioners most often engaged in business were regular officials of the Archbishop.

Three sets of Articles[1] or of Injunctions[2] used in Visitation have been quoted extensively here. The Injunctions of Archbishop Grindal in 1571 have been used in various sections of the text to mark the standard set up by ecclesiastical authority; the texts may indicate how far it was, or was not, carried out successfully. The Articles, or Questions, issued by a Prebendary are more unusual; no others of this type have yet been found at York. Like all the Prebendaries of York at that time, this Canon treated his prebend as a 'peculiar jurisdiction', that is, as independent of the Ordinary's jurisdiction, and possessed of its own rights of independent jurisdiction and visitation, its own Ecclesiastical Courts and officers, and power to issue marriage licences, etc. The third set is of Questions issued for the Chapter of Durham, and for Darlington Ward; they are inserted here because of their marked anti-Roman character.

An index of the great collection of papers and files from the Ecclesiastical Courts is now in process of construction; beginning

[1] The term is used with two main senses, that of Visitation Articles (as on pp. 6, 12), or, if found in the records of the Ecclesiastical Courts, of the points on which the counsel for either prosecution or defence proposed to argue. 'Articles of Information' to the Archbishop or to the Ecclesiastical Commission belong to the latter class. The document in which these 'articles' were set out is often called the 'libel'. Visitation Injunctions were usually set out in the form of 'articles' or paragraphs, and are sometimes alluded to as 'Articles'.

[2] Chiefly used for the detailed instructions, arranged in heads or paragraphs, issued after a Visitation as a result of the findings in the Visitation, as corrections of the past and directions for the future. The term is also used for the orders of the judge or judges in the Ecclesiastical Courts, including the Ecclesiastical Commission.

with a document dated A.D. 1302, the papers are now indexed completely down to the year 1599, with a few others of later date found as strays. The attestations in these files are often of much value for their full detail, and information given incidentally. They have been used in quotation, and in four examples in entirety for their general interest. Several 'informations'[1] or petitions to the Ecclesiastical Commission have found their way amongst these Cause Papers, and some use of them is made.

In general, statistical problems or statements have been declined here, not only because the subject requires much more detailed treatment and evidence than space permits, but also because the evidence itself, on so many of the more important points, is so scanty or so uncertain. For example, it might be asked, To how many parishes, or to how many clergy, do these Visitation papers refer? It would be extremely difficult to answer the question with any degree of confidence. One of the Visitation Books, R. VI. A. 5, of 1575, gives a total of no less than 1,145 parishes or chapelries in the area, including Chester, a total far higher than estimates sometimes given, which range about 650 parishes; this latter number is in all probability considerably too low. To fix the number of chapelries existing in any given year is impossible with any certainty, and equally difficult is it to decide the number of incumbents. Even if the total of rectors and vicars were not above 650 or 700, many of them no doubt had a curate, and some had two, or even more, who served in the parish church or in dependent chapelries. All of these would be cited or summoned to a Visitation, any of them might appear in the 'Comperta'. But if it be desired to assess the proportion of the criminous to the non-criminous, the fixing of reliable figures will be of the utmost difficulty, if not impossible. Even the Institution Books and Registers will not help much here, for in so many cases chapelries and curacies (in the modern sense) were ignored. A similar weakness attends the valuable lists of clergy examined by

[1] A way of supplying reports on ecclesiastical misdemeanours to the Archbishop or Commission other than that by Visitation presentments. The precise method or regulations, if any, are not clear; the 'information' might come from any person, but was usually from an incumbent or parish clerk rather than from a parishioner. Most of the 'informations' as they have survived have been put into shape as 'articles' by a lawyer.

the Archbishop's chaplains in 1575. They are printed here entire, but they give no indication at all to show what proportion of the total number of clergy was examined, although clearly the number examined was a minority, or the reasons why these clergy were selected for examination. Conjecture would hardly be profitable where it is so unfounded.

It may be stated that this book is designed to take a place in a scheme of the writer which aims at making more widely known to students the richness of the collection of archives at York. Hitherto, this vast accumulation has been too little accessible for research, but the policy of the present Registrar is to give readily every facility for access by serious students, and this calls for a more exact knowledge, more widely published, of the contents of the archives.

NOTES

In the texts, the apostrophe 's for the possessive has been omitted, to keep nearer to the original: "Quenes maiesties Injunctions", etc.

'The said', 'aforesaid', 'dictus', 'antedictus', 'predictus', have been omitted except where clearness of meaning required retention of these words.

'He' is sometimes substituted for 'this examinate' or 'this respondent'.

A.D. 1561–4. R. VI. A. 1. This book is so primitive in form, and raises so many uncertainties, that it can hardly be considered one of the series. It contains much which is not Visitation, and also a large section recording the examination of clergy and schoolmasters in 1564. It has not been used to supply any texts except in relation to this last subject.

A.D. 1567. R. VI. A. 2. Diocese of York including Nottingham. A Court Book; presentments in quotation only. The number of parishes represented is small.

A.D. 1575. R. VI. A. 5. Diocese of York. Presentments only. Probably a majority of the total number of parishes.

A.D. 1578. R. VI. A. 7. Diocese of Chester. Presentments, with some quotation from the Court Book.

A.D. 1590. R. VI. A. 9. Diocese of York. Area and parishes about those of R. VI. A. 5.

A.D. 1590. R. VI. A. 12. Diocese of Chester. Presentments only.

A.D. 1595. R. VI. A. 14. Whole Province. Presentments and a few Court Book quotations. Large number of parishes.

A.D. 1595. R. VI. A. 15. Diocese of Chester. Presentments.

A.D. 1598. R. VI. D. 1. Archdeaconry of York only. Presentments. Probably a majority of parishes.

CHAPTER I

THE PROBLEMS AND THE PROCEDURE

It would be fair to expect that a series of volumes such as the Visitation Books should give some indication of progress and show whether a general policy pursued over some forty years had or had not been successful in attaining its objects; if indeed there was a policy in the Church of England which aimed at more than meeting the problems of the moment as they arose, these Books should declare whether that policy was in fact a success or a failure. Again, some indication may be expected of the relation between the policy of ecclesiastical authority and that of the State—the policy of the Government as it affected the Church—and also some reflection of the impact on parochial life of great contemporary movements. Be it said at once that in some of these respects the Visitation Books and even the records of the Ecclesiastical Commission will be found strangely defective. One omission is quite astonishing in its completeness, and that is the almost entire absence of reference to heresy; even incidental allusions are of great rarity, and proceedings against heretics, especially with any statement of the charge, almost unknown. Similarly, the documents must be considered unsatisfactory in their evidence on one of the most vital topics in the Elizabethan period, that of recusancy. Any discussion dealing at all fully with the growth, the progress or even the existence of recusancy must be declined here, mainly because the evidence of the records used must be regarded as insufficient for sure analysis or definite conclusions. Certain statistics may be compiled, but their value is decreased by the fact that the documents do not distinguish clearly between recusancy, which was papist, and non-communicating, which was due to the puritan extreme of reform. In fact, the interpretation of the Visitation documents generally is open to much doubt and divergence of opinion. On the face of the evidence, the first ten years of the reign gave close attention to the destroying of superstition and found recusancy no serious problem at all, while the latter part of the reign had little need to concern itself with superstition but was faced by a growing body of recusancy. Yet the Act Books of the Commission, while they entirely support this view about the early part of the reign, and about superstition in the latter part, show a tough struggle with

I

recusancy in the period 1570–80 and a marked success against it in the years which followed. As a broad general conclusion, the Visitation Books suggest that in 1567, when the series really begins, we enter upon a stormy period, when grave problems were everywhere around, and serious irregularity of many kinds, but by 1590 or 1595, when the series ends for this reign, hardly anything remained of a graver nature except the problems of recusancy[1] and of the neglectful rectorial farmer;[2] all else had been reduced to petty offence.

1. VISITATION ARTICLES FOR A PREBENDAL PECULIAR

A.D. 1576   [Visitation Miscellanea, R. VI. E. Uncalendared.]

Artycles to be enquyred upon in the visytacion of the right worshipfull Mr. Edmunde Bunnye Bachelor of Divinitye Prebendary of the Prebende of Wystowe in the Cathedrall Churche of Yorke holden at [blank] the [blank] day of [blank] in the year of our Lord God a thowsand fyve hundreth seaventye and sixe.

Firste whether your Vicar or Curate upon everye Sondaie and holie-daie and upon Weddensdaies and Frydaies do at convenient howres reverentlie and distinctlie saye or singe the Common Praier accord-inge to the Lawes of this realme turninge his face towards the people as they may best heare the same, and do mynister the two holie sacraments that is to say Baptisme and the Lord's Supper accordinge to the booke of common prayer.

---

[1] Always used in the sense of one who refuses to attend church at all, as distinct from one who attends at least occasionally but refuses to communicate. It is important to note that no distinction is suggested or made in these documents between extreme Puritans and Papists, both of whom might be described as recusants, although there is a slight inclination to assume that Papist will be under-stood. The term is rarely found in the earlier books of the Elizabethan series.

[2] Even in medieval times it was not unusual to make a lease of the greater or rectorial tithes of a parish, that is, to 'farm' them, to a layman, but this practice increased enormously after the Dissolution of the monasteries. The increase in cases of tithe brought by lay rectors or farmers after 1540 and before 1570 in the Ecclesiastical Courts as against those brought by all rectors between 1302 and 1539 is almost in the proportion of four to one; between 1540 and 1560 there were 135 cases brought by lay farmers against parishioners out of 520 cases of all kinds before the Courts. A majority of these leases or 'farms' had been granted in the first place by the Crown.

Item whether doth your vicar or curate teache and instructe the youth of the parishe in the Lord's praier the articles of the faith the tenne commaundements and to answer to the questions of the catechisme.[1]

Item whether hath he admitted to the holie Communyon any notoriowse offender or any furthe of charity before repentance and reconciliation first made or any such as can not by hart saie the Lord's praier the articles of the faith and the ten commaundements.

Item whether he hath maried any persons without bannes of matrymonye betwene them thrise asked or any persons within the degrees of consanguinity or affinity forbidden by the lawes of God, and set furth in a table for that purpose.

Item whether doth he upon Sondaies and holidaies duelie reade the homilies setfurth by auctoritie when there is no sermon.

Item whether he doth proclame bydd or observe or suffer the parishoners to observe any holiedays or fastinge daies heretofore abrogated or not appointed by the new kalendar or hathe the people any knoledge thereof by any indirect meanes.

Item whether doth he well kepe a Regester booke of all weddings burialles and Christenings within your parishe.

Item whether doth he serve two Cures, or serve any Cure in this Jurisdiction without licence of the ordinary.

Item whether doth your vicar or curate kepe any alehowse[2] tiplinge howse or taverne in his vicaredge or dwelling howse, or sell any ale beare or wyne, or kepe any suspected woman in his howse, or be himself an incontinent liver or geven to dronkennes or idlenes, or be a haunter of alehowses or suspected places or a hunter

---

[1] In the Diocese of York there was a tradition dating at least from the time of Archbishop Thoresby (A.D. 1353–73) if not earlier requiring the clergy to instruct the people, especially young people, in the Creed, the Commandments, and other matters later embodied in the Catechism, in the vernacular, and to question them on their knowledge.

[2] There was apparently a wide tendency to supply ale in vicarages, and the attitude of authority was generally, but not always, to disapprove. Those who came to church from a distance and remained close by between the morning and the 'evening' services would need some place of refreshment, and supervision was presumably better in the vicarage. Ale was, of course, the staple drink, and almost every house brewed its own ale.

1-2

a hawker dycer carder[1] swearer tabler[2] or otherwise geve any evell example of lief and if so wherein.

Item whether have you in your Church or Chapell a convenient place erected wherein the mynister maie stande and reade devyne service to the people with his face towards them and so as they may the better heare and understand him.

Item whether have you in your Church or Chapell a booke of common praier withe the newe Kalendar and a psalter to the same the English bible in the large volume, the two tomes of homilies, a table of the tenne commandements a convenient pulpit well placed, a comelie and decent table for the communyon with a fayre lynnen cloth to lie theron, a comelie communyon cupp with a cover of silver, a decent large surples with sleves a chest for the regester booke and a stronge chest for the poor mens boxe and all other things necessarie in and to the premisses.

Item whether in your Church or Chapell all altars be utterlie taken downe and clere removed, and the altar stones be broken defaced and bestowed to some common use, and the rode lofte[3] taken downe unto the crosse beame and the bords and beames which were thereof sold to the churches use.

Item whether is the bodie of the churche or chapell well repaired in lead tile slate glasse iron and timber and other necessaries and whether is the same church or chapell cleanlie kepte and decentlie, and whether is the churchyeard well fenced or not.

Item whether is there any person or persons in your parishe that hath in his kepinge any masse bookes or forbidden Latyne service bookes, or any vestements albes tunicles stoles phanons pixes handebells sacring bells sencers crismatories crosses candlesticks holie water stocks or fatts,[4] Images or any other reliques or monuments of superstition or idolatrie, or whether any such be reserved or secretlie kept in any place in the said parishe.

Item whether therebe any parishioner that admitt or suffer in his

[1] A player at cards, which might lead not only to waste of time, but also to quarrels.

[2] Probably, from the context, a player at 'Tables', a form of backgammon.

[3] See the quotation given on p. 202.

[4] The common occurrence of this phrase suggests a basin or 'vat' for holy water set on a pedestal.

howse or backside anye to eate drinke or plaie at cards tables bowles or other games in tyme of devyne service, preachinge or reading of homilies on the sondaies or holiedaies.

Item whether there be any person or persons within your parishe or chapelrie that do absent them selfs from the church and not resort to devine service on Sondaies and other holiedaies or any that doth not receive the holie Communyon according to the lawes of this Realme at least yerelie at the feast of Easter.

Item whether there be anie that walke talke or otherwise un-reverentlie behave them selves in devine service tyme or any that in service tyme use gamynge, or to sitt abrode in the strete or church-yeard or in any taverne or alehowse upon sondaies or other holiedaies in devine service tyme.

Item whether there is any in your parishe that weare beads,[1] or praie upon beads or knotts, or upon any Latyne prymer[2] not allowed or that burne any candelles in the church superstitiouslie or that do resort to any popishe preist for shrifte or auriculer confession, or any that superstitiowslie weare any crosses, or saie De Profundis or other prayers for the dead.

Item whether is there any in your parishe that be either blasphemers of the name of God, great or often swearers, adulterers fornicators incestuouwse persons bawds or recevers of naughtie or incontinent persons, or harborers of women with child not beinge maried, or any that be suspected of such falts or crymes, any dronkards or ribalds, or that be malicious contentyowse or uncharitable persons slaunderers of their neighbours railers scolders or sowers of discord betwene neighbours and what be ther names.

Item whether is there any in your parishe that have maried within the degrees of consanguinitie or affinitie, any maried without bannes askinge thre tymes, any maried that is precontracted,[3] any that have been maried and live asunder, and who they be.

[1] Rosaries.
[2] There was a double objection to the use of this simple elementary book of prayers and devotions: it was a relic of the 'old religion', and it was in Latin and therefore not suitable for intelligent use by the simple laity.
[3] Precontract with one person was a bar in Canon Law to any later contract of marriage with another person. A common cause of litigation in the Ecclesi-astical Courts. A good illustration is on p. 72 below.

Item whether is there any of the clergie or laitie in your Parishe that be favorers of the romishe and forren power, letters[1] of true religion, hearers or saiers of Masse or of any Latyne service, preachers or setters furth of popishe doctryne, mainteyners of sectaryes, disturbers or mislikers of devine service, receivers of any vagabounds or popishe preists, or mainteyners of the people in ignoraunce, and perswading them to stubbornes or mislikings of the godlie procedings of the Queenes Majestye in matters of Religion.

A.D. 1587

Articles of Inqeierie for the Visitation at Wistow.

Articles exhibited in the Visitacion of Mr. Edmund Bunnye Batcler of Divinitye Prebendarie of Wistowe holden at Wistowe the viiith daie of June 1587.

For the Clergie

INPRIMIS whether your parsonn[2] Vicar or Curate doth reverentlie plainlie and distinctlye at conveniente tyme of the day aswell upon Sondayes and holy dayes as also upon Weddensdaies and Frydaies singe or say divine service and celebrate the Sacraments in such manner and forme as is appointed in the boke of Common prayer sett furthe by aucthoritye of Parliamente.

ii. Item whether your parson [etc.] at such tyme as he sayethe the communion or commemoration or ministrethe the Sacraments doth weare a cleane and a decent surples with large sleeves or no.

iii. Item whether your Parson [etc.] doth diligently teache the youth of youre parishe upon Sondayes and holydayes the Lordes prayer the Crede and the tenne commaundements and also the catechisme or no.

---

[1] Those who hinder, obstruct or oppose.
[2] PARSON is used regularly in these documents to equal in meaning rector, that is, the incumbent who received the greater or rectorial tithes; VICAR, for the incumbent, often employed by a rector to take his place in performing parochial duties, who received the minute tithes and fees; CURATE, the cleric in charge of a parish, or chapelry with 'cure' of souls. The last term is also found in the modern sense of an assistant or subordinate to a rector or vicar.

iiii. Item whether your Parson [etc.] doth admitt to the holy communion any excommunicate person or any beinge out of charitie or any beinge under the age of xxiiii yeares which cannot say the catechisme or no.

v. Item whether your Parson [etc.] doth solemnize matrimonye betwixte any persons unles the bannes be lawfullie asked thre sondayes or hollydayes before the same or no.

vi. Item whether youe have had iiiior sermons preached in your churche this last yeare and by what preachers they were made.

vii. Item whether any do serve as curate within your parishe which hath not a licence under the ordinarie his seale so to do or no.

viii. Item whether your Parson [etc.] doth read an homelie everie Sondaie and holydaye or noe.

ix. Item whether your Parson [etc.] beinge unmaried dothe kepe in his house any woman under the age of LX yeares and above XIIII unles she be his verie nighe kinswoman or no.

x. Item whether your Parson [etc.] doth kepe a register boke wherein he writeth the names of suche as be christened maried and buried or no.

xi. Item whether your Parson [etc.] be a dizer tabler Carder swearer or dronkerd or useth the companye of lewde persons or noughtie women or is vehemently suspected to live incontinently with any other man's wife or useth to resort to any suspected houses or places.

xii. Item whether your Chauncell Queare parsonage or viçaredge house and other houses thereunto belonginge be well repayred or no and if not then present in whose defalte.

For the Laitie

i. INPRIMIS whether have you in youre parishe churche all maner of books and other things necessarie for the administringe of divine service viz. a booke of common prayer with the newe Kalendar and a Psalter to the same a Bible of the largest volume the two tomes of homilies the table of the tenne commaundements a convenient pulpitt a decent table with fare clothes to cover the same a

Communion Cuppe of silver with a cover and a decent surples with large sleves or no.

ii. Item whether the bodie of youre churche and the steple of the same be well repayred and the windowes thereof well glasened without any broken plate or holes in the same or no.

iii. Item whether your church and church yearde be well and cleanlie kepte and the churche yearde walls well and stronglie fenced or no.

iiii. Item whether there be any in your parishe that use buyinge or sellinge walkinge or talkinge in youre parishe yearde in tyme of divine service or any that use to sitt stand or walke in the church-yearde or nighe the same when service is in sayinge or no.

v. Item whether there be any man or woman in your parishe beinge comed to yeares of discretion hath not receaved the wholye communion within your parishe Churche iii. tymes this last yeare namelie at Easter last and if there be any sutche presente their names.

vi. Item whether there be any within youre parishe which have absented them selves from youre parishe churche upon Sondaies and holy dayes or no, and how long they have so absented them selves.

vii. Item whether there be any within your parishe which are excommunicate and howe longe they have so remaned.

viii. Item whether there be any victulers or aylewives in your parishe that suffer any resorte of people into their houses or backsides either to eate drinke or playe at cardes tables [1] dize or bowles in tyme of divine service and if there be any suche presente their names and also the names of suche as do resorte thether.

ix. Item whether there be any scholemaster in youre parishe which doth teache either privilye or openlie without a sufficient licence from the ordinarie or no.

x. Item whether there be any maried man in your parishe that doth live from his wife or she from him or any that are maried together the bannes of matrimonye beinge not thre solemne dayes

---

[1] A form of backgammon. 'Tabler', on p. 4 above, is one who plays at Tables.

asked before, or any that are maried furth of their owne parishe Churche or no.

xi. Item whether any man or woman have quarrelled brauled or chidden in the Churche or churche yearde or hath offered to fight or drawe any weopen in the same or no.

xii. Item whether there be any in your parishe that refuseth to pay youre parishe clerke his wages or any other duties or cessments to your Churche or to the poore.

xiii. Item whether there now be or at any time within this twelvemonthe last past have bene in youre parishe any fornicators or adulterers or any man or woman either maried or unmaried which are judged or suspected to have lived in fornication or adulterye together and if there be any suche presente their names and where they nowe remaine.

xiv. Item whether there be any woman in your parishe which is withe childe or hathe borne a childe in fornication and hath not named the father thereof then by vertue of youre othes who have hard named or suspected to be the father thereof.

xv. Item whether there be any man or woman in youre parishe which hath a child begotten in fornication or adulterie within theis vii yeares last past and after the gettinge or bearinge thereof did flee furth of youre parishe before he or she did pennance for the same and now is comed into your parishe againe.

xvi. Item whether there be in your parishe any Dronkards swearers Banners[1] scoulders or slaunderers of their neighbors or any usurers or no.

xvii. Item whether there be in within your parishe any bawdes or receyvers of noughtie companye or suspected persons into their houses or do harboure or have harboured any woman begotten with childe furthe of matrimonye and have suffered them to departe unpunished and if there be any such presente their names.

xviii. Item whether your churchwardens do geve in their accountes at the ende of theire yeare and whether they continue in office any longer then one yeare or no.

---

[1] Those who ban or curse.

xix. Item where there be any fornicators or adulterers within your parishe which have bene putt to pennance by the deane of this deanrie since Easter last past was a twelvemonth and what be there names.

xx. Item whether there be any somoner or under-sommoner which have taken any bribes or rewards of any fornicators adulterers or other offenders within your parishe for bearinge with them or overseinge[1] their offences or for any other thinge whatsoever declayringe the name of the sommoner or undersommoner which toke the bribe or rewarde and the name of him her or them of whome he toke it and howe muche the same bribe was.

2. DURHAM INJUNCTIONS, 1559

For comparison with these Injunctions by Grindal and Bunney may be given some extracts from Injunctions issued at Durham. Although they show sufficient points to establish their affinity to the general type of Elizabethan tradition in Injunctions, they present interesting points of individual difference, especially in their marked anti-papist emphasis.

Book of Chapter business used by Tobie Mathew when Dean of Durham. [York Diocesan Registry, R. VI. C. Delta, f. 50.]

INIUNCTIONS geven the xxvth daie of September. In the first yere of the Reigne of our sovereigne Ladie Elizabeth by the grace of God....By William Lorde Evers Henrie Gates knighte Edwyne Sandes Doctor of divinitie and Henrie Harvie Doctor of Lawe Commissioners emongest others appointed by the Quenes Majestie of her highnes visitacion in the diocese of York Duresme Carlill and Chester To the Deane Subdeane Chauntor Chauncellor Threasorer Archedeacon Prebendaries Petticannons Vicars and all other Ministers of the Cathedrall Churche of Duresme....

2. Item they shalbe also present at all Sermons preached within the Churche and Lectures of Divinitie, and shall cease from all other divine service during the tyme of the same.

4. Item They shall make a Librarie in some convenient place within their Church within the space of one yere next ensweing this visitacion and shall lay in the same Sainct Augustine Basill Gregorie

---

[1] Now = overlooking.

Nazanzene Hierome Ambrose Crysostome Ciprian Theophylact Erasmus and other good writers workes.

6. Item they shall everie daie at their tables in tyme of their meales reade in Englishe some parte of the holie scripture, to thyntente they having reverent communicacion therof, may utterly avoide al other sclanderous and unfructfull talking.

10. Item That you shall have your divine service at due and convenient howres in your Church and that you shall besides the same your ordinarie morninge praier and service have everie working daie at six of the clock in the morneing the common morninge praier with the English Latine [i.e. Litany] and suffrages in place and steade of the morow Masse, to thintent that the schollers of the Gramer schole, and other weldisposed artificers may daylie resort therunto. . . .

11. Item That the Ordinarie for the tyme being shall att all tymes convenient call the Petticannons of the Church before him, and examyne them how they profitt and spend their tyme. . . .

15. Item ye shall lay in the Queere as you maie convenientlie provid two Bibles of the largest volume in English for the Ministers to use and two other of like sort in the bodie of the Churche in suche meet and convenient places as every other person comming thither maie have recourse unto the same, And likewise one Booke of the paraphrases[1] in the bodie of the Cathedral Church and an other in the Queere.

16. Item That ye shall have weekelie at the least thrise everie weeke a Lecture of Divinitie in Englishe in the Cathedrall Church to bee read at ix of the clock in the forenoone in your Chapiter house openly so that all people maie comme to it And that ye shall appoint somme learned man to reade it And shall geve him xx li. a yere stipend and that all the prebendaries and Petticannons shalbe present at everie Lecture, onles therto somme lawfull excuse.

17. Item That everie preest within your Church under the degree of a Battcheler of Divinitie shall have att the least of his owen the whole Bible in Englishe, and the Paraphrases of Erasmus. . . .

---

[1] The first [second] tome or volume of the Paraphrases of Erasmus upon the newe testament, on the Great Bible text, published in folio by E. Whitchurche, who also printed the Prayer Books of Edward VI, in 1548 and 1549.

3. DARLINGTON ARTICLES, 19 ELIZ.

[Ibid. f. 90.]

ARTICLES to be enquired upon by the Jurates and sworne men within Darlington warde within the Diocesse of Durham mynistred unto them by the Right Reverend Father in God Richard by devine providence Bishopp of Durham and other his associates the Quenes highnes Commissioners For the hearing ordering and determyning of Causes ecclesiasticall within the saide Diocess of Durham...at Durham the last daie of September in the xixth yere of the Raigne of the Quenes Majestie that now is, as followeth.

The first Article, with eight dependent paragraphs, orders true present-ment about the observation of the Book of Common Prayer, in accordance with the Act of Parliament 'intituled An Acte for the Uniformitie of Common Prayer and Service of the Churche'. The sub-headings generally are against those who in particular ways 'deprave or despise' the Book of Common Prayer; by speaking against it, by using other forms especially of celebrating the Holy Communion. Sub-heading 3 enquires 'WHETHER any other persons either ecclesiasticall or temporall in any interludes plaies songs rimes or by other open wordes have declared or spoken any thinge to the derogacion...'. The fifth asks 'WHETHER any preest mynister or deacon have bene by any person letted or interrupted in any Churche Chappell or oratorie to singe or say common prayer' after the forms of the Book.

The second Article passes on to inquire about offenders against the Act of Supremacy of 1 Eliz., the third similarly concerning those against the Act of 5 Eliz., 'intituled an act for the assurant of the Q. Majesties Roiall power over all states and subiectes within her dominions....'. The fourth requires presentment of all 'the extollers and advauncers favorers manteners abetters or defendors of the aucthoritye or iurisdiccion of the Byshopp of Rome and of that malignant churche and of the impious idolatrous and blasphemous Religion of the same'. Articles 5, 6 and 7 refer to breaches of Acts of 1 Edw. VI, 3 Edw. VI, 8 Eliz. and 13 Eliz. Article 8 is strongly anti-Roman:

ITEM you shall dewlie enquire and trew presentment make of all and singular persons that either have browght over and delivered abrode anie bulls pardons agnus dei dispencacions pictures beades reconciliac. from the Pope the sea and court of Rome or from anie datario penitentiarie minister or messinger of the same or any sedicious bookes, impugninge the religion nowe in this Realme most godlie received established and professed, and the Q. Highnes supream iurisdiccion ecclesiasticall within the same, and also of all that use retein kepe or extoll the same, or that use to pray on beades, Popish practases[1] primers,[2] or that use any other supersticious prayers or sayings as the Ladies psalter the Lordes psalter or any popishe orisons or saings (as they be called) or that fast or hier others to fast any supersticious fastes (as those of olde called our Ladies fastes St. Katherins faste St. Sithes fast St. Runans faste the blacke faste etc. or that be suspected so to doe.

Article 9 calls for the names of those advancing doctrine contrary to the Thirty-nine Articles of 1562.

10. ITEM whether there be any parsons vicars curates or other person ecclesiasticall that wear laie apparell great ruffes great bumbasted breches, skalings[3] or scabulonious[3] clokes or gownes after the laie fashion and contrarie to the Advertisements and Injunctions or that be common haunters of ale howses, tavernes, or drunkardes, or that be reputed to be common users of unlawfull games as cardes dyse table playinge, bowling or suche unlawfull or prohibited games or that refuse to wear the surplice in the church at ministracion of sacrements and saing of devine service, or that doe neglect the same....

14. ITEM whether there be any...curate that hath admitted and receyved to the holie Communion any notorious offendors... banners...knowen usurers...or any that cannot perfectly say the cathechisme the Lordes prayer the Articles of the Christian faith and the x Commaundments of almighty God contrarie to the iniunctions...and whether there be any of yeares of discrecion that have not receyved the holie Communion in there parishe churches or chappells at Easter last and also at least thrice yerelie....

---

[1] Probably for 'portases'. The 'portas' or 'portiforium' was the Roman Breviary.
[2] A book of simple prayers and elementary instruction. Often used as a children's lesson book.
[3] No certain meaning is known for either of these terms.

17. ITEM whether there be any that have use or disperse abrode any Lovain bookes[1] or any other bookes sett furth either within this Realme or els where by Doctor Harding Saunders Rascall[2] or any other sedicious Englishe fugitive and disloyall subiect, impugninge the Queenes supream and imperiall aucthoritie ecclesiasticall or the sincer religion of Christe established....

20. ITEM you shall enquire...of all that openly or privatelie defend hold or mainteyne any erronious or hereticall opinions and likewise of all sckismatiks puritanes or precisians (as some tearme them)...of all that have or kepe any sedicious bookes intituled an admonicion to the Parliament or any suche other bookes impugninge the Booke of Common Prayer....

23. ITEM whether all...curates be diligent in teaching the cathechisme to their parishioners, whether they use any communions or commemoracions for the deade or at Buriatts of the dead whether they say service upon any abrogated holidaies or suffer anie ringing on All Saincts daie at night....

26. ...enquire of all sorcerers coniurers charmers[3] blessers[4] or medeciners, as they be called, of men women children or cattaile for the worme or any other maladie whatsoever....

31. ITEM whether your severall parishe churches and chappels be furnished with and have all necessarie bookes and other furnitures... and whether they be knowen or suspected to have or kepe any vest-

---

[1] Louvain was one of the most active Continental presses in issuing books written by the Roman seminarists in attacks on English writers, particularly Dr Jewell.

[2] Of Thomas Harding's books against Jewell two were printed at Antwerp (1565, 1566), and three at Louvain (1564, 1567, 1568). Nicholas Sanders published controversial books at Louvain in 1565–8. Rascall is no doubt for John Rastell, a Jesuit, who wrote books and tracts, two of them definitely attacking Jewell: *A confutation of a sermon pronounced by Mr. Jewell* (Antwerp, 1564), and *A treatise entitled Beware of M. Jewell* (Antwerp, 1566). See also p. 149, n. 1.

[3] Those who use charms. The sense here is probably of use for the purpose of healing.

[4] Not all the activities of wizards, witches and the like were supposed to be ill intentioned. Much application was made to such persons for deliverance from bewitching by 'ill-looking', 'forspeaking', or other malevolent activities causing disease or misfortune.

ments tunicles massbooks grailes etc images crucifixes pixes[1] paxes[2] or any other suche cursed and execrated abhominable monuments of supersticion poperie and idolatrie.

32. ITEM whether there be anie that use to make curtesey and do reverence to anie crosses of wood or stone or to bowe there knees to suche, or in passing by to leave them on there right handes of purpose and for reverence sake.

33. ITEM of all minstrells and Jeasters to use to singe popishe supersticious songs or bawdie ballades full of filthie ribawldrie or anye sedicious songs or rimes in commendacion or defence of popery or of any rebells or fugitives.

4. VISITATION OF 1567

For the Visitation of 1567 one book only has survived in the Registry, that of the Archbishop's Court of Audience which dealt with the presentments arising out of the Visitation. As this quotes usually what can be only the original terms of the presentments, the loss of the latter is the less serious. This volume shows plainly the state of chaos and disorder into which parochial affairs had fallen in some districts, and also enables us to see how ecclesiastical authority proceeded to deal with these irregularities. The fact that it is particular districts which are most seriously at fault may indicate that the chief weakness or inefficiency lay with Archdeacons or Rural Deans, and that to some extent discipline had broken down in diocesan organisation at these points. There may be evidence here of the degree of dislocation and lawlessness which was the result of the violent political and religious changes since the death of Henry VIII, and of the uncertainty and confusion which were due directly to these changes.

This Book for 1567 has been chosen to illustrate these matters rather than the Book for 1561–6, which is concerned so largely with the examination of schoolmasters, and besides is less suitable by reason of certain internal problems of its own. The legal forms used are too numerous and too technical to allow of explanation in detail; they have been abbreviated

[1] The 'pix' was a metal case for the Reserved Sacrament, hung over an altar, or set in a 'tabernacle', and covered with a veil.
[2] The 'pax' was a metal plate, kissed by the priest and then passed to the congregation, for giving the 'Kiss of peace'.

wherever possible. The heading used, 'Officium dominorum[1] contra Tho. Abbott...', shows that the cases were dealt with summarily by the Archbishop's Commissaries sitting as judges in his Court of Audience for Visitation.

[York, Diocesan Registry, R. VI. A. 2, f. 1.]

Acta in Visitacionis negotio Reverendissimi in Christo patris et domini domini Thome permissione divina Eboracensis Archiepiscopi Anglie Primatis et Metropolitani jure suo archiepiscopali Anno Domini 1567 Suaeque Translacionis anno septimo.

Die Mercurii Vicesimo viz. die mensis Augusti A.D. 1567 Infra Ecclesiam Cathedralem et Metropoliticam Eboracensem Loco Consistoriali ibidem Coram Reverendo in Christo patre et domino domino Richardo permissione divina Sedis Nottingham Episcopo Suffraganeo et venerabilibus viris Magistris Joh. Rokeby LL.D. et Waltero Jones LL.B. dicti....Archiepiscopi pro dicte sue Visitacionis execucione Commissariis legitime et sufficienter deputatis Judicialiter pro tribunali sedentibus....

[Ibid. f. 9 v.]

Officium dominorum[1] contra Chris. Graunger vicarium de Cuckney. Super actu comparicionis Quo die horis et loco...comparuit personaliter cui domini objecerunt that he hayth not had any quarterly sermons and the homylies in his paryshe churche according as he is appoynted by the quenes majesties Injunctions quam objec-

---

[1] The 'Office of the Judges' was found usually in one of two forms in the Ecclesiastical Courts: *Officium Dominorum Promotum per A.B. contra C.D.* This is the heading to an ordinary form of suit, where the Office is 'promoted' or called into action by A.B. or more usually by his 'proctor' or counsel, to establish his case against C.D. *Officium Dominorum contra E.F.* This is the heading for a suit 'on mere motion', 'ex mero motu', where the judges exercise jurisdiction spontaneously, 'unmoved' by any 'promoter'. This form is used especially in cases of contempt, and often after an 'information' or a presentment. Other forms commonly found are: *In Causa Mota ex Parte G.H.* Here G.H. sues *ex parte* for some relief or guidance, without naming a 'respondent' or defendant. *J.K. contra L.M.* An ordinary suit or action between parties. Not always easy to distinguish between this and the first form of these four. Matrimonial causes usually in the last form.

cionem confessus est for that he cannot preache [1] et igitur submisit se correccioni dominorum Et tunc domini monuerunt et injunxerunt that he shall fromehencefurth be resident of his cure and also that he shall diligentely apply his bookes and study and do the beste he can to instructe and exorte the parishoners in the worde of God by readinge of the homylies or otherwise and also that he shall iiii times in the yere declare to the parishoners that all forren powers ar justely taiken away.

[Ibid. f. 10.]

O.d.c. Joh. Blythe Rectorem de Kyrketon...comparuit...cui domini objecerunt that he hayth been oftentimes so drunke that he could not say his service and many Sondays and holly dais he hath done no service in his parishe churche by reason of his drunkennes quam objeccionem negavit Et ulterius domini objecerunt eidem that he hayth babtised children upon the workedays cui objeccioni respondendo dicit that one time he hayth babtised a child upon a worke day et igitur submisit se correccioni hujus Curie et ulterius... that he hayth not preached or caused to be preached his quarterly sermons quam objeccionem confessus est et submisit se etc. Et tunc domini assignaverunt eidem Rectori ad purgandum se [2] quinta manu

---

[1] An unusual statement, but even by its rareness throwing some light on the question whether the smallness of the number of licences issued to preachers was due rather to the fact that most of the clergy were unfit to preach than to the requirement that those to whom a licence was issued were unusually well qualified. The general trend of the evidence is to the latter explanation, but it is curiously difficult to find evidence showing what, to the mind of those issuing the licences, was sufficient as proof of suitability as a preacher. Learning was certainly one of the major qualifications; no doubt orthodoxy was another. It was not unmixed zeal to hear sermons which caused some Puritans to complain of lack of preaching, but after all, there were homilies, and William Stead's evidence (see p. 230) shows that it was not usual to stint preachers for time.

[2] [Com]purgation was the clearing one's self of an accusation before a judge. Canonical compurgation is the form found in the Visitation and Court proceedings, and was used only where the accused had put in a plea equivalent to 'not guilty'. The accused took oath that he was clear of the fact 'objected', and brought in a required number of honest neighbours, not above twelve, as ordered by the Judge, to swear upon their consciences and belief that his oath was true, or even that his general good conduct made his guilt unlikely. The accused was usually reckoned as one of his own compurgators; se sexta manu meant on the oath of himself and five others.

viz. duorum clericorum et trium laicorum proxime vicinorum suorum die Mercurii proxime post festum S. Michaelis...et ulterius ...ad audiendum voluntates suas super confessata eodem die.

[Ibid. f. 31 v.]

O.d.c. Robt. Cressey Rectorem de Headon...habet plura beneficia incompatibilia. Excusatur.

[Ibid. f. 32.]

O.d.c. Joh. Swinscoe vicarium de Headon. Est quoque vicarius de Eastdraiton...he being institute in the vicarag of Headon and having possession of the same was also institute in the vicarage of Eastdrayton and likewise inducted in the same quam objeccionem confessus est et submisit se correccioni dominorum judicantium et tunc domini decreverunt dictam vicariam de Headon vacantem fore et vacari ad omnem juris et facti effectum.

O.d.c. dnm. Joh. Pereson clericum, Rectorem de Warsop. he is not resident upon his benefice nor hathe not bene of longe; nor he doeth not destribute any thinge to the pore of the parishe; the saide parson haithe other lyvinge in the South Countrye. [*Rest of entry blank.*]

[Ibid. f. 32 v.]

O.d.c....dnm. Willm. Walton clericum vicarium de North-wheatley....is also vicar of Westmarkham and parson of Barle-burghe in Darbie shire And he haithe not preached his quarterly Sermons and beinge not resident upon his benefice haith not destri-buted the fourtie parte of the same to the poore of the parishe....
[A representative] allegavit quod Willm. Walton clericus est tanta infirmitate detentus quod absque gravi periculo corporis sui ad hanc curiam...accedere non potest....Denuo citandus...[on Friday before St. Luke next].

O.d.c. dnm. Tho. Hulley clericum curatum de Welley...[he] is excommunicate and is not admitted to serve....He shall serve no cure within the dioces of Yorke and also that he shall repaire to his benefice of Assher in Darbyshire and there be resident at or before Lady Day in Lent next comying sub pena juris.

[Ibid. f. 33.]

O.d.c. Leon. Stafforde Rectorem de Carleton in Lyndricke...
haithe mo benefices and is not resident and ther haithe been no
sermons this many a daie. [*Blank.*]

[Ibid. f. 33 v.]

O.d.c. dnm. Willm. Pulleyne cler. Rectorem de Billestrope...
haithe mo benefices then one And he haithe not preached his quarterly
sermons never sence he was parson at Belestrope...dicit that he hath
two benefices viz. Faringdon and Billesthorpe within the dioces of
York for the which he is lawfully dispensed with all as appeareth
by his dispensation now exhibited And whereas yt doth appeare ir
his dispensation that he was parson of the parsonage of Monsley
within the dioces of Norwich therefore he is now assigned to bring
and opteyne a certificat frome Norwich sealed with the ordinarye
his seale there, that he neyther was nor presentlie is parson of the
parsonage of Monsley....And further did monishe and enjoyne
[him] that frome hensforth he shalbe diligent in serving of his cure
at Billesthorpe both in reding the homilies and other devyne service
setforth by publique auctoritie playnly and distinctely as also in
preaching his quarterly sermons in his churche of Billesthorpe....

[Ibid. f. 34 v.]

O.d.c. Hug. Pulleyne vicarium de Marneham. Est etiam vicarius
ecclesie parochialis de Laxton....Personaliter comparuit cui domini
objecerunt that he is vicar not onely of Marnham but also of Laxton
quam allegacionem fatetur esse veram et allegavit quod habet
pluralitatem habere easdem et exhibuit eandem pluralitatem sub
sigillo ad facultates sigillato et per dominam nostram Reginam con-
firmatam...[quam] domini receperunt et decreverunt pro valore
ejusdem Et tunc Pulleine petiit eandem dispensationem registrari...

[Ibid. f. 35.]

O.d.c. dnm. — Thurland Rectorem de Cromwell. They have been
destitute of a Curate this thre yeares last and for want therof have
had no dyvine service nor Sacramentes ministred etc. and their

children ar not taught and all things are furthe of order.[1] [He did not appear; the case was postponed.]

O.d.c. Mr. Matth. Torte Rectorem de Hockerton. He haithe an other benefice in Lincolne shire and the youthe within their parishe ar not taught etc. Nota quod oportet eum comparari apud Sowthwell.

[Ibid. f. 35 v.]

O.d.c. Mr. Willm. Burnell ar. proprietarium Rectorie de Winkeburne. He ought to finde theim a Curate and haithe founde them no Curate theise two yeares but haithe sometymes set some of his owne men to rede them service without aucthoritie and throughe his defalt they have had no sermons nor homylyes red in their Churche nor none to teach the youthe within their parishe. [Blank.]

O.d.c. dnm. Joh. Holme Rectorem de Northclifton. He is not resident upon his benefice nor doeth destribute the xltie parte to the pore and he sufferethe his Chauncell to fall into utter ruine and decay and haith not preached any of his ordinary sermons within theise thre yeares.... [Blank.]

[Ibid. f. 37.]

O.d.c. dnm. [blank] vicarium de Sireston. He is not resident nor haithe not destributed the xltie parte etc. nor haith not maid any his ordenary sermons theise eight yeares and the Chauncell is in utter decay and like to fall downe. [Blank.] Vacat hic quia prius exoneratur.

O.d.c. Joh. Barker Rectorem de Shelton. He is not resident upon his benefice nor doethe not his service in dew tyme and order as he owght. [Admitted the charges. Ordered to reside or to obtain a licence for non-residence.]

[Ibid. f. 37 v.]

O.d.c. Anth. Mosfurthe vicarium de Stoke. He haithe not preached nor caused to be preached his quarterly sermons and he sufferethe the vicarage house to be in great decaye. Vacat hic quia prius exoneratur.

[1] Are out of order.

O.d.c. Joh. Sye vicarium de Farneffeilde. He is also vicar of Blytheworth and haith not preached nor caused to be preached his quarterly sermons...cui domini objecerunt that he is not onely the vicar of Farnefeilde but also the vicar of Blytheworth and that he doith use to say the service at Blethworth so spedely and quickly that the paryshoners ther assembled cannot understand the same and that he doyth not rede the homylies nor mayketh his quarterly sermons as he is appointed by the quenes majesties [sc. Injunctions] and also that he is a quareler and that he dwelleth upon a temporall ferme[1] Cui objeccioni respondendo dicit that he is vicar of Farnefeild and also vicar of Blethworth and that he hayth no dispensacion for the same nor hayth not preached his quarterly sermons and sometimes he haith said his service at Blethworth hastely of intente he mighte do service also at Fernefeilde but he sayth he hayth red the homylies diverse times in boyth the churche and he sayth he is no quareler but he dwelleth of a temporall ferme Et tunc domini injunxerunt eidem vicario ad obtinendum dispensacionem pro eisdem duabus vicariis...et ad exhibendum...alioquin ad dicendum causam quare ab eisdem deprivari non debeat Et ulterius...that frome hencefurth he shalbe diligent to maik or cause to be maid his quarterlie sermons and also the homylies and that he shall behave hime self soberlie and quietly emongst his neighbors and se his cures diligently served.

[Ibid. f. 38 v.]

O.d.c. dnm. Joh. Sympson vicarium de Radfurthe. He is a verrey busy[2] felowe and he is also vicar of Basforde and doethe not his quarterly sermons preached at eyther of the said churches. [Denied only the 'busy felowe', and was ordered exactly as John Sye.]

O.d.c. Anth. Wycliffe Rectorem de Kirkbie in Asshefeilde. He is also parson of Kirkbiewhiske. [Produced evidence that his case had been judged elsewhere.]

---

[1] The offence here was that the vicar was not resident in his vicarage, but had taken a lease of property which was not ecclesiastical at all and was living there. A 'farm' in the modern agricultural sense is a temporal farm.

[2] Possibly here, as often in Marian documents, for a Puritan, or extreme reformer.

[Ibid. f. 39.]

O.d.c. dnm. Chris. Parker vicarium de Mansfeilde in Sherwood. He is also vicar of Tattersall in Lyncolneshire and haithe been absent from his benefice this two yeares duringe which tyme they have had no quarterly sermons nothing destributed to the poore nor any thinge done which he ought to doe. [He did not appear.]

O.d.c. dnm. Leon. Mitchell Rectorem de Eperstone. He is not resident and destributethe nothinge to the poore and omitteth his quarterly sermons. The Chauncell of the Churche the parsonage and howses belonginge the same ar in great decay. [Exoneratur, because heard before the Ecclesiastical Commissioners.]

[Ibid. f. 39 v.]

O.d.c. dnm. Willm Grene vicarium de Arnall. He haith utterly neclected his quarterly sermons and he sufferethe his vicarige to fall into extreame ruyne and decay and is also a common dronkerd and a companyon to Juvelles[1] and dronkerdes and usethe verrey oft to rayle with his neighbours verrey shamefully And likewise did receyve to the holly Communyon one Margaret Taylior beinge owt of Charity to the evill example and great dainger of others...respondendo dicit that he hath preached his quarterlie sermons and he confesseth that his vicaredge is in ruyne and decay but he uterly denieth all the reaste of the objections. [Compurgation ordered, and done 26 November of that year.]

[Ibid. f. 40.]

O.d.c. dnm. Ric. Brande Rectorem de Screton. He doeth not maike nor cause to be made his quarterly sermons and the parsonage in most parte of the same and other howses belonginge the same ar in extreame decay and verrey ruynowse. [Blank.]

O.d.c. dnm. Joh. Normavell Rectorem de Clifton. He is also parson of Elston And he beinge presente doeth not use to communicate when his Curate doeth minister the Communion. [Did not appear.]

---

[1] Apparently the correct reading, but the meaning is not known.

[Ibid. f. 40 v.]

O.d.c. Mr. Ric. Walker Rectorem de Goteham. He is also parson of Leake and haythe an other benefice in Cheshire and one or two in Stafforthshire and doethe not maike or cause to be maid his quarterly sermons. [Did not appear.]

O.d.c. dnm. Nich. Saxton Rectorem ecclesie parochialis de Widmerpole. He usethe to saie the Communion for the dead as he did at the Buryall of one Willm. Calverd at his deathe. Hoc negotium expeditum est per Mr. Walterum Jones aput Sowthwell ut supra.

[Ibid. f. 41.]

O.d.c. dnm. Rog. Smyth Rectorem de Cotgrave. he haithe an other parsonage called Holme Perpoint. Hoc negotium expeditum est per Mr. Walt. Jones ut supra.

O.d.c. dnm. Brian. Sandforthe Rectorem de Hawkesworth. he haithe an other benefice in Darbie and is not resident upon his benefice nor doeth not destribute the xltie parte emongest the poore of the parishe as he ought to doe...apparet Rectorem perquisitum fuisse et non inventum....

[Ibid. f. 41 v.]

O.d.c. dnm. Oliver. Leycetor Rectorem de Byngham. he is also vicar of Kirkebie Wharfe in Yorkeshire and haithe not preached in his Churche any quarterly sermons this thre yeares...perquisitum et non inventum....

O.d.c. Willm. Allerton clericum Rectorem de Eastwood. [A long and detailed charge alleging repeated adultery, brawling, haunting of ale houses and other offences, including the usual failure to preach. To the last he replied that 'he hayth had sermons when he coulde get preachers viz. two or one sermons in the yere'. For the rest, he was ordered to make compurgation 'se sexta manu' and 'absolutus est ad cautelam usque ad eundem diem'.]

[Ibid. f. 52 v.]

O.d.c. Tho. Farnell Rectorem de Aston. He is not resident upon his benefice but serveth cure at Letwell in the prebend of Laughton and doeth not destribute the xl parte of his benefice to the poore and the Chancell of the same Churche throughe his negligence is in extreme decay and so is the parsonage howse.

[Ibid. f. 53.]

O.d.c. Robt. Salven cler. Rectorem de Barneburgh. He is not resident nor doethe not destribute the xl parte of his benefice to the poore nor doethe or cause to be taught the children of his parishe the Cathichisme...respondendo dicit that he is not resident upon his benefice howbeit he sayth he is Chaplaine to my lorde of Darby and for the most parte haythe given his attendance upon honorable lordship in household and he sayth he doyth destribute the xltie parte of his benefice and that he hayth had his quarterly sermons Et tunc domini assignaverunt eidem Rectori that he shalbe attendant upon my said lorde of Darby as he is bounde by the Acte of Parliament or els to be resident upon his parsonage as the law requireth upon paine of the lawe and that [he] be diligent for his quarterly sermons.

O.d.c. Anth. Blayke cler. vicarium de Doncaster. He is also parson of Whiston and of Barnet and vicar of Saint Donstones in the West of London and haithe a benefice also in Warwickeshire called Rookebie and a prebend in the Churche of Yorke. [Confessed. Ordered to show his pluralities.]

[Ibid. f. 53 v.]

O.d.c. dnm. Joh. Tunholme Rectorem de Bramwithe. He doeth not preache his quarterly sermons And he haith evill intreated the Deane and other officers and haithe slaunderously reported the visitors of this visitation ex relacione decani.

[Ibid. f. 54.]

O.d.c. Mil. Walker vicar de Campsall. He is also vicar of Arkesey And the cure at Campsall is verrey negligently served. [Confessed that] he hayth no dispensacion Et tunc domini assignaverunt eidem Walker ad introducendum dispensacionem pro eisdem duobus beneficiis die veneris prox. post synodum Pasche sub pena juris and that in the meane time he shall se the cures diligently served.

O.d.c. Anth. Iveson cler. Rectorem de Burghwalles. He is also vicar of Carnaby. [Postponed.]

[Ibid. f. 54 v.]

O.d.c. Hen. Mallyverer Rectorem de Thirnscoghe. He is also vicar of Anderby with steple in the dioces of Chester. [He showed his dispensation.]

O.d.c. Joh. Wainehowse Rectorem de Kirkesmeton He is also vicar of Lancaster and of Walsame in Northfolke and is purposed to have an other benefice besydes theise And also he doethe neglecte his cure at Smeton and doeth not se the same furnyshed with a sufficient Curate he haithe not preached his quarterly sermons nor seen the homylies read in his parishe. And likewise haithe been suspected to lyve incontinently with one Perkins wif of the said towne and with certeyne other light women comers and goers thyther And moreover kepeth in his howse one Francis Lancaster a woman of evill Conversacion and an incontinent lyver. [Postponed to the next week, when he showed dispensations for three of his benefices, and denied all the other charges. He was ordered to make compurgation on Wednesday after St Andrew's Day; there is no further record.]

[Ibid. f. 55.]

O.d.c. dnm. Willm. Jackson Rectorem de Darfelde. He is not resident upon his benefice. [Did not appear.]

O.d.c. Geo. Aslabie vicarium de Tickhill. He doethe suffer his vicarage to fall into extreme ruyne and decay...respondendo dicit that he hayth bestowed asmuche of his vicaredge as he is able and as the lyvinge will beare notwithstanding the same is in decay because yt is suche a greate house Et tunc domini decreverunt Commissionem fieri Decano Doncastrie to vew the same vicared [and] to appoint suche house of the same as shalbe sufficient for the lyvinge and that suche other howses therof as ar superfluous may be pulled downe wher-with the other may be sufficiently repayred et ad certificandum de gestis....

[Ibid. f. 55 v.]

O.d.c. dnm. Tho. Robynson Rectorem de Kirksandall. He is verrey negligent in servinge the Cure and redinge the homylies by reason he takethe upon to serve the Cure at Barnebie upon Dunne...

he shall not serve the Cure at Barneby any longer then Christenmas upon paine of the lawe.

O.d.c. dnm. Joh. Tyas vicarium de Ecclesfelde. He is also parson of Treton. [Ordered to show dispensation.]

[Ibid. f. 56.]

O.d.c. Tho. Herryson Rectorem de Hymsworth. He sufferethe the Chauncell of his Churche to fall into extreme ruyne and decay... dyd confesse that his parsonag is partely in decay but he hayth had workemen upon the same this sex wekes...ordered to repair it before Martinmass and to certify.

[Ibid. f. 102 v.]

O.d.c. dominos Tho. Blackburne Ric. Tirrie Ninian Atkinson Chris. Bawdersbie Joh. Browmflet alias Carver Clericos vicarios seu curatos ecclesie parochialis de Rippon. The said vicars beinge comaunded and enjoyned by the Right Reverend father in God Richerd by the permission of God Busshope of Notingham and Mr. Walter Jones Bachelor of the Lawe in the diocesane visitacion of the most Reverend father in God Thomas Archebushope of York to reade or cawse to be redde the Lessons at Evenninge and Morninge prayor in the bodie of Rippon Churche that the people might heare the same and Likewise the Epistle and Gospell and the homilies and theie have refused so to do And the said vicars do not communicate together when the Communion is ministred in the said Church as theie ought to do And the said vicars on a nighte toke the keies of the Churche from one John Daie the Sacristane ther, and that night all the imageis and other trumperie were conveighed furthe of the said Churche and bestowed by the said vicars where it is not knowen and where unto the said vicars the dressinge of the said Churche apperteinethe they yet suffer the Stones and Rubies[1] of the altares to remaine in divers closetts in the said Churche yet not caried awaie And the said Mr Blackburne and the rest of the said vicars did never after anye homilie or after anie devine service exhort the people to remember the poore Item ther is in a howse within a vawte of the

---

[1] Apparently for 'rubbish', or perhaps 'rubbles'. The word is written 'rubles', below.

said Churche yet remaninge reserved vi great tables of alablaster full of imageis and xlix books some antiphoners and suche books as ar Condemned by publique auctoritie...respondendo dicunt as to the first objection theie aunsweare that theie do sometimes reade the Lessons as theie were enjoined in the bodie of the Churche as ther boks will serve them and dalie in the quere, and as for the Epistle and Gospell and homelies theie do not reade them in the bodie of the Churche For that theie hard no suche Commaundement. And for the communicatinge togethers on Sondaies when the Communion is ministred theie do sometimes being in the Churche communicate together all at once and sometimes not And the third objection theie do expresselie denye And for the Rubies and alter stones theie do confesse some bottom of alters yet to remain ther which they will conveighe And theie do aunswere they do oftentimes after the homilies and devine service exhort the people to remember the poore [to f. 109] Et tunc domini iniunxerunt eis that theie shall not faile everie Sondaie and everie other holiedaie allowed by the booke of Common Praior Cawse and se both the Lessons at the morning praior and the epistle and the gospell at the Communion or Commemoracion to be openlie plainlie and distinctlie redde in the pulpit in the bodie of the Churche of Rippon in suche convenient place as the people maie most convenientlie assemble to heare the same and that also they do conveighe and take downe the Rubles of the alter stones yet remaninge untaken awaie and do make uppe the same againe handsomelie.... [A day appointed for further hearing; Brownflet excused public appearance because 'senex et impotens'.]

Further charges at Ripon [Ibid. ff. 102 v et seq.]

...c. Tho Blackburne...est Rector etiam ecclesie parochialis de Londesburghe necnon Magister Hospitalis Sancti Johannis in Rippon.

...c. Ric. Tirrie...haithe bene longe suspected to live incontinentlie with a woman...[to plead by a proctor,[1] as 'ex relacione curatorum ceterorum...est impotens et senex'].

[1] The term is used with two quite distinct meanings: for prosecuting or defending counsel in the Ecclesiastical Courts, as here, or for a person responsible for gathering and managing the fruits of a benefice or a demesne or a manor, sometimes almost in the sense of a steward or bailiff.

...c. Joh. Birkbie clericum (et vicarium ecclesie parochialis de Rippon)...est Rector etiam ecclesie parochialis de Moremonkton necnon Capellanus Domine Latimer Necnon he is of verie dissolute lieffe and lewde conversacion and usethe veine undecent apparell namelie great britches cut and drawen oute with sarcenet and taffitie, and great ruffes laid on with laceis of gold and silk And of late toke upon him to minister or saie devine service in the Churche of Rippon upon a holiedaie in the assemblie of the people in his Cote without gowne or Cloke with a long sword by his side And he is also vehementlie suspected to be a notable fornicator, and he haithe divers times in the night time bene taken abroade in the towne of Rippon by the Wakeman and other officers with lewde women, and he useth to daunce verie offencivelie at alehowseis and mariags in the presence of common people to the verie evell example of others and the great slaunder of the ministers. [He denied the whole of the charges, and was ordered to make compurgation.]

[Ibid. f. 105.]

O.d.c. Joh. Jackson Clericum parochialem ecclesie parochialis de Rippon The said Jackson usethe still to make bread for the holie Communion with the picture of the crucifixe and other pictures upon the same contrarie to the quenes Majesties Injunctions...he usethe manie times to scoffe and scorne at the quenes procedings in the state of religion quam objeccionem denegat et quod facit panem ut prius quam fatetur....

[Ibid. f. 105 v.]

...c. Edm. Browne Clericum. The said Sir E.B. is commonlie reputed and taken for a misliker of Christs Religion nowe established in this realme and lurketh about Rippon and is commonlie harbored at the howse of one Roberte Kettlewood...non est inventus....

[Ibid. f. 148 v.]

...c. Joh. Jacksonne Clericum parochialem ecclesie de Rippon... domini iniunxerunt eidem that he do from henceforthe use and behave him as becomethe a faithfull and obedient Subiecte unto the Quenes Majestie her Magistrates and the lawes of this Realme of

Englande And that he do deface such moylds and prints as he haithe in his custodie and do reforme his makinge of breade and do make the same in suche manor and order and as he is bounden by the Quenes Majesties Injunctions and as therin is prescribed and not otherwise sub pena juris etc. et sic dimiserunt eundem ab hac instantia.

[Ibid. ff. 186 v. et seq.]

O.d.c....gardianos de Easington. The bible and paraphraseis ar not fullie serviceable no collection for the pore, They have xxxs. in ther hands which was given to the pore mens boxe by one John Overton iii yeres sence which they deteine. [They confessed, and were remitted to the Ecclesiastical Commissioners.]

...c....gardianos...ecclesie de Kilnesey. They do reserve a holie water stock and two tabernacles.[1] the pore mens box is without locks ther is no collection for the pore, no Registre booke.... [Referred to the Ecclesiastical Commissioners.]

...c....gardianos...ecclesie de Skefflinge. Robt. Laughton a yere and a half sence did give a cloth to the Communion table not yet delivered, a holie water stock an image with a crosse that the Roode hanged on is reserved, an alter yet standing, the pulpit undecentlie kept, no collection for the pore, nor chest for the Registre boke.... [Confessed; remitted as above.]

...c. Robt. Mell vicarium de Holimme. He is also vicar of Withornsee and parson of All Halowes in Peaseholme (York)....

...c. (gardianos) de Holimme. Ther is no sufficient Bible no pulpit no collection for the pore nor pore mens boxe...dicunt that ther Bible to ther knowledg is sufficient for they ar not learned to examyne the same And they saie they have a place convenient for the pulpit in the said Church but no pulpit And that they have no pore mens boxe for that ther parishe is pore and nothing to put into the same.... [Ordered to reform these things and to certify by the Rural Dean of Holderness, and referred to the Commission.]

...c. (gardianos) de Withornsee. A holie water stock is reserved, no collection for the pore, no pore mans boxe, nor no sufficient

[1] A case for the Reserved Sacrament. Sometimes made to contain a Pix.

Registre...dicunt ther was a stock in the Churche which is defaced.... [The rest they confessed and were ordered to reform and to certify....]

...c. Edm. Bowes cler. vicarium de Owthorne. He omitteth his sermons, useth the Communion for the deade, suffereth the Chauncell to fall into decay and seeth not a sufficient Bible provided...domini monuerunt eum that he do enstruct the yowthe the cathechisme read diligentlie the homylies and the sermons discharged and diligentlie execute his office as he ought to do et sic domini dimiserunt eum ab hac instantia.

...c. Tho. Bellard cler. Curatum de Welwick. He haithe used somtimes to minister the Communion with ii persones and somtimes one contrarie etc....dicit eandem non esse veram savinge that somtimes he haithe ministred the Communion with ii persons. Et tunc domini propter ejus in ea parte contemptu suspenderunt eundem Bellard ab officii sui exercitio necnon a ministracione sacramentorum et sacramentalium infra diocesim Ebor. donec legitime fuerit restitutus....

...c. (gardianos) de Welwick. The Bible is not serviceable, ther is one Image of John two holie-water fatts pictures painctings a Cope with imageis, crosestaves candlesticks clappers [1] a gilden tabernacle [2] reserved and kept no wekelie collection for the pore...dicunt that ther was suche imageis and other superstitiowse monuments as is obiected of which thay had no knowledge at the Visitacion but nowe they ar burnt and defaced Et tunc domini monuerunt eos to bring in two witnesses to depose of the defacing of the said superstitious [monuments] die Lune post Purificacionis Marie And if they be not defaced to bring them in that day to the Court before the Commissioners for ecclesiasticall cawseis.

...c. (gardianos)...de Halsham. Ther is an alter standing ther is no collection for the pore the pore mens box is without locks ther is no Registre boke ther is a holiewater stock reserved.... [To the Commissioners.]

...c. Nich. Coke cler. Rectorem de Rosse. He is also parson of Bridgeford in Nottinghamshire, and being not resident at Rosse destributeth not the xlth parte....

[1] Used instead of bells in Holy Week.
[2] Perhaps not for 'gilt' or 'gilded', but 'belonging to a gild'.

30

...c. (gardianos) de Rosse. The holie water stocke pictures paintinges in the Rode lofte is reserved, ther is no collection for the pore, no pore mens boxe no Registre boke is kept and the Communion boke is rent and not serviceable...dicunt that the holie water stock is defaced and conveighed awaye they know not whether and that in dede ther ar paintinges in the rode lofte...domini monuerunt eos that they do reforme all the premisseis detected against them [before the Purification] and that they or thone of them do appere before the Quenes Majesties Commissioners for ecclesiasticall cawseis the Mondaie then next folowinge and bringe in certificate under the deanes hande of Holdernes of the reformation therof and further to do and receive as to justice shall apperteyne.

...c. (gardianos) de Burton Pidsey. The Communion boke is torne a holie water stock a cope with imags upon it vi banner staffes xi banner clothes an amese[1] the Sepulchre[2] and Pascall[3] is reserved.... [To deface and to appear before the Commissioners.]

...c. (gardianos) de Tunstall. They have no Paraphrases Ther ar pictures paintings and tabernacles reserved no pore mans box no collection for the pore nor no Registre boke...dicunt ther is no paintings nor tabernacles in ther church but all is defaced.... [Referred to the Commission.]

...c. Mich. Bolton clericum et Geo. Bolton parochie de Headon. They ar men which utterlie mislike the estate of Religion now established and never use to come to the church but do speake verie unseamelie words against Christes word and the ministers therof and disswade the people from the same.... [Did not appear; excommunicated.]

...c. Willm. Bolton eiusdem parochie. He useth to praie upon a Latine primer and did not communicate at Easter last...he receiveth into his howse Michaell Bolton and George Bolton two papists...dicit that they beinge his brethren naturall doth receive them as nature requireth into his howse and giveth a meales meat or night lodginge and not otherwise And he saiethe he had a primer

---

[1] A vestment worn on the neck: the amice.
[2] Probably the 'Easter Sepulchre'. Sometimes made portable and not part of the fabric of the church.
[3] Probably the great Paschal Candle.

in Latin and Englishe which when he perceived to be contrarie the lawes he cast away.... [Referred to the Commission.]

...c. (gardianos) de Preston. The Rode Loft is full of paincted pictures ther is no pore mens boxe nor no collection for the pore They have no Communion boke but a King Ed. boke...dicunt that the pore mans boxe haith indede no key, and they confesse they have no Bible of the last edicion And for the collection of the pore they saie it is executed dewly howbeit ther is some pictures in the rode loft.... [Referred to the Commission.]

[Ibid. f. 202 v.]

...c. (gardianos) parochie de Hombleton. Ther is paincted pictures upon the Rode lofte...dicunt that ther ar pictures in the Rode Lofte but they ar defaced... [ordered] that they or one of them do deface the said painctinges on thisside the feast of Candlemas next and certifie....

[Ibid. f. 203.]

...c. Joh. Sawle clericum...that he did minister the Communyon with beare...dicit that he in dede did minister the Communion with beare, but it was onelie for necessitie and want of wyne...domini...suspenderunt eundem Johannem Saule ab officii sui exercitio necnon a ministracione sacramentorum et sacramentalium infra aliquam parochiam sive capellam infra diocesim Ebor. donec legitime fuerit restitutus....

[This entry inserted here after several earlier formal entries of proceedings without a specified charge. Sawle was Vicar of Hatfield.]

[Ibid. f. 203 v.]

...c. (gardianos) de Garton. Ther is paincted pictures on the Rode Lofte no collection maid orderlie for the pore a Communion boke of King Edward all torne and rente...dicunt...that they have in dede no other boke but a boke of Kinge Edwards time But they saie they did not knowe but that it is sufficient for so they were let understand by ther curate....

[Ibid. f. 205.]

...c. (gardianos de) Riesse Ther is no pulpit no pore mans boxe the Bible is not sufficient but torne no paraphraseis a Communion for the deade...dicunt that they in dede at the Visitacion had no pulpit but sence they have maid a newe one and also sence that time have maid a pore mans boxe and they confesse ther Bible wanteth some leafes and the paraphraseis they can not get for moneye....

...c. (gardianos de) Siglesthorne. A Bible not of the largest volume the paraphraseis is torne and rente a Communion booke of King Edward time...dicunt that theye beinge not learned nor understandinge ther dewtie in this behalf did not perceive or know but that the Bible whiche they have alredie is sufficient howbeit they do confesse ther Communion boke is of Kinge Edwards edition.... [To reform and certify.]

[Ibid. f. 205 v.]

...c. Nich. Jackson Vicarium de Mapleton No sermons is maid the paraphraseis is torne and defaced the Registre boke is unperfectlie kept he did leave his Cure and roume awaye for the space of two yeres And he is a giver of evell example of lieffe to others a quareler a dronkerd and a player at tables.... [He denied and was ordered to make compurgation.]

[Ibid. f. 206.]

...c. Steph. Keed vicarium de Skipsey Ther is no sermons and the Registre boke is unorderlie kepte the second tome of homelies is torne ther is an old vestment the Bible is torne and rent.... [Admitted the vestment; emphatically denied all else except 'that the Bible is partlie torned'. Ordered to reform all before Candlemas and to certify.]

[Ibid. f. 209 v.]

...c. (gardianos de) Waghen. Ther is the pictures of Marie and John with a picture of Christe in the Rode Lofte a vestement of buschion[1] with ii tunicles of blewe for ii boyes a Superaltare a Lenten clothe[2] painted with a crosse nailes speres and suche like a stole a Fanyll[3] the Communion table gilded and painted with divers

[1] I.e. Fustian.
[2] More likely a frontal for an altar, or the Lenten Veil, than a veil for pictures, etc.
[3] I.e. Fanon or Maniple, a vestment worn on the left wrist.

33

Imageis the Bible torne in certain places, paincted pictures of Christofer and others on the churche walles the churche windowes ar in decaye...dicunt that ther is no Imags in ther churche but suche as be defaced except suche as be in the toppe of the churche which no man can tell what they be And what vestements and other superstitious monuments ar reserved for that the Churchewardens next before them haith them in ther custodie and will not deliver them but by an Inventorie And for the church windowes they ar in decaye Whereupon the judgeis did decre a lettre to the Deane of Holdernes to see the defaltes of that parishe reformed.

[Ibid. f. 210.]

...c. Joh. Lewson clericum vicarium de Swyne. He omittethe his ordinarie Sermons and sufferethe his vicaradge to fall into decay. [Ordered to reform.]

...c. (gardianos de) Swyne. The Bible not of the largeste volume the paraphrases is torne and lackethe almost v chapitors ther is no Collection for the pore, the churehwardens levie not the xiid. of suche as absent them selfs from the churche ther is a crosse of woode standinge over the northe Ile with a scutchon having the figure of v woonds and other superstitious things therin the body of the churche is in decay.... [To reform and certify.]

[Ibid. f. 211 v.]

...c. (gardianos de) Capellanie de Skirley. The holie water stone not defaced paincted pictures in the Rode Lofte, the collection for the pore not orderlie, the pore mans boxe not sufficient no paraphraseis the Bible not of the largest volume the Communion boke bene of King E. edition they lack the second tome of Homylies... dicunt that the fatte was defaced before the Visitacion And they confesse that ther is in dede some paintinges in ther church and that they have no other boke but one of King Edwards edicion And that they do want the first tome of homilies and paraphraseis of Erasmus.... [To reform before the Purification and to certify.]

These extracts from Holderness give perhaps one of the most brilliant pictures of the appearance of parish churches in the early part of Elizabeth's reign. It should be noted that the destruction of paintings and furniture had already begun and proceeded considerably.

5. Parallel Extracts for Comparison.
The Measure of Success after
Thirty Years

The usefulness of this comparison must be relative, and dependent upon the comparative reliability of Visitation Books. The volume indexed as R. VI. A. 14, of 1595 and 1596, is the last of this series of Visitation Books with the exception of R. VI. D. 1 for 1598, which is a book for the Archdeaconry of York only. This volume, R. VI. A. 14, covers an exceptionally large area of the whole province, and for this reason, and also because it is in much detail, may be taken to afford a fair indication of the success or failure of authority through the Visitation machinery, so far as Visitation Books by themselves can show this. The quotations given here are, therefore, as full as possible in the space available, and are chosen from those parts of the province which in earlier years had been found least satisfactory, namely the Archdeaconry of Nottingham (see 1567), the Deanery of Cleveland or the Deanery of Holderness, or the Diocese of Chester in all the Registry records.

At this point, it may be convenient to insert a comment on the reliability of these records, particularly as they affect the district of Holderness, although anything like a general note on the interpretation of Visitation documents cannot be attempted here. What is said at this point must refer also to material given on pp. 29, 30, and following. Holderness was a district then considered remote, and difficult of access by reason of poor communications, and was long prone to the survival of remains of the 'old religion' and to irregularities. It was a comparatively backward deanery, where the ecclesiastical measures of the time had slow effect, and is thereby the more suitable as an indication of the success or failure of those measures. When the records for 1567 are compared with those for 1568 and for 1595, remarkable changes are found, especially relating to the survival of 'monuments of superstition'. Indeed, the contrast between 1567 and 1568 is so strong as to look suspicious, and provoke the suggestions that the Visitation in the latter year was somewhat perfunctory, or that the churchwardens in that year had learned how to be more artful in concealing or not returning in their presentments what they wished to keep but the authorities wished to discover and to destroy. This is a matter of serious concern to the valuation of these records generally. Against the view suggested, it may be pointed out that the 1568 Book is a 'Comperta' Book, like that for 1567 but unlike that for 1595. It would be difficult to show that either of these Visitations of 1567 and 1568 was perfunctory, since the presentments in anything like completeness have not been preserved. The possibility of deliberate negligence by churchwardens cannot be ruled out. But such omission by churchwardens would require for success the connivance of practically the whole of the parishioners, since no more than one dissentient parishioner would be needed to lay the necessary information to the authorities. The danger of leakage was no doubt a deterrent in some cases. But assuming complete or almost complete connivance by the parish and the churchwardens working together, and a knowledge progressively more complete of what it was necessary to hide if the parishioners, or churchwardens, or both, wished to preserve their vestments, books, and other 'monuments', and especially if they had an incumbent who was sympathetically inclined to the old ways, it would not be difficult to return with impunity defective present-ments. More than one of the texts quoted here hint more or less plainly at such carelessness or connivance, as for example, the entry for Askrig on p. 152, or for Aysgarth on p. 225. On the other side, there was always the risk of the single informer, who might set in motion a formidable machinery of punishment which might be troublesome and even painfully severe. There is also another source of evidence which gives weight to the presumption that authority was in general successful and the Visitation records therefore to be taken, again in general, at something like their face value. This is found in the Books of the Ecclesiastical Commission of York. These show that in the period about 1570–80 the Commission reinforced the whole Visitation system of correction and of detection by setting up, first, small Commissions 'in eyre', and later, permanent local Commissions for chosen centres, with special juries and apparatus, who were to detect or to receive information from any source about those very offences which the churchwardens or parishioners have been supposed ready to conceal. There is no doubt at all that these Commissions and juries did their work thoroughly. Some of their original returns have survived, and these in addition to the record of their work which is found in the Act Books of the central Commission at York leave no doubt at all of one pertinent fact, that little indeed of 'monuments of superstition' was found by them which had escaped previous visitations. To this extent, the evidence is against anything like wholesale concealment, negligence or connivance, or perfunctory visitation. The truth, as usual, is probably somewhere between extremes; there was indeed concealment in the parishes; authority failed of complete success. But the advantage, in the long run, was so heavily on the side of authority that the evidence of the Visitation records may be taken in general as it stands without much subtraction or correction. A final assessment is made more difficult by the fact that we must compare 'Court' volumes with 'Comperta' volumes, and by the omissions which are inseparable from the nature of Visitation records.

The most serious of all these omissions is that which concerns 'recusancy'. There is a marked absence of reference to recusancy in the earliest Visitation

Books, but no indication what this means. There is no indication of the reason for the prevalence of recusancy in certain districts, as the Diocese of Chester or the Deanery of Cleveland; weakness in Bishop or Arch- deacon or even Rural Dean might have far-reaching effect here, and the uncertainty is increased by the absence of indication whether Papists and Puritans were both counted as recusants; both undoubtedly refused to attend their parish churches. The Visitation Books give no guidance here. There were definite centres of recusancy, some of which were due to the influence of a powerful local family; this is shown more clearly by the Commission Act Books than by the Visitation Books.

One further point may be advanced. The Visitations recorded in these texts were almost exclusively archiepiscopal. The Archbishop's Visitation, whether Primary or Ordinary, put a stop to all other Visitations for the time being. But in the year before, and in the years succeeding, the parishes were visited by their Archdeacons (or Prebendaries). Records of these visitations have survived but rarely, yet it might well be that the Archbishop in his Visitation found fewer presentments to correct, for example, of fornication, because the local offenders had been corrected recently in an archidiaconal visitation of some thoroughness.

The districts selected from the Presentment Book for 1595–6 are those with a general reputation for recusancy or 'superstition'.

A late Tudor Visitation Book, A.D. 1595 and 1596
[R. VI. A. 14, ff. 12–15 v.]

Maxfelde alias Macclesfelde Decanatus.

Moberley.	The perambulacion is not used in this parishe. Mr John Cawdwell parson ther who useth but sometymes to weare the surplesse.
	Two fornicators.
	They presente Hughe Cherrye for workinge on the Sabbothe day as hedginge and suche lyke and he dothe contynually use it beinge a riche man which is very offensive.
Wylmeslowe.	[3 men and a woman] alehousekepers kepe companyes drynkinge in theyr houses in tymes of devyne servyce.
	3 fornicators etc.

Alderley.	Edwarde Hollinshede parson ther dothe not usually weare a surplesse.
	John Bodon undertoke the reparacion of the decayes of theyr churche and hathe not re-payred the same Fra. Hobson and Tho. Dayne yonger are churchewardens.
	Ellynor Symcocke dyd not communicate at Easter last, a common scolde and a disquyeter of her neighbors.
	1 fornicator.
Macclesfelde.	Adam Padley and his wyfe do not come to the churche, and 18 named for moral offences.
Bosley.	They do not presente any thinge.
Syddington capella.	Robte. Drake maryd under a hedge by John Warde a straunger without any knowne lycence.
[Ibid. f. 13.]	
Chelforde capella.	They do not presente any thinge amisse.
Goosworthe capella.	2 fornicators.
Poynton Capella.	They presente nothinge.
Prestburye.	6 presentments of adultery or the like.
Marton Capella.	They present nothinge.
[Ibid. f. 13 v.]	
Dysley capella.	They wante a surplesse Mr. Loghe shoulde provyde one.
Chedley.	2 fornicators.
Motterame.	Margery Boothe wydowe comethe not to the churche. [Two persons] not knowne to be maryed, yet if they be maryed the same was without bannes askinge or lycence.
Stopforde.	7 named for adultery.
Northerdon.	They presente nothinge.
Taxall.	They do not presente any thinge.

Mydlewyche decanatus.

[Ibid. f. 14.]

Churcheholme capella.

They presente wydowe Carter, for not commynge to the churche.

Brereton.

John Thorley ther parson appeared not in the Visitacion, he is vycar of Byddulphe in Staffordeshyre where he is resydent, not knowne to be dispensed withall to holde twoo benefyces And theyr parsonage howses are in very greate decaye in the parsons defaulte.

1 fornicator.

Swettenham.

They presente the wyfe of Mr. Henry Manwayringe for not receyvinge the holly communyon att her parishe churche.

Lawton.

Mary Layton wyfe of Willm. Layton gent. a recusante.

Ther was a May pole sett uppe upon Lawton grene upon a Sabbothe or holly day, where a pyper and dyvers youthe were playinge, and dauncinge, the pypers name is Henry Dowse.

Goostree capella.

Eliz. Wylson wydowe dyd not communycate att Easter last past.

Eliz. Waynewryghte wyfe of Thomas Waynewryghte a scold and a disquyeter of her neighbours.

2 fornicators.

[Ibid. f. 14 v.]

Asburye.

The lady Egerton, Cycele Buckley my ladyes mayde do not come to the churche.

12 named for moral offences.

Willm. Walker presented for a dronkarde.

Ellenor Lees chylde was christened furthe of theyr parishe churche neither was she churched after her chyldbyrthe in the defaulte of John Moston of Damporte who harboured her.

Lytle Budworthe.	1 suspected adulterer.
Sanbache.	11 named for adultery etc.
	Robte. Anger was disobedyente to the churchewardens when they desyred him to come into the churche in tyme of devyne servyce.

[Ibid. f. 15.]

Whytegate.	The chauncell of theyr churche is in great decay in the defaulte of Mr. Holcrofte.
	2 fornicators.
Over.	Alyce Starkye wyfe of John Starkye esquyer and Amye her doughter have not come to the churche this last yeare.
	2 fornicators.
Warmyngchame.	The chauncell of theyr churche is not in good reparacion in the defaulte either of Willm. Lyngarde the parson or of Mr. Thomas Marburye farmer of the parsonage.
Davenham.	A married couple living asunder.

[Ibid. f. 15 v.]

Mydlewyche.	Mr. Randulphe Parker preacher ther appeared not in the Vysitacion[1] neither was ther shewed any lycence for him to preache in this province.
	17 named for adultery etc.

Part of Retford Deanery, A.D. 1596. [ff. 74–8]

[Ibid. f. 74.]

Southwheatley.	Nil.
Kirton.	Nil.

---

[1] One of the important purposes of Visitation was to make clergy exhibit their letters of Orders and of Presentation and Institution, and preachers or lecturers, readers, parish clerks and schoolmasters their licences.

Estdraiton.	Ther chauncell in decay in defalt of the Chapter of York.
	Tho. Lambe doth not repair to his parish church according to thinjunctions.
Harworth.	[Three men] received not at Ester last in ther parish church.
	John Turner for harboring a woman delivered of child.
	Barth. White and uxor Gillott for withholding clerk wages.

[Ibid. f. 74 v.]

Bole.	Nil.
Claworth.	Martin Stringer gent. and Eliz. his wife refused to communicate in ther owne parish this last Ester.
Blith.	John Scrobie a notorious recusant.
	John Pullen of Stirropp hath maried his owne wifs sister.
	Robt. Wright excommunicate for not returnyng his pennance.[1]
	John Nailer deteyneth[2] xxiiiis. given to the church and pore.
Westmarkham.	The Chauncell of the church and ther vicaredg houses are not in good repair.
Elkesley.	The Chauncell and vicaredg howses are in great decay.
	Stephen Modie vicar ther.
Welley.	[Blank.]
Walkringham.	John Townend excommunicate for fornication with Dorothie Dow. She is penanced.

[1] When the Court imposed a penance, the offender was always ordered to bring back at a stated day a certificate signed by the vicar and wardens of the church where the penance was done. See p. 50, n. 1.

[2] Probably as executor of a will which made a bequest to the poor.

Sturton.	Ther decaied chauncell is to be repaired by the Chapter of York.
	Robt. Fitzwilliams gent. for inclosing part of the Church yerd to his owne use.

[Ibid. f. 75.]

Westretford.	Grace Scott widow doth not communicate as she ought to do she is a scold and disquieter of her neghbors.
	Robt. Golland thelder liveth not with his wife.
Tuxford.	1 excommunicate 1 fornicatrix.
	Katherine Reynes an excommunicate person did not receive at Ester last.
Carbarton.	Mr. Barton ther vicar weareth not the surples at any time.
Clarebrough.	Robt. Harison liveth from his wife.
Scrobie.	Nil.
Littlebrough.	2 fornicators.
Headon.	2 fornicators.

|Ibid. f. 75 v.]

Sawnby.	2 fornicators.
Messen.	Ther chauncell is in great decay. Willm. Hill fermer of the parsonage is thought to be bound to repair it.
Rampton.	John Rayner ther vicar doth not use the signe of the crosse in Baptisme.
	Ther parsonage houses be in great decay Mr. Clayton parson.
	Ther Bible is in some ruyne. They want one Tome of homilies, a psalter and injunctions.[1]
	1 fornicatrix.
Westdraiton.	Nil.

[1] The Queen's Injunctions of A.D. 1559.

Bevercots. Ther Chauncell is not in good repair.

Fra. Chapman ther vicar is not resident nether distributeth to the pore.

Misterton. 8 named for fornication or suspicion of it.

1 suspected bigamist. 2 common drunkards.

Simon Hall excommunicate being presented for not mending a glasse window.

[Ibid. f. 76.]
Nortoncuckney. 2 fornicators.

Bawtrie. Ther chauncell windowes decaied in defalt of Sir Jervas Clifton heires.

2 men refuse to pay cessements. 2 fornicators.

Ollerton. Willm. Gibson and his wife live not together.

Edwinstow. Ther church is not sufficiently repaired.

Jo. Chadwick for railing against the church-wardens in the Church and churchyerd.

Alex. Motley refuseth to contribute to the repair of the church.

Robt. Collingham practizeth phisick and chirurgie by what auctoritie they know not.

4 women stand excommunicate.

[Ibid. f. 76 v.]
Egmanton. Chris. Sandburie, Margt. Thawke vidua fence not ther part of the churchyerd.

1 adulterer.

Northwheatley. Edwd. Gowland and Marie his wife drunkerds.

3 adultery etc.

Walesby. Ther chauncell is in decay in defalt of the Earle of Shrewsburie.

Wilfrey Hurst and Cuth. Both for chiding in the church.

5 women named as common scolds.

Laneham.	Willm. Ellis for seldome comyng to church.
Awsterfeild.	Anne Milnes uxor Edwardi did not communicate at Ester last.
[Ibid. f. 77.]	
Northleverton.	Nil.
Gameston.	Mr. Birkhead ther parson did church a fornicatrix and suffered hir to depart unpunished.
	Rowland Haworth servant to Mr. Tho. Markham is defamed with [her].
Boughton.	Ther Chauncell is in decay in defalt of the Church of Southwell.
	Willm. Ward refuseth to contribute to the cessement made by common assent.
Estretford.	Peter Topcliff and Gregorie Kirchivall his servant did not communicate.
	Ric. Ibatson an excommunicate person came to the church and railed of John Mason a churchwarden who willed him to depart.
	Willm. Oxenford his wife did not communicate since Ester was xii monethes. she is of evill report for adulterie.
	2 suspected adulterers.
Mattersey.	Mrs. Nevile widow hath not communicated this twelve monethes.
[Ibid. f. 77 v.]	
Heyton.	Alice Daniell uxor Thome is a swerer and´a disquieter of hir neghbors.
	[Three men] did take parcell of the belframe and imploied it to ther owne use.
Estmarkham.	Nil.
Apesthorp.	Nil.

Askham.	Ther Chauncell is decaied in defalt of the Deane and Chapter of York.
	Ric. Swift for disquieting his neghbors.
Worsopp.	Mr. John Long refuseth to contribute towards the repair of the church.
Carleton.	2 women excommunicate persons.
Grove.	Nil.
Everton.	[Two men] fence not ther part of the church-yerd.
	Charles Sheaperd wife liveth from hir husband.

[Ibid. f. 78.]

Fynyngley.	Nil.
Bilsthrop.	Nil.
Stokham.	Nil.

Visitation of the Chapter of Southwell [ff. 86 and 86 v.]

[Ibid. f. 86]

The aunswere of Mr. Grace to tharticles exhibitid in his Gracs Visitation.

To the first article nil.

2. They have books necessarie and a communion Cupp but other ornaments they want.

3. They want two vicars [1] of ther number by reason of late removing of two.

4. Residence is kept by Mr. Cooper and Mr. Claiton.

5. Thomas Barker one of the vicars was latelie convicted of fornication and punished for the same.

6. Nil.

7. Ther vicars and singing men have often served without ther chorall habite.

[1] Here means Vicars Choral, whose chief function it was to sing services for and in the place of their respective Canons or Prebendaries who employed them, in their Cathedral or Collegiate church.

8. Ther Chapters and capitular acts are orderlie done and kept.

9. Nil.

10. The greater number of ther prebendaries do not preach ther appointed sermons, by them selfs nor others. He nameth not who they be that have offended.

[Ibid. f. 86 v].

Capitulum Suthwell. Mr Copers answers

1. He answereth affirmativelie.

2. That church hath Bibles and Books of Common Prayer and a Communion Cupp but no Coops[1] or other ornaments.

3. They now want some vicars chorall, which they are desirous to interteyne so they be of honest lif. Vide originale.

4. Residence is kept by him and Mr. Cleiton.

5. Sir Thomas Barker one of ther vicars hath bene latelie convicted and punished for fornication.

6. Nil.

7. Ther vicars and singing men have sometimes bene in the Quear at service without surples but not in any contempt.

8. Capitular acts are dulie kept.

9. He knoweth not what to answere.

10. Ther is great negligence of prebendaries absent for preaching sermons.

Typical entries for York Churches. [ff. 99 and 99 v.]

[Ibid. f. 99.]

St. Nicholes withoute Walmegate.   Peter Vessay pays not the clarke wagies viz. xviii d.

All Halowes in Northstreete.   Brian Wharton did not communicate at Easter beinge oute of charitie.

Geo. Colyer and Willm. Raynowlds did not communicate at Easter.

[1] I.e. Copes.

St. Diones in Walme-
gaite.

Isabell Lee wife of Doctor Lee Alice Carlill recusantes excommunicate.

1 adulterer.

[Six men] excommunicate for not payinge there duties to the churche.

Miles Gray excommunicate for not coomynge to churche.

John Plumpton excommunicate for woords againste his neighbours in the churche.

Verie manie persons presented for not payinge there lays to the churche. There names ar contayned in a schedule annexed to the presentmente. Vide schedula.

[Ibid. f. 99 v.]
St. Georgies
    Nayburne.

Joane Palmes wife of John Palmes esquire do not coom to churche nor communicate.

Geo. Palmes esquire Henrie Mayson Anne his wife Marie Launder John Thornes schoolemr. non communicantes.

St. Helenes.

Presentements by John Sim.

James Bartrame beinge churchewarden dothe kepe a servante excommunicate.

Peter Waslin kepes a woman in his house that coomes not to churche nor communicates. [And three others, for the same offence.]

St. Elens in Stain-
gaite.

Edeth Sharpe wife of Richarde Sharpe a recusante.[1]

Roger Gillote behinde with his cesmente viz. viiid. by John Symes reporte.

John Sim harbored twoo fornicators and suffred theme to departe unpunished.

_____

[1] See footnote on p. 2.

St. Martins in Micklegate	Anthonie Hartefurthe there parson is non residente and maikes not distribucion to the poore.
	Mr. John Sawre remaynynge at command with Mr. Alderman Richardson a recusante.

Clevelande Decanatus [ff. 148–55]

[Ibid. f. 148.]

Stokeslay.   Nil.

Welberie.   2 recusants. 2 suspected fornicators.

Egton.   35 recusants, two couples of them 'not knowne to be maried'.

[Ibid. f. 148 v.]

Whitbie.   32 recusants, 4 non-communicants.

Chris. Staynhows dothe commonlie receive recusantes there ar dyvers metinges at his house and it is suspected soom preeste is thereaboutes.

James Hebburne kepethe a schoolemr. a popishe recusant withoute licens.

Chris. Marsingall butchar usethe to sell meate in service tyme.

[Ibid. f. 149.]

John Boyes and Chris. Blenkarne kepe open shops and sell marchandize in service tyme.

Widowe Lelome ailwife suffers drinkers in her house in service tyme. Widowe Willie for the lyke.

6 presented for adultery etc. 1 scowlde.

2 non-communicants, 7 fornicators.

Kirklevington.   John Gibson for not payinge his clarke wage.

Robte. Dosser refusethe to pay schoole wagies.

Robte. Walkar he repayres not his parte of the churche wall.

48

[Ibid. f. 149 v.]

Huton Rudbie.	3 recusants. 1 fornicator. 2 excommunicate.
Skelton.	12 recusants. 11 named for fornication.
Brotton.	The Chancell is in decay.
	7 recusants. 1 non-communicant at Easter. 1 fornicator.

[Ibid. f. 150.]

Eshedell syde capella.	8 recusants.
Danbie.	7 obstinate recusants. 3 recusants who 'have not communicated this laste yere'.
	Willm. Phillips dothe kepe his childe frome baptisme. He will pay no cesmentes to the chappell cessed by his neighbours.
	1 suspected of incontinency.
Hinderwell.	5 recusants. 11 fornicators and two harbourers.

[Ibid. f. 150 v.]

	3 excommunicate, and 6 who 'do not pay there cesments due to the churche'.
Ingleby subter Arneclife.	Nil.
Myddleton cum Hilton.	1 recusant.
Ugglebarbie.	4 recusants, apparently all in one household.
Ormesbie.	The chancell is in greate decay which is verie hurtefull and offensyve to the churche.
	Willm. Wilcocke is slacke in coomynge to the churche, he did not communicate at Easter and as thay thinke is excommunicate. 2 fornicators.

[Ibid. f. 151.]

Kildaile.	4 fornicators. 1 scold.
Westerdaile.	1 non-communicant at Easter.
Ayton.	4 adulterers.
	John Topham for not payinge his cesmente towards the buyinge of a Byble.

Loftehouse.	5 obstinate recusants in one family. 2 recusants. 1 fisherman an excommunicated recusant.
Inglebie under Grenehawe.	Nil.

[Ibid. f. 151 v.]

Hawnebie.	Nil.
Wylton.	2 non-communicants. Tho. Thomson reaped his corne upon the Sabothe day. 3 fornicators. 1 harbourer.

[A marginal note says of one of the non-communicants: '5 Julii 1596 comparuit personaliter dictus Bulmer who offered himselfe redy and willinge to receive the Communion Unde Mr. Joh. Benet LL.D. iniunxit ei to receive at the next Communion at Wilton et ad certificandum[1] sub manibus ministri ibidem...'.]

Kirkebie in Clevelande.	2 men and 2 women slanderers of their neighbours. 4 fornicators.
Aislabie.	1 recusant.

[Ibid. f. 152.]

Acclame.	1 recusant, 1 who refuses to pay his cessments, 1 railer against her neighbours.
Seamar.	1 excommunicate, 2 suspected of adultery.
Marske.	2 fornicators.
Eston.	Ther chancell is in greate decay. 2 excommunicates.
Upleatham.	6 fornicators.

[1] In certain cases in the Courts, where the judge ordered particular action by the defendant, as to communicate on a certain day, or to do a certain penance on named days and in certain places, the sentence usually ended with an order to certify of the performance of the act or penance ordered, confirmed by the signature of one or more witnesses, of whom the incumbent of the parish was generally one. Failure to bring in this certificate at the appointed time was 'not returning his penance'.

[Ibid. f. 152 v.]

Wharleton.

The Byble is not sufficiente.

4 named for adultery. 8 recusants.

Easington.

2 non-communicants at Easter. 3 named for suspicion of adultery.

The entries for the rest of this Deanery show little variation from the above.

Eastriddinge Arch[idiaconatus], Holdernes. [ff. 168–75 v.]

[Ibid. f. 168.]

Attenwicke.

1 fornicator.

Lisset capella parochie de Befurth.   Nil.

Northferibie.

The chancell is in greate decay in defalte of Mr. Tho. Crumpton.

2 fornicators.

Tho. Applebie of Feribie occupies the goods of Chris. Thorneton and Judeth his wife dyinge intestate, withoute auctoritie.

Skecklinge cum Burstewicke.

2 recusants. 2 non-communicants. 3 suspected of incontinency etc. 1 drunkard.

Raphe Jeffrayson parishe clarke is not sufficiente to discharge his place.

[Ibid. f. 168 v.]

Rosse.

2 fornicators.

Geo. Nightingale refuseth to pay clarke wagies.

Barmeston.

2 living suspiciously together.

Gowsell.

2 suspected of fornication.

Sutton.

3 suspected of fornication.

Ottringham.

2 fornicators.

Henrie Wallis for not payinge his lay to the churche viz. iis.

[Ibid. f. 169.]

Dunnyngton.

Edw. Donkon clarke there curate servethe twoo cures viz. Dunnyngton and Nunkelinge. so he is lycensed.

Kirkellay.

Robt. Rysom of Willarbie received the Communion at Easter beinge excommunicate.

Mris. Anne Ellarkar wife to Mr. Raphe Ellarkar esquire James Ellarkar gent. of Hawdingeprice did not communicate at Easter.

Ric. Lilfurthe of Anlabie a common prophaner of the Sabbothe day beinge a bakar he travels to the mill and to Hull to sell breade on the Sabboth.

Nicholes Gallaway a sleper in service tyme.

Edmunde Myles parishe clarke dothe not behave him selfe dutifullye in his office.

2 fornicators and 1 drunkard.

The churche yarde is undecentlie used with geese and swyne in defalte of Mr. John Harrison.

Elsternewicke.

Nil.

Hollim.

There is a faire kepte in the churche yarde once a yere and so haithe bene tyme oute of mynde.

[Ibid. f. 169 v.]

Owthorne.

The chancell is in utter ruyne and decay and verie lyke to fall and to endanger a great parte of the bodie of the churche. Sir Chris. Hilyard fermer of the tiethes of Frodingham Chris. Jobson proctor [1] of Runswell John Constable proctor of Waxam Roger Harlande proctor of Owthorne all which townes ar in the parishe of Owthorne.

---

[1] See footnote on p. 27.

2 fornicators. 3 drunkards.

Chris. Hancocke Willm. Richardson and Nicholes Colman churchewardens in anno 1594 did not maike there accompte of a cesmente by theme gathered towchinge a bell. Robte. Matcham Marke Russes Willm. Burdas do not pay there tax towards the mending of a bell.

Willm. Richardson withhoulds frome the parishe iis. beinge parte of a cesmente laide for the churche.

Nich. Colman Chris. Hancocke Willm. Richardson churchewardens in anno 1594 withoulds frome Edmunde Jackson vis. iiiid. and frome Willm. Farebarne xs. which thay disbursed aboute the castinge of a bell.

Rowthe.

John Thomson of Frodingham for denying to pay an assesmente to the poore duringe his abode at Rowthe.

1 fornicator.

[Ibid. f. 170.]
Kayingham.

The chancell is in decay and so haithe bene manie yeres paste it is to be repayred by the L.Arch. of Yorke his Grace it haithe bene manie tymes heretofore presented in severall Visitacions withoute anie reformacion. The decayes yerelie increase and oneles the same be spedelie repayred it will fall to the grounde and so require greate chargies to be builded upp again which may be saved by lookinge to it in tyme. Thay humblie desire soom order for the survay and amendemente thereof.

Custance Thomson did not communicate at Easter she coomes not to the churche. 3 persons excommunicate.

Willm. Thomson haith not decentlie covered his wyves grave.

Mr. Bethell for not paying his lay havinge goods within the lordeship of Kayingham.

Willm. Thomson clarke is not sufficiente to serve.

2 incontinent persons.

Ryes.   Nil.

[Ibid. f. 170 v.]
Trinities in Hull.   John Hewit coomes but seldoom to the churche. John Mawde excommunicate these 2 or 3 yeres. 2 fornicators.

Awdbroughe.   Dorothie Williamson wife of James Williamson an obstenate recusante. 2 fornicators.

Swyne.   4 persons stand excommunicate. 8 fornicators.

[Ibid. f. 171.]
Wawne alias
  Waughen.   No hospitalitie nor anie contribucion to the poore in defalte of Mr. Palmer chancelor or Mr. Paylar his fermer.

The chancel is in decay in defalte ether of Mr. Palmer or Mr. Paler his fermer.

Geo. Martin negligente in coomynge to churche.

Willm. Maykins suffers certain persons to drinke in his house in service tyme.

Geo. Martin for leadinge of wood on the Sabothe day in tyme of devine service.

Laur. Smithe and Isabell his wife and Isabell Harrison did not communicate at Easter at their churche.

Willm. Kirkebie yoongar denyes to pay his cesmente to the reparacion of the churche.

Ric. Compton intermeddles with Margarete Kirkemans goods withoute auctoritie.

Willm. Kirkebie the yoongar for drinkinge in the Ailhouse in prayer tyme.

6 for adultery etc.

[Ibid. f. 171 v.]

Marton.

John Wells Margarete his wife and Willm his servante recusantes.

Emote Wells and Richarde Wells did not communicate at Easter.

Eastehaitfeeld capella parochie de Sigles-thorne.

Thay had but one sermon the laste yere in defalte of Mr. John Seele ther parson.

The chancell is in decay in defalte of the said Mr. Seele.

Eliz. Daykins non communicante.

The bodie of the churche or chappell is in decay.

Tho. Hancocke Wm. Reay gardiani.

Sculcotes.

Nil.

Wethernewicke.

Geo. Jackson a common drunkarde and disquieter of his neighbours.

Easington.

Mr. Johns vicar dothe not signe children in baptisme with the signe of the cros.

he usethe not the perambulacion in the rogacion weeke.

he cited dyvers men to Yorke contrarie to the order of lawe.

he kepes the register booke in his owne house contrarie to order.

he dothe not were a surples usuallye.

[Blank] Cockes wife of John Cockes did scoulde with her neighbours.

Willm. Brownes wife kepte companie in her house in tyme of devine service.

[Ibid. f. 172.]

John Nunyngton dothe use the ailhouse comonlie.

Mr. Joanes dothe use cardes with disquietnes in the ailhouse.

John Shipley Willm. Applebie and 3 or 4 moe plaid at bowles on Whitsonday in the churche yarde.

Beforde.	Nil.
Marflete.	[*Blank.*]
Siglesthorne.	Mr. Seele there parson is not residente nor kepes hospitalitie.

He haithe 2 benefices Siglesthorne and Bolton juxta Bollande.

One of the syde Iles is in decay in defalte ether of Mr. Archedeacon Remyngton or Mr. Hillarie Daykins.

Tho. Robinson now of Bransburton and laite of Catfosse refusethe to pay his cesmente to the repaire of the churche and other necessarie uses of the parishe beinge xxiii d.

Thornegumbalde. Nil.

[Ibid. f. 172 v.]

Hilston.

The chancell windowes ar in decay in defalte of Mr. John Dringe there parson.

Henrie Segs Robte. Barret and Willm. Meedlay for brawlinge in the churche yarde This Segs was the begyner of bothe the quarels.

Drypoole.

Anne Harrison wife of Ric. Harrison and Agnes Atkinson scoulded in the churche yarde to the offence of the congregacion.

Bransburton.	2 fornicators.
Hesell.	5 fornicators and 3 scolds.

[Ibid. f. 173.]

Garton.	Nil.
Sudcotes.	Nil.
Nunkeelinge.	Thay had but twoo sermons in defalte of Mr. Raphe Creswell.
	Eliz. Creswell wife of Raphe Creswell a recusant.
	Raphe Creswell non communicante.
	Walter Errington did not communicate at Easter.
	1 fornicator.
Wyesteade.	3 fornicators.
Tunstall.	3 suspected of incontinence.

[Ibid. f. 173 v.]

St. Maries in Hull.	Nil.
Hompton.	Nil.
Burton Pidsay.	Thay had but twoo sermons this laste yere Hugo Martin vicar.
	2 suspected of incontinencie before mariage.
Catwicke.	Nil.
Sprotlay.	Jane Cliffe do not coom to churche nor communicate.
	2 fornicators before marriage.
Humbleton.	Elin Smithe wife of Robte. Smithe for scouldinge with Walter Gartham the quenes officer and others.
	2 fornicators.
Pattrington.	Mr. Humphrey Hall parson dothe use huntinge in the feelde dyvers tymes. 20 July 1596 Mr. Jo. Benet LL.D. iniunxit eidem Mr. Hall not to frequent huntinge offensively sub pena juris.

The chancel in decay in his defalte. Monitus est...per Mr. J. Benet ad reparandum cancellum citra festum S. Michaelis et ad certificandum....

2 fornicators.

[Ibid. f. 174.]

Leaven.

Tho. Greneburie and Anne his wife Fra. Scott wedowe did not communicate at Easter.

3 fornicators accused.

Wethernesay.

The chancell in greate decay.

8 fornicators.

Preston.

Mich. Coonstable and Marie his wife non communicants.

5 suspected or accused of adultery etc.

[Ibid. f. 174 v.]

Mappleton.

Thay had no sermons this laste yere in defalte of Mr. Archdeacon Remyngton.

Kilnesay.

2 fornicators 1 harbourer.

Halsham.

Willm. Moore clarke there parson is not residente kepes no hospitalitie distributes not to the poore.

The chancell verie ruynous in his defalte.

Janete Munkman an ould wedowe a recusante excommunicate.

4 named for fornication.

Northfrodingham.

2 non-communicants. 5 suspected of incontinence etc.

The charge against Joh. Tomson for assessment at Rowthe is repeated here.

[Ibid. f. 175.]

Wellwicke.

1 woman recusant. 4 fornication. 2 excommunicate.

Bilton.

Nil.

Hornesay.

4 accusations of fornication, 2 before marriage.

Ulroome.

Nil.

Skipsay.	The chancell is in greate decay. Mr. Miles Sands fermer of the parsonage.
Hedon.	Stephen Harries stands excommunicate for recusancie.
	2 fornicators and 2 before marriage. 1 scold.
	John Colman abused the preacher and church-wardens.
[Ibid. f. 175 v.]	
Wyeton.	Nil.
Riston.	2 fornicators.
Skirlay.	2 fornicators.
	Raphe Harpham led pease on a Soonday in the after noone.
Pawle.	The chancell is in greate decay.
Skefflinge.	Tho. Wintringham did not communicate at Chrestenmes but did mocke and flowte at them that did receive. reported by Mr. Jones but not sene by them.
	Thay wante a Byble. Jo. Spilsbie Wm. Howdell Chris. Smithe gardiani.
	James Flinton for playinge at cards in service tyme at Ric. Thwaites house.
	Joh. Sheparde denyes to pay the clarke wagies.
	4 named for adultery etc. and 1 harbourer.

The most surprising reformation in this volume is at Ripon, shown on the last folio of the book, ff. 183 and 183 v. Apart from eight recusants in Ripon itself and the immediate neighbourhood, three scolds and one fornicator and one who 'suffers unlawfull persons to drinke at unlawfull tymes in his house in the nighte to the disquietinge of his neighboures', the town had nothing to show, and even in the Church, where formerly there had been so much amiss, the only faults were 'they wante a surples in the churche', and 'the bodie of the churche in decay', for both of which 'Robte. Dawson fermar' was named as responsible. There were four men 'that absente theme selves oute of the churche in tyme of sermon', and one 'bakar' 'kepinge market in tyme of service and sermon'.

The only marked increase which the series of books can show is in recusancy; in all else, even in plurality and in the neglect of the chancel by the farmer, there is improvement.

CHAPTER II

THE CHURCH

1. THE CHURCH AND THE SERVICES

(a) *Whitewashing the Church*

A.D. 1571 Archbishop Grindal's Injunctions to the Laity, No. 5 [Reg. Grindal, f. 157 v.]

ITEM that the churchewardons shall see that in their churches and chappels all aultars be utterlye taken downe and clene removed even to the foundacon and the place where they stood paved, and the wall whereunto they ioyned whited over and maide uniforme with the reste so as no breache or rupture appeare....

A.D. 1586 [Visitation Book, R. VI. A. 9, f. 172 v.]

Almonbury: '...the Chauncell is not whyted nor paved in suche decent sort as it ought to be....'

But this was not entirely a post-Reformation use. A Vicar of Hutton Cranswick in 1548 (Reg. S.V.), after ordering 'Dirige and Messe' for himself, left ten shillings 'for weshinge and whitinge of oure Churche within'.

(b) *The Floor strewn with Straw or Rushes*

A.D. 1583 [Ecclesiastical Commission, Act Books, R. VII. A. 10, f. 229.]

The churchwardens of Bolton Percy were commanded to certify this day of there repairing nedeful places in the body of there church and of amending stalls and strawing the church with rushes.

A.D. 1594 [Visitation Books, R. VI. A. 13, f. 90 v.]

Wadworth: 'Contra Mich. Cockson gen. proprietarium Rectorie. He refuseth to deliver strawe for strawinge the churche which of anciente tyme the fermars have usuallye founde and provyded for that purpose.' [He was enjoined to deliver it as usual.]

20 May 1524   Lease of Rectory of Burton Pidsea   [R. As. 16a/5.]

...and all the said terme shall fynd strewyng accustomyd to the churche by all tymes accustomyd....

A.D. 1728   [Visitation Corrections, R. VI. E. 70.]

Petition from the Vicar and churchwardens of Gargrave to the Archdeacon of York:

...We beg leave to set forth to you that there has been an ancient immemorial custom within our parish for the housholders thereof yearly to bring or send rushes into the Church for the people to kneel upon in time of divine service, and to acquaint you that this custom has within a very few years last past dwindled away by degrees into an entire disuse, by reason of which there is now scarce any thing at all within the seats of the Church but the bare ground itself: We believe this to be the cause of a great many people's not behaving themselves in such decent sort as becomes the worship of God, and also of many more absenting themselves from the Church in the winter season.

(c) Forms of Service

3 Feb. 1563/4   [Ecclesiastical Commission, Act Books, R. VII. A. 1, f. 97.]

In causa inter Joh. Webster clericum contra Chris. Jewetson de Bubwithe.....in tyme of devyne service when Joh. Webster clerke had red the Epistle and Gospell and red the Acte of Parliament published and set furthe for the reliefe of the poore and was mindinge to have gone forwards with the redinge of an homelie....

9 Feb. 1567/8   [Ibid. R. VII. A. 3, f. 175 v.]

...c. Joh. Doddinge...of Eastrington. The said Doddinge is detected to be within orders [1] and that he refuseth to procede and further that he is of corrupte judgement in matters of religion and that he useth at the recitall of the Commaundements to say Lorde have mercy upon us and encline our harts to kepe thy lawe and not theise lawes puttinge a difference as it were betwixte the said wordes and teacheth his scolers to do the lyke and he is suspected to have in his chamber certeyne olde books and many other monuments of idolytry and superstition....

[1] I.e. ordained Deacon but not Priest.

A.D. 1575   [Visitation Books, R. VI. A. 5, f. 61 v.]

Siggeston: 'They have not the recitinge of the Lords praier the articles of the belief and the tenne commaundements after the Gospell.'

[Ibid. f. 77 v.]

Cheryburton: 'Their minister (Tho. Davie not licenced here) serveth the cure also at Etton and maketh such hast that he omitteth the reading of the homilies the recitall of the x commaundements the Crede and the Lords praier on Sondaies and holiedaies when they have no sermons.'

[Ibid. f. 78.]

Thomas Davye ther Curate doth not reade the threatenninge against synners in their churche neither doth he teache the youthe of their parishe the Cathechisme.

A.D. 1567   [Ibid. R. VI. A. 2, f. 1 v.]

Gringleye: '...c. Jac. Burton clericum Vicarium de Gringleye... according to the Quenes majesties Injunctions in that behalf haethe not maid his quarterlie sermons in his said churche and that he haithe not disswaded his parishoners from the usurped powre or auctoritie of the Busshope of Rome.'

[Ibid. f. 9 v.]

...c. Chris. Graunger Vicarium de Cuckney... [enjoined] that he shall iiii times in the yere declare to the parishoners that all forren powers ar justely taiken away.

[Ibid. f. 137 v.]

...c. Jac. Laiton vicarium de Helmesleye He haithe not discharged his quarterlie sermons nor never at anye sermon or exhortacion maid unto his parishoners haithe perswaded them against the usurped auctoritie of the busshope of Rome. [He denied the charge.]

(d) *Perambulations*

27 May 1578 [Ecclesiastical Commission, Act Books, R. VII. A. 9, f. 155.]

...c. Roger Menithorpe clerk Curate of Old Malton...respondet that he went in the perambulacion upon the Ascention daie and did say gospells at certen stations in the feilds whiche he will amend and not so use hereafter....

[Visitation Books, R. VI. A. 13, f. 168 v.]

Skeckling: '...c. Oliver Richardson. He detains viiis. which was geven yerelie to suche as wente the perambulacion in the parishe for drinke. he occupieth the land oute of which it was geven...ostendit quasdam cartas sive evidencias quibus visis et inspectis dominus dimisit eundem nisi gardiani hanc causam in Curia Consistorii contra (eum) prosequi voluerint.'

(e) *Altar Table*

3 Oct. 1564 [Ecclesiastical Commission, Act Books, R. VII. A. 1, f. 172.]

The Rector of Harswell and one of the churchwardens certified 'that they have clensyd the place where the alter stode and sette uppe a decent table etc.'

[Ibid. R. VII. A. 5.]
Attached to f. 147, which is of 5 Oct. 1570, a small slip of paper, with:

Churchwardens of Richmond. [Names of four men.]

There wanteth there a communion table, and use for it an old chyste, and the table of commaundementes....

The churchewardens of Massam and Kyrkbye.

At Kyrkbye all the monuments of idolatrye be undefaced and the crosse standing in the roodelofte and no byble neither other bookes that are apointed to be in the churche.

At Massam there be divers things lacking in the churche to wytt a Communion table and certayne bookes for the churche and neither punishment nor presentment for those who come not to the churche at all in both the parishes....

(f) *Covering for the Communion Table*

A.D. 1575 [Visitation Books, R. VI. A. 5, f. 9.]

Fuyston: 'They want the paraphrases of Erasmus, and a coveringe of buckrome for the Communyon table whiche heretofore hath bene founde alwaies by the howse of St Robertes nighe Knaresburghe before the suppression of the same beinge persons [1] ther and now come to the Quenes Majestyes hands who theye saye ought to prepaire and provide the same.'

[Ibid. f. 40.]

Brafferton: 'They want Erasmus his paraphrase and a decent coveringe of buckrame or silke for the Communion table, and a psalter. and locks for the cheste.'

Similar entries for Bolton Percy, Rufforth, Horton, and Bossall.

[Ibid. f. 23 v.]

Calverley: 'The pulpitte and the clothe for the Communion table ar not in decent order but in decaie. Gardiani...ar sent for.'

The references to this matter in the Visitation Book for Chester in 1578 are numerous and explicit, e.g.:

[Ibid. R. VI. A. 7, f. 38 v.]

Eccles cum capella de Ellenburgh. They have no coveringe for the cleane kepinge of the Communyon table.

One of the parishes in this Visitation gives almost a compendium of the possible charges against a parish:

[f. 29 v.]

Weverham: 'They want a Communion booke a Bible of the largest volume the first tome of the homilies.

Ther is in the church an altare standing undefaced.

There lacketh a lynnon clothe and a coveringe for the Communyon table a chest for the poore and keping of the Register in The parishoners refuse the perambulacion.

---

[1] I.e. parsons, or rectors.

The people will not be staied from ringinge the bells on All Saints daie.

They frequent alehowses in service tyme.

Great talkinge used in the churche.

No levyinge for the poore of thabsents [1] from the churche.

Morres Daunces and rishe bearings used in the Churche.

Jane [*blank*] an old noonne [2] is an evell woman and teacheth false doctrine.

They refuse to communicate with usuall breade.

None come to the Communion iii tymes a yeare.

They refuse to bringe in ther yowth to be cathechised.

Crosses ar standinge in the churche yeard.

The Vicar weareth not the surplesse.

[Five moral offences.]

There is a pece of an altare standing in Mr. Irelands quier.' [3]

(g) *No Chalice*

A.D. 1575   [Ibid. R. VI. A. 5, f. 39 v.]

Topcliffe: 'They want a Communion cuppe....'

[Ibid. f. 88.]

Harpham: 'They want a silver cupp but they meane to provide one before Lammas next.'

[Ibid. f. 18 v.]

Gargrave: 'Brian Robinson had a chalice and a pixe of silver which was the parishes, and it was never restored by him again.'

---

[1] Those absent.   [2] Nun.

[3] A side chapel or part of the quire or transept used and reserved as a private pew by Mr Ireland and his family. A well-established practice in Tudor times. The right to hold such a pew could not be based legally on descent in a particular family, but on occupation of a particular house combined with an obligation to keep the pew and 'quier' in good repair. This was distinct from the right to occupy a pew in the chancel, which was reserved properly to the lay rector, or, sometimes, to founder's or benefactors' kin.

(h) *Wafers*

A.D. 1571 [Ecclesiastical Commission, Act Books, R. VII. A. 5, f. 208.]

...c. Hen. Loughe clerke curate of Bridlington.... Et monitus est insuper ad confitendum publice in ecclesia sua that the use of the printed caks by him used were vaine and taken away by the quenes auctority and hereafter not to use the same....

A.D. 1571 [Ibid. R. VII. A. 6, f. 54 v.]

The case of Leon. Atkinson of Masham.

See p. 151. See also the entry for Ripon in the 1567 Visitation, p. 28, and for Weverham in 1578, p. 65.

(i) *The Provision of Bread and Wine*

(i) *By the people*

A.D. 1586 [Visitation Books, R. VI. A. 9, f. 90.]

Cropton: '...c. Geo. Potter et Geo. Sheles. They refuse to provid bread and wyne for the people to communycate.'

[Ibid. f. 196 v.]

Darrington: [Two men] 'refuse to pay eyther of them iiid. for bread and wyne beinge cessed.' [They were dismissed on proof of having paid.]

(ii) *By the Rector*

A.D. 1575 [Ibid. R. VI. A. 5, f. 34 v.]

Barnebye upon Donne: 'The said Mr. Whalleye refused to finde breade and wyne at Easter last contrarie to a custome in that behalf heretofore observed.' [He was 'fermor or proprietarie' there.]

[Ibid. f. 54 v.]

Gysburne: 'The Archbishopp of Yorke his grace (as they present) beinge parson here standeth charged to allowe iiii markes yerelie towardes the costes of bread and wyne which somme hath not bene paid these vii yeres or therabouts.'

(j) *The Real Presence*

1 June 1573   [Ecclesiastical Commission, Act Books, R. VII. A. 7, f. 103 v.]

Willm. Tessymond was not satisfied in conscience to communicate. He believed 'eucharistiam post consecrationem verum corpus Christi in se continere et ulterius dixit ecclesiam Romanam fuisse et esse Christi ecclesiam'. [He was re-committed to York Castle.]

(k) *Irregularities*

A.D. 1567   [Cause Papers, R. VII. G. 883.]

Charges against Ric. Levett, a priest of Beverley Minster, of celebrating Masses, etc. He 'did or at the least wayes sawe divers hostes consecrated and laid up in a pixe or box to be preserved', kept superstitious books, implements and vestments, and was a favourer of the usurped power and abrogate religion. He admitted that he had been a priest at Beverley 'ever sence the begynyng of the reigne of the Quenes Majestie that now is and before in lait quenes Maries in her tyme etc.', completely denied the saying of Masses or laying up of consecrated hosts or keeping of books etc., but 'trueth it is that I had in a box certayne syngyng breads remanyng in a chest of myne by the space of eight yeres to be ended at Saynct John the Baptiste next ensuyng...and the same breads did remayne in the box all the said tyme...of a foileshenes symplecitie neclegence slouthfulnes and for lake of grace, and not for suche uses as they ware first ordayned for...'.

30 July 1582   [Ecclesiastical Commission, Act Books, R. VII. A. 10, f. 174 v.]

Matilda wife of Joh. Wilson of Bilton 'after she had received the sacramentall breade did convey the same furth of her mouth into her handkerchief'. [She confessed it and was ordered a penance.]

A.D. 1583   [Ibid. f. 217 v.]

Eliz. Coulson servant of Mr. Joh. Palmes of Naburne ar. confessed that 'by reason of a payin in her syde and a coughe she then had she putt owt the sacramentall bread of her mowth for which abuse she was sent to the custody of the sheriffs of York per warrantum ibidem remanenda quousque etc.'

The clue here is probably in the woman's connection with the recusant family of Palmes of Naburn. The reason is clearer in Cause Paper R. VII. G. 284, of 1570, where the Curate of Shereburne in Hartfurth Lythe reported that Mrs Kath. Lacye on Easter Day 1569 'did sitt downe amongest the rest of the parishoners being then presente and redy to receyve the Communyon to whome when he had ministred the sacramentall bread and so gone from hir orderlie unto one by one untill he had ministred the bread unto a dousen persons as he supposed, and lokyng backe behynde him did well se and perceyve Mrs. Lacye who had receyved, taike furth of hir mouthe the breade... and did conveye the same behinde hir, which thing when he did perceyve he did returne backe towards Mrs. Lacye and did ask hir what she mente to conveye the Sacrament in such order'. He also called a churchwarden to note what she had done, and afterwards saw her 'treade the same bread under hir fote'. On successive days Mr Lacye and Mrs Lacye called to offer different explanations of the incident. Mrs Lacye was well known as an opponent of the established religion 'now sett furth by publique auctoritie, affirmyng that hollie bread was good, and the world was good when the same was used, and that praying to Our Ladye and the other saynts was good and she wold use the same, and that she wold use the ypocryticall use of maikynge crosses upon the founte stone at such tyme as she cometh into the churche to be purified of hir children, and she denyeth to offer any offering except she shuld kisse the patten of the chalyce or the Communion booke...'.

A.D. 1575   [Visitation Books, R. VI. A. 5, f. 45.]

Alne: 'The chauncell called Katherine quere is in decaie divers waies in defalt of Mr. Ric. Ellerker of Yowton.

Mr. Anthonie Ellerker of Yowton disturbed the Vicar on Easter Daie last in tyme of his celebratinge the Communion.

Item Ric. Ellerker his brother being then churchwarden ther made the like disturbaunce.'

A.D. 1598   [Ibid. R. VI. D. 1, f. 65.]

Mexbrough: 'Anna Morley for abusinge her selfe on Easter Day last in chidinge with Francis Wattson the minister when he was ministringe the Sacraments to herselfe with others.'

(l) *Administration to Improper Persons*
[Ibid. f. 10 v.]

St Crux (York): 'Tho. Hingeston curate there for contempt in ministering Communion to an excommunicate person.'

68

[Ibid. f. 27 v.]

Kildwicke (in Craven): 'Willm. Harrison clerk our Curate for that he ministred the sacraments to Alice Laycoke being excommunicate.'

A.D. 1567   [Ibid. R. VI. A. 2, f. 26 v.]

...c. dmn. Joh. Herrington clericum curatum de Clayworthe... he haythe receyved one Richerde Storres being a man of evell lief to the holly Communion at Easter laste...dicit that he receyved [him] to the Communion at Easter last past but he sayth he did not know hime at that tyme because he was but newly comed into that paryshe....

A.D. 1575   [Ibid. R. VI. A. 5, f. 11 v.]

Thorner: 'John Barker communicated not at Easter last becawse he was oute of charity with an other man.'

[Ibid. f. 28 v.]

Bristall cum Tonge: 'One Eliz. Cordingley a woman distracted received not the Communion sence she fell distracted.'

[Ibid. f. 40.]

Bossall: 'Mr. Thwaits his wyfe received not the Communion at Easter last for that she is madde.'

(m) *Holy Baptism*

(i) *Use of Surplice and of Sign of Cross*

A.D. 1586   [Ibid. R. VI. A. 9, f. 181.]

Emley...Steph. Shele clericus vicarius ibidem sometymes ministreth the Communyon and baptiseth children, not wearinge his surplesse: he refuseth to sygne suche children as he baptiseth with the syne of the crose....

A.D. 1590   [Ibid. R. VI. A. 10, f. 169.]

Ganton: 'Contra Willm. Langdale rectorem He refuseth to baptise signo crucis and to wer surples.' [He was admonished to do both as by law and her Majesty's injunctions he is bound to do.] 'Which the said Mr. Langdale did promis to do.'

A.D. 1594   [Ibid. R. VI. A. 13, f. 51 v.]

Gigleswick: 'Contra Mr. Chris. Shutt vicarium he dothe not baptize children with the signe of the Crosse....Admonished to minister the sacrament of baptisme to some one child with the signe of the Cross before Christmas next in Gigleswick Church...and to certify.' [Other uses of the sign of the Cross forbidden.]

A.D. 1575   [Ibid. R. VI. A. 5, f. 76.]

St Maries in Beverleye: 'John Warde dyd not receive at Easter last and useth crossinge contrarie to the Injunctions.'

17 March 1570/1   [Ecclesiastical Commission, Act Books, R. VII. A. 5, f. 237 v.]

Against Willm. Allen, Alderman of York: 'Forasmuche as before the Commissioners he affirmed that by the signe of the Crosse made on his forheade or other parte of his bodye with his hande he is stronger against the assalts of the Devell and perilles of the worlde, and also that he is enstructed therby to remember Christs passyon Therfore for the takinge away of suche superstition and the removing of suche abuse the Commissioners did judicially enjoyne him from henceforthe not to use suche crossinge...either pryvatelie or publi-quelie under payne of the lawe.'

(ii) *A Further Note on Holy Baptism*

27 May 1578   [Ibid. R. VII. A. 9, f. 155.]

Articles presented against Rog. Menithorpe clerk curate of Old Malton. He answered: 'that he chrestened a child on the workedaye latelie and divers other children at other tymes but onelie suche as ar weke. Ad secundum respondet that he dyd chresten Dobbyes childe but did not dipp it in the water but powred water upon hit heade....'

(n) *Marriage*

A.D. 1571   [Ibid. R. VII. A. 6, f. 92 v.]

...c. Tho. Dicconson of Lethame. He was maried in Latyne service as is suspected. [Referred to the Bishop of Chester.]

15 Oct. 1574 [Ibid. R. VII. A. 8, f. 10.]

Two persons for marriage without banns, 'contra tenorem libri communis orationis etiam in Com. Lancastrie¹ in ecclesia aliena ubi eorum neuter moram trahit nec traxit'. [They were committed to York Castle.]

[Ibid. f. 32.]

The same two persons appeared again, when it was alleged 'that they were maried in a parlor or chamber within the dwelling howse of Sir Miles Caryer Curate of Downeham Chapell within the parishe of Whalley in Lancashire or in some other howse site and situate within the towne of Downeham speaking and pronouncinge the words of matrimonye specified and conteyned in the boke of Common prayer after the Curate solemnisinge the matrimonye betwene them after the order of the booke of Common Praier, at which tyme a ringe was delivered and received between them after the order of the said booke. And the Curate did pronounce them to be lawfull man and wife after the order of the booke of Common Prayer.' [Witnesses were heard, and the parties were dismissed.]

(o) Banns

A.D. 1571 [Visitation Books, R. VI. A. 3a, f. 137.]

...c. Ric. Shawe and Janet Semyer of Royston. The bands of mariag being asked betwixt them yet he refuseth to marie hir and have so continewed a yere togethere. [Ordered to marry before the Feast of the Purification, and to certify.]

A.D. 1575 [Ibid. R. VI. A. 5, f. 35.]

[Two couples at Conisburghe] 'have bene either couple thrise asked in the churche together half a yere since and ar not maried whereat some ar displeased thinkinge they will not marrye'.

---

¹ The Act Books of the Ecclesiastical Commission show that much attention was paid to the possibility that marriages according to the Roman rite, or by vagrant or domiciled Papist priests, were celebrated in Lancashire between persons who lived in Yorkshire sufficiently near to the Lancashire border to be able to slip over easily and unnoticed.

[Ibid. f. 80 v.]

Bubwith: 'John Smith and Janet Smith have bene asked in the churche and have kept howse together for one half yere, and the parishoners thought they wold have maried together but ar now broken of and the man gone but his goods remain ther still.'

A.D. 1578   [Ibid. R. VI. A. 7, f. 30.]

Chester, Knottesford: '[Seven couples] have maried without bannes askinge some [in] feilds some in Chapells and some in prophane places yea it is doubted whether they be maryed at all.'

(p) *The Form of Betrothal*

A.D. 1584   [Cause Papers, uncalendared.]

A cause for 'breach of promise' between Margt. Clarke of Bridlington, widow, and John Elyot of the same, widower, who alleged that he was drunk at the time of the supposed betrothal. The chief witness was the Curate of Bridlington, who stated that Elyot said to him: 'Sir Roberte you are welcome sytt ye downe and I will gyve you a pott of ale for you must aske me in the churche on Sonday next With whome quoth this examinate Marry quoth he With Margaret Clerke. Wel quoth this examinate But I would here her speake and therupon John sent for her and she came forthwith to whome John said Margaret my wyfe[1] sitt you downe you are hartely welcome, for I meane to make you my wyfe, and kyssed her and dronke to her, to whome she said Sir I thanke you most hartely if so be that you be so perswaded in your harte as you speake it, who answered that he was, and althoughe some say that I will

[1] This passage is a good illustration of the relation between the betrothal-contract, banns and actual marriage. The contract was made with the form of 'verba de presenti', 'I take thee...', which made the ceremony a binding contract; this contract was not to be dissolved, even if marriage did not follow. On the contrary, a betrothal by 'verba de futuro', 'I will take thee...', could be dissolved if the marriage was not consummated. The priest here expected that the contract would precede the calling of banns, and the man made sure of a valid contract by taking the woman to live with him, in addition to his 'verba de presenti'. Difficulties arose most seriously when the contract was made between children, sometimes of less than ten years of age, a practice which although less common than in medieval times had not disappeared in Tudor days.

turne tomorrow, yet I will never turne. Then quoth [I] unto them Joyne hands together in the feare of God seinge that you are contented to be man and wyfe together and say this after me, and [he] toke [her] by her right hande and saide unto her after [me] I John take the Margaret to my handfest wyfe to have and to holde from this day forwarde for better for worse for richer for poorer in sicknes and in healthe, to love and to cheryshe till death us departe accordinge to Gods holly ordinaunce and therto I plight the my trouthe, and so they drewe handes and ioyned them together agayne and she said unto him…and so they drewe handes and he kissed her againe… and ymedyately hereupon he caryed her from thence to his owne hous in Brydlington and gave her possession of his hous and his kylne…and toke the persons aforesaid with him to be witnesses therof….'

(q) *Burial*

For notices of Communion for the dead and ringing of bells for the dead, see the extracts from the 1567 Visitation Book and the note of Grindal's Injunctions.

The Visitation Book for Chester in 1578, R. VI. A. 7, has many references to these practices, e.g.:

[Ibid. f. 8.]

Tilston: 'Rafe Leche useth praier for the deade and willeth the people to praie for them and saie a pater noster and de profundis for the deade when the people do rest with the dead corps.'

[Ibid. f. 16 v.]

West Kirkby: 'Two men presented for "ringinge upon mourninge daies at the twelvemonthes ende".'

Trinityes in Chester: 'The parish clerk "rings mo peales at funerals than is decent".' [Similarly at Manchester and Walton.]

[Ibid. f. 31 v.]

Midlewiche: 'There is to much ringing for the deade.'

(r) *Burial Fees and Mortuaries*[1]

A.D. 1598 [Visitation Books, R. VI. D. 1, f. 27.]

Horton: 'Joh. Bushell and Robt. Whitington beinge poore men did bury Tho. Benton in the Church yeard.'

[Ibid. f. 28 v.]

Kirkby Malloughdaile: 'Robt. Kinge our Curate for buringe Tho. Siggeswicke in the Church yeard being excommunicate yett he not knowinge of the premisses.'

[Ibid. f. 33 v.]

Slaidburne: 'James Parker for not payinge ii s. for his father and mothers graves in the Church being an accustomed duety.'

[Ibid. f. 59.]

Tickhill: 'Alex. Minskippe for not payinge a mortuary for Tho. Lyllyman his wifes first husband and also for not payinge an other for his wife deceasyd.

Joh. Jackson administrator of Geo. Grene defunct for not payinge iii s. iiii d. for his burial in the Church. Joseph Woodroffe for not payinge iii s. iiii d. for his childs buryinge in the Church.'

The usual fee at Fislake seems to have been 'vi s. viii d.' [f. 57].

2. ATTENDANCE AT CHURCH

(a) *Grindal's Injunctions for the Clergy*

[Reg. Grindal, f. 156.]

20. Item for the puttinge of the churchewardons and sworne men better in remembrance of their duetye in observinge and notinge all suche persons of your parishe as do offende in not comminge to divine service, ye shall openlye everye Sondaye after ye have reade the seconde lesson at morninge and eveninge prayer, monishe and

---

[1] A mortuary was a gift or bequest due from a man—or sometimes a woman—before death, to the parish church, in recompense of personal responsibility for tithes and offerings or dues unpaid in his lifetime, or from his executors after his death, as a sort of compounding for those lost by his death. In the latter case, the mortuary was usually taken to be the 'second-best beast' or other possession at the time of death.

warne the churchewardons and sworne men of your parishe to looke
to their othes and chardge in this behalfe and to observe all who
contrarye to the lawe do that daye offende, eyther in absentinge
themselves negligentlye or wilfullye from their parishe churche or
chappell, or unreverentlye use them selves in the tyme of divine
service, and so note the same to the intente theye maye eyther present
suche offenders to the Ordinarye when they shalbe required thereunto or levye and take by way of distresse to the use of the poore
suche forfeitures as ar appointed by a statute [of 1 Elizabeth]....

(b) *Further Machinery for Enforcing Attendance*

24 Oct. 1577 [Ecclesiastical Commission, Act Books, R. VII. A. 9, f. 107.]

This daie and place beinge called and appearinge before the said
L. Archbishop and L. President and other her Majesties Commis-
sioners aforenamed Mr John Dyneleye L. Maior of the Cittie of
Yorke, Willm. Birnande esquire Recorder of the said Cittie and
Joh. Harbert one of the Aldermen of the same, And beinge judiciallie
interrogate by the Commissioners what execution hath bene had
and done of that good lawe or ordinance made the xvth daie of
Januarie last by the Maior Aldermen and other magestrats of the
same Cittie againste such as do refuse to come to the Churche the
Maior answered thereto that of divers of such offenders distresses ar
taken and of other some sureties for payment of the penalties set
downe to be payed for such offenders but the distresses be not solde
nor any further thinge done, and so where some slackness hath bene
in the execution of the aforesaid lawe or ordinaunce the Maior did
then and there saye it should be amended hereafter And then beinge
as it seamed of good mynde and purpose to see due execution of the
lawe or ordinaunce in verie dede he the L. Maior did then and there
beseche the advise of this honorable Courte tochinge such as be in
warde by appointement of this Commission whether he should take
distresse or levye the forfeiture of any such or not Whereunto this
honorable Court thought good to answere him Not for the tyme of
such ther imprisonment but in tyme of libertie aswell for tyme past
as for to come And to thende that this Courte may understande the
better what execution had of the lawe, that direction may be taken

for remedie of the slacknes of the same in tyme to fore and assiste
to the punyshement of such offendors The Maior is appoynted on
Tewesdaie nexte to exhibite a catalogue unto this honorable Court
of all the names of such as have bene presented unto him for not
cominge to church with certificate what hath bene doone against
everie such in waie of their punishments for their offences And the
Recorder and Alderman Harberte have promised to further the due
execution of the Lawe in all they can And so they were for this tyme
dismissed.

31 Aug. 1580   [Ibid. R. VII. A. 10, f. 29 v.]

To the churchwardens of Wheldrake for the time beinge.

Understanding by credible enformacion that manie of the
parishioners of Wheldrake forgetting ther duetie towards God
and neglectinge the good lawes and statutes of this realme are verie
slack in coming to devine service and sermons delighting more in
ther owne ease and securitie then in the service of thalmightie, and
minding the reformacion of such offendors and the edificacion and
due instruction of the people in Godds trueth, We have thought
good to will and require yow and nevertheles in her Majesties name
and by vertue of her highnes commission for causes ecclesiasticall to
us and others directed straitlie to charge and commaund yow that
yow and everie of yow being for the time being churchwardens at
Wheldrake aforesaid do hereafter diligentlie note and observe who
doth or shall within your parish offend in the premisses and that (all
parcialitie and affection set aparte) yow do your duty hereafter in
levieng from time to time of the goodes of everie person that shall
without lawfull cause be absent from devine service upon anie
Sondaies or hollydaies for everie offence xiid. according to the
statute in that behalf provided and employ the same to the use of
the poore of your parishe accordingly And for the better execution
of this good law we do hereby also charge and commaund in her
majesties name and by vertue of her highnes said commission all
headboroughes bailiffes constables and all other her majesties officers
and loving subjectes whatsoever within the province of Yorke to be
aydinge and assisting to yow in the said premisses not fayling hereof
as yow and they will answere to the contrarie at your perills And

that if anie person or persons shall obstinatelie offend in this behalf yow do present them and certefy ther names and offences unto us from time to time that we may take further order with them for there punishment according to ther demeritts. Geoven at Bushopthorpe the xxxth of August in the xxiith yere of her majesties raigne.

Ed. Ebor.   H. Huntington.   Ma. Hutton.   Joh. Gibson.

Notices of absence from Church are rare in the Visitation Books of 1561, 1567 and 1571.

A.D. 1575   [Visitation Books, R. VI. A. 5, f. 43.]

Thirske: 'Gyles Tailior cometh not to the churche.

John Stevenson a vagarant cometh not to the churche.

Willm. Scrowton is negligente in cominge to his parishe churche on the Saboth daies and dyd geve opprobriowse words and answeres to the churchwardens for executinge their office calling them knaves.

John Wyseman presented to absent him from the Churche on the Saboth daie who said he wold come when he wold and thought best.

Chris. Burton presented for plaienge at Showlay bourde[1] the first of Maie last in service tyme.'

[Ibid. f. 86.]

Skarburghe: '...Gregorie Pacocke one of the churchwardens was absent from morninge prayer untill the Epistle was readd, and likewise was absent at the evenynge prayer on Sondaie the xiith of June wherebie he gave evell example....

Robt. Lacie one of the baliffs came not on Sondaie the xiith of June to evenyng praier till the readinge of the seconde Lesson....

[Thirty-three men named.] All these presented for cominge slowlie to the Churche Morninge praier beinge half doone and have bene demaunded their fynes and refuse to paie the same making light accompte of the same. Sondaie the xixth of June 1575.

John Dickson presented for delivering of malt the same Sondaie a litle before Morning praier and carried it on horsebacke to a bote....

[Fifteen men named] presented for being absent on Sondaie the xixth of June at evenynge praier during the tyme whereof they were shootinge.

[1] Perhaps better recognised as Shovel Board.

Brian Tailior presented for plaieing at cards the said xixth of June in the evennyng praier tyme in Willm. Jeetsons house with the wife of the said William.

Davy Steward [and three others] presented for plaieng at cards in evennyng praier tyme the said xixth of June. . . .

[Six men named] presented for being absent from evennynge praier on Sondaie the xixth of June aforesaid.'

The rise in later years is very marked. The figures for 1590 are: Bulmer Deanery, 21 persons named for non-attendance; Ainsty, 39; York City, 4; Beverley and Harthill, 35; Howdenshire, 10; Holderness, 10; Ryedale, 4; Dickering, 3; Buckrose, 0; Cleveland, 0. But in the same year, Cleveland had 105 'recusants'; Ainsty had 33; York, 10; Beverley and Harthill, 10; Howdenshire, 14; Holderness, 2; Ryedale, 5; Dickering, 5; and Buckrose, 1.

In 1594 the figures are: York City, recusants 15, other absentees, 5; Ainsty, 29 and 3; Craven, 11 and 4; Pontefract, 13 and 10; Doncaster, 2 and 7; Bulmer, 37 and 3; Ryedale, 3 and 2; Allertonshire, 6 and 5; Ripon, 7 and 7; Snaith Peculiar, 14 and 1; Howdenshire Peculiar, 0 and 3; Cleveland, 105 and 32; Harthill, 6 and 1; Hull and Holderness, 3 and 5; Buckrose, 1 and 0; Dickering, 1 and 1; Ripon, 55 and 0. In these figures, those for recusants represent individual names, for absence single entries, which may contain several names. For comparison the number of entries for all 'moral' offences may be given; these include all such charges as fornication, adultery, etc. They are, in 1594: for York, 26; Ainsty, 61; Craven, 85; Pontefract, 123; Doncaster, 72; Bulmer, 45; Ryedale, 44; Allertonshire, 11; Ripon, 16; Snaith, 2; Howdenshire, 14; Cleveland, 83; Harthill, 52; Hull and Holderness, 64; Buckrose, 17; Dickering, 32.

3. RECUSANCY AND NON-COMMUNICATING

Allusion has been made already, pp. 1, 2 and 35 above, to the difficulty of forming any definite conclusions from the material supplied by the Visitation records for the history of recusancy, especially as there is so little indication of the precise meaning attached to the term. But some rough statistics may be compiled, which may give general information or at least material for comparison.

A.D. 1575 [Visitation Books, R. VI. A. 5.]

Although it cannot be said that this book pays no attention to recusancy and non-communicating, yet distinctly more interest is taken in the supply of sermons and the state of churches and chancels.

The figures are given, in all the following cases, by Deaneries, and the number after each Deanery name represents the number of parishes in the Deanery from which presentments, or 'omnia bene' reports, are entered:

York City (27 parishes): recusants, 0; non-communicants, 10.

Ainstye (46): 0 and 9.   Alderton (11): 0 and 3.
Craven (26): 1 and 8.   Buckrose (20): 0 and 4.
Pontefract (41): 0 and 8.   Hull (5): 0 and 4.
Doncaster (65): 0 and 7.   Holdernes (39): 0 and 3.
Bulmer (47): 0 and 9.   Beverley (21): 0 and 3.
Ridall (34): 0 and 4.   Harthill (35): 0 and 0.
Clevelande (49): ? 2 and 4.   Howdenshire (10): 0 and 0.
Dickering (34): 0 and 5, and 50 at Scarbrough absent from one service or part of a service, but not non-communicants.

The most remarkable entry is on f. 105:

Saxton: 'Joh. Belhouse wife beinge excommunicate for Recusancie was buried in the churche yarde by the forcible meanes of Joh. Belhouse her husbande.'

There are no entries here for the Diocese of Chester or for the Archdeaconry of Nottingham.

A.D. 1578 [Diocese of Chester only, Ibid. R. VI. A. 7.]

Deanery of Macclesfeld (11 parishes): recusants, 0; non-communicants, 2.

Malpas (7): 1 and 3.   Layland (7): 7 and 6.
Namptwiche (12): 0 and 19.   Amoundernes (19): 9 and 34.
Bangor (4): 0 and 8.   Furnes (9): 0 and ? 20.
Wyrrall (14): 0 and 2.   Cowpland (32): 0 and 0.
Chester (24): 4 and 39.   Lonsedall (14): 1 and 7.
Frodesham (17): 0 and 0.   Kendall (10): 0 and 13.
Midlewiche (13): 0 and 0.   Richmond (47): 1 and 8.
Manchester (24): 0 and 17.   Cattericke....
Warryngton (19): 3 and 96.   Burrobridge (19): 0 and 5.

This year has some of the most interesting entries:

[Ibid. f. 19 v.]

Trinityes in Chester: [Six men and women] 'refuse to communicate oneles they have singing breads or wafer breade albeit the parson minister with usuall breade and singing cakes.'

[Ibid. f. 47.]

Hytonne: [Two women] 'come not to the churche not communicate they are (as it is sayd) in bondes to appere at Lancaster at the next assyzes for the premisses.'

[Ibid. f. 47 v.]

Prescott: [Seventeen men and women]: 'They do not come to churche nor communycate, they are presented to therle of Darbye.'

[Ibid. f. 58.]

Standyshe: 'Eliz. Tetlowe a mydwyfe absenteth her selfe from the churche receyveth not the communyon goeth upp and downe the country with chyldren to be baptysed of popyshe prestes.'

[Ibid. f. 58 v.]

Croston: [Six men and women] 'have harde masse as is notoryouslye reported done at [Willm. Mawdesley alias my Lorde of Croston] his hous upon Mydsomer day last past done by a ronagate parson called as he nameth him selfe John Beggar alias Lee, and the said persons do not come to the churche nor receyve the Communyon.'

[Ibid. f. 93.]

Kyrkeby Kendall: 'Ther be dyvers chappells in the parishe wherin ther is no servyce sayd because ther resorteth therunto no company. Some chappells have Communyon cuppes of sylver and some of pewther.

Many have been maryed and many have communycated which cannot say the Cathechisme beinge under xxty yeres of ayge.'

A.D. 1590   [Diocese of Chester, Ibid. R. VI. A. 12.]

Catterick Deanery (24 parishes): recusant, 1; non-communicants, 27.

Richmond (27): 7 and 91.		Kendall (24): 0 and 24.
Rippon (5): 0 and 12.		Lonsdale (16): 3 and 19.
Borobrig (21): 13 and 52.		Furnes (10): 0 and 4.

Amoundernes (15): 56 (at least) and 50.

Blackburne (15): 80 recusants, 30 of them at Whalley, where 'not one of them did communycate sence Archb. Gryndall his Metropoliticall Visitacion dyvers tymes complayned upon sence that tyme but no Reformacion'. 11 non-communicants.

Lealande (7): 10 and 33. Frodsham (15): 1 and 1.
Manchester (21): 1 and 21. Malpas (8): 20 and 2.
Waryngton (19): 132 and 21.
Wirralle (15): 3 and 2. At Neston (f. 88): 'Alice Whitmoore wife of William Whitmoore a recusante / he doth not communicate.'
Bangor (4): 8 and 12. Maxfeelde (13): 4 and 1.
Chester (26): 19 and 14.
Namptewyche (12): 28 and 4, including at Churcheminshall Tho. Simkin who 'often absenteth him selfe from the churche for wante of apparell'.
Middlewiche (13): 2 and 3.

A.D. 1595 and 1596 [Almost the whole Province, Ibid. R. VI. A. 14.]
Chester (17 parishes): recusants, 5; non-communicants, 9.
Wyrrall (15): 1 and 3. Richmond (33): 140 and 19.
Bangor (4): 17 and 0. Catterick (26): 22 and 9.
Malpas (7): 10 and 3. Burrobrig (21): 150 and 12.
Namptwyche (12): 1 and 12. Kendall (20): 0 and 2.
Maxfelde (18): 0 and 4. Londesdale (16): 14 and 2.
Mydlewyche (13): 1 and 6. Furnes (10): 0 and 1.
Frodesham (14): 0 and 5. Cowpeland (30): 0 and 1.
Manchester (23): 6 and 29. Amondernes (16): 132 and 44.
Warrington (26): 211 and 80. Retford (60): 1 and 18.
Blackburn (15): 91 and 20. Newark (41): 1 and 9.
Leyland (8): 34 and 29. Southwell (24): 0 and 4.
Nottingham and Byngham (90): 2 and 17.
York City (30): 15 and 21. Buckrose (29): 6 and 0.
Ainstie (56): 44 and 33. Dyckering (31): 1 and 3.
Craven (26): 7 and 11. Harthill (67): 19 and 9.
Pontefract (37): 19 and 24. Holderness (64): 10 and 11.
Doncaster (78): 21 and 27. Howdenshire (9): 19 and 2.
Bulmer (58): 74 and 22. Snaithe (2): 13 and 0.
Ridall (41): 18 and 12. Allertonshire (14): 27 and 1.
Clevelande (47): 165 and 15.

This book gives a total of parishes and chapelries for the whole area of no less than 1,145, but it will be noticed that there is great variation in the numbers represented in the various Visitation Books, so that an accurate total is difficult to reach.

4. BEHAVIOUR IN CHURCH

(a) *Walking and Talking*

[Archbishop Grindal's Injunctions to the Laity, Injunction No. 15.]

ITEM that the churchewardons and sworne men shall not suffer anye persons to walke talke or otherwise unreverentlye to behave themselves in anye churche or chappell, nor to use any gaminge or to sitt abroade in the stretes, or churche yeardes, or in any taverne or ailehouse upon the Sondayes or other holye dayes, in the tyme of divine service, or of anye sermon, whether it be before none or after none, but after warninge once given shall punishe both them and all others that negligentlye or wilfullye shall absent themselves from divine service or come verye latelye to the churche upon Sondayes or holye dayes, havinge no lawfull lett or hinderance, and those also that without anye juste cause shall departe out of the churche before the divine service or sermon be done...the churchewardons shall levye and take of every one that wilfullye or negligentlie so shall offende the forfeiture of xii d. for everye suche offence, And shall also present them to the Ordinarye....

A.D. 1571 [Visitation Books, R. VI. A. 3 a, f. 37 v.]

Officium dominorum contra Joh. Kelsey parochie de Ottringham in Holdernes...domini objecerunt that he wente furthe of the Churche in tyme of devyne servyce in contempte therof and talked in the churche porche and being warned by the churchewardens to come into the churche he said he wolde not.... [A penance assigned.]

[Ibid. f. 161.]

...c. Geo. Hunter parochie de Wakefield. For talking in the churche in tyme of devyne servyce. Referred to Mr. Deane.

...c. Tho. Speaghte parochie de Wakefield...for unreverent talke in the churche in the tyme of devyne servyce...respondendo dicit that one tyme being in his parishe churche he did goo furth of the same, upon a necessarie cause, and one of the churchwardens wold know the cause and he made aunswer And thow shalt knowe, if thou will see...penance by declaration in Wakefield Church ordered on the following Sunday.

[Ibid. f. 162.]

...c. Joh. Grene parochie de Wakefield for walking and talking in the churche...fatetur unde domini monuerunt eundem quod faciet declaracionem culpae in ecclesia de Wakefeld die dominica proxima.

A.D. 1575 [Ibid. R. VI. A. 5, f. 19.]

Hortonne: 'Thomas Bentham a Tailor hath gone out of the churche in service tyme, and hath with light words obstinatelie refused to come in at the request of the churchwardens.'

[Ibid. f. 30 v.]

Fishlake: 'John Briggs dyd go oute of the Churche in service tyme with one John Bryan, and talked about a private bargain betwene them.'

The offence is not a common one. Less than a dozen cases were presented in the whole diocese in all the Visitations between 1567 and 1598. But the entry in the Commission Books for York Minster suggests perhaps a greater frequency.

(b) *Against Walking in Sermon Time*

4 Jan. 1579/80 [Ecclesiastical Commission, Act Books, R. VII. A. 9, f. 251 v.]

An Order for the reformynge of thabuse of walkinge and talkinge in this Cathedrall churche of Yorke duringe the tymes of sermons and lectures preached and red within the same.

WHERE divers evill disposed persons heretofore have and yet do use unreverentlie to walke and talke within this Cathedrall and Metropolitaine churche of Yorke in tyme of sermons and lectures preached and redd within the same to the manifeste contempte of the woorde of God the lett and hinderance of the preachinge and hearinge thereof and the most pernicious example of others to offend in the lyke We the quenes majesties Commissioners appointed for causies ecclesiasticall within the Citie dioces and province of Yorke undernamed for the reformacion of suche abuse and the stablishing of quiet order to be used and contynewed in this Churche in that behalfe do geve streighte charge and commaundement in her majesties name and by vertue of hir highnes commession to us and others directed that no person or persons do hereafter presume either to walke in anie place of the said Churche or to withdrawe theme selves frome the place of preachinge or redinge into anie parte thereof for talke or conference frome or after the beginning of the salme to be soonge before the sermon or lecture untill the endinge of the salme to be soonge after the same upon paine of imprisonment and other punyshment at the discrecion of us or anie thre of our associates to be imposed upon everie offender in that behalfe And for the better observation of this order we further will and require and by vertue of hir majesties said commission streightelie charge and commaunde the vergers of this Churche that they and everie of theime at the tymes of suche preachinge and redinge frome tyme to tyme geve there diligente attendance in this Churche and without parcialitie note and furthwith presente to the moste reverend father in Christe Edwine by Gods providence Archebushop of Yorke primate of England and Metropolitain or to us and others his graceis associates in the said Commission the names and surnames of all and everie the offenders in the premisses and there severall offencies in that behalfe that further order may be taiken with them accordinge to there demerites to the advancemente of vertue and repressinge of vice and the vergers not to faile hereof as thay will answer to the contrarie at there perill Yeven the fourte day of Januarie 1579 in the xxiith yere of hir majesties most prosperous reigne. God save the quene.

Signed by eight Commissioners.

(c) *Brawling and Disorder*

A.D. 1567 [Visitation Books, R. VI. A. 2, f. 112 v.]

...c. Joh. Wamesley of Hodtherhouse in Mitton Parish...excommunicate sence Martynmas last, and that notwithstandinge on Midsomer daie last past presumed to come into the churche and beinge rebuked by the churchwardens did resist against them and offered to have foughten with them.

[Ibid. f. 63.]

...c. Robt. Jonson juniorem de Flamburghe He is presented to have misused him selfe in his pastymes in the churche yarde...[he confessed] that he one tyme did pitche the barre[1] in the churche yearde and otherwyse he saieth he did not offend. [Penance ordered.]

[Ibid. f. 92.]

...c. Joh. Jetter de Marske...disturbed the mynister in sayinge devyne servyce so that the minister lefte of redinge for lacke of audience.[2] [A declaration penance was ordered.]

A.D. 1575   [Ibid. R. VI. A. 5, f. 13.]

Acaster: 'Simon Tanfeld a dronkarde drue his knife and porred[3] with it at Ambrose Jackson in Acaster church upon a Sondaie sence Easter last.'

[Ibid. f. 59 v.]

Yarome: 'Henry Harrison of Yarome presented that he did fighte with one Chris. Mathewe Clarke on Easter daie last paste after that he had received the holie Communion to the disturbance of the whole parishe and contrarie to Gods Lawes as the presenters thinke.'

[Ibid. f. 31.]

Bolton-upon-Dearne: 'Thomas Shepparde did argue in the churche with the Constable about a light horse.'

There were three offences of this kind in the 1586 Visitation. It was equally rare in 1590.

[Ibid. R. VI. A. 10, f. 75.]

Wighill: '... [nine men named] dyd daunce after Percivall Graves of Walton a pyper on Sunday the thirde of May last in servyce tyme.' [Penance ordered to be done in the churchyard before the Vicar and six honest persons.]

---

[1] A sport akin to 'tossing the caber'.
[2] Perhaps meaning 'because he could not be heard'.
[3] 'Porre', to strike at with the intention of provoking. A 'por', a fire-poker.

A.D. 1598   [Ibid. R. VI. D. 1, f. 12 v.]

Guyesley: '...c. Joh. Lacocke...for a man of very crooked and unreverent behavior usinge beastly and shameles speeches in matters of religion both privily and openly in the Church before the preacher and havinge bene admonished still continueth and maiketh a iest of his owne vainnesse.'

[Ibid. f. 21 v.]

Leeds: '...c. Willm. Matthewe for brawlinge often tymes in the church.'

[Ibid. f. 26.]

Carleton: '...c. Willm. Hargraves for disturbinge of divine service and the minister forbidinge him; he the said Willm. bad the minister come downe furth of the pulpitt if he would the which he was forcyd to doe before he would stay himselfe.' [This he denied on compurgation, and was dismissed.]

[Ibid. f. 64 v.]

Harthill: '...Margaret Bell (abiit) for maikinge disorder in the Churche with Isabell Nedam one of the churchwardens wives.'

13 Feb. 1565/6   [Ecclesiastical Commission, Act Books, R. VII. A. 2, f. 86.]

...c. Chris. Dobson, three others and Oswald Atkinson. It was objected 'that they have plaied at the foote ball within this Cathedrall Churche of Yorke. To which objection they awnsweringe confessed that the foote ball was broughte into the Churche by Dobson and thereupon Oswald Atkinson did take the ball from him in the churche and there was but one stroke striken at the same in the Churche. Wherefore the Commissioners did order that Oswald Atkinson shalbe sett in the Stocks at the churche side upon Sonday nexte at nyne of the clocke before nowne and ther to sytt in the stocke by the space of one hole houre and at the houre ende be tayken furthe and laid over the stocke and have six yerts with a byrchen rod upon his buttocke and that Chris. Dobson shall have lykewise sex yerts upon his buttocke with a byrchen rod....' [The Vergers and Apparitors were to see this carried out.]

(d) *Disputes over Pews*

One of the most fertile causes of disturbance in the parish church was individual property in pews or stalls. It may be said generally that in pre-Reformation times what may be described as property in pews was mainly restricted to the chancel, where such persons as the rector, the farmer of the rectory, the founder of the church or of any part of it with his family and kin, and also persons of local importance by some inherited or feudal right, expected to have the private use of a pew or stall. In many cases, chapels in aisles or transepts were regarded as almost the reserved property of particular individuals or families.[1] Seats in the nave of the church receive little attention before the Reformation. This, of course, is not conclusive as to the frequency of their existence, but it may be stated quite confidently that there was a great increase in the erection of private pews in and after the reign of Edward VI. The distribution of monastic lands and the astonishing increase in lay farmers of Rectories on the one hand, and the marked social changes which were beginning to make themselves felt throughout the whole life of the country on the other, or both working together in association, produced this development, and before long we find custom passing towards law, that the person who paid certain parochial rates or held certain property not always freehold in the parish or manor, or held an official position especially as churchwarden, had a prescriptive right or claim to a pew or stall for himself and his family in the parish church. This was a new manifestation of privilege, but it soon became and long remained a source of trouble and dispute. In a period so almost violently class-conscious as the Tudor age, it is not unexpected that the pew should become a mark, an outward and visible sign, of social precedence, and then that disputes often bitter and stubborn should arise over the right to have a particular pew in a particular part of the church, or even any pew at all.

A.D. 1575 [Visitation Books, R. VI. A. 5, f. 35 v.]

Barneby upon Donne: 'Ther is great dissention amongs the parishoners about ther stalls.'

A.D. 1590 [Ibid. R. VI. A. 10, f. 73.]

Pannall: 'Edwd. Lethome dyd misuse Tho. Wardeman in his owne seate in the church att service tyme and thruste him furth of his seate by vyolence.'

[1] See footnote 3 on p. 65.

[Ibid. f. 125.]

Marfleet: '...Agnetem Acie and Ellis Arrott for unreverent behaving themselfs in church in strugling about a stall.' [Penance ordered.]

A.D. 1598   [Ibid. R. VI. D. 1, f. 18 v.]

Thorner: 'Robt. Herrison for pullinge by force Chris. Austroppe out of his stall before prayer tyme on the Saboth day.' [Excommunicated.]

[Ibid. f. 28.]

Kirkby Malloughdaile: 'Willm. Anderson son of Willm. Anderson for maiking disorder in the Churche in tyme of divine service and pullinge Hen. Anderson furth of his stall.'

A.D. 1571   [Ecclesiastical Commission, Act Books, R. VII. A. 6, f. 35 v.]

Forasmuche as contention haith bene moved of late betwixte the parties and others for stalles and seates in the quere called the Ladye quere in the Southsyde of the Chancell of the Churche of Normanton by reason of certeyne armes sett upon the stalles ther And that neither the Ladye quere nor the stalles be of any great antiquitie but buylded within the memorie of man and consideringe also that the same stalles be farre from the pulpit and not commodiouslie sett for suche as frequent the same stalles to here the worde of God preached and other devyne servyce saide Therefore yt is ordered that all the stalles within the Ladye quere shalbe taken up before the xv daye of August next comyinge by the churchewardens of Normanton and set up in some other convenient place of the churche as to the discretion of the churchewardens shall be thought mete provided alwaies that neither any armes heretofore graven upon any stalles in the Chapell or any other armes heretofore to be graven shalbe suffred to be sett up or to stande in or upon any stall or pewe within the Church or Chapell leaste like contention growe hereafter by that occasion It is also further ordered that the gentlemen and gentlewomen being nowe by this order removed from the Ladye quere shalbe convenientlie placed neare the quere and the husbande men removed and set lower, and that no stalles be sett in the Ladie Chappell hereafter, onles yt be formes in the lower parte thereof for servants Provided also that yt may be lawfull for anye that are disposed to build them selves newe pewes in the Churche so that no armes be sett in or upon the same, for the cause above rehearsed.

A dispute between two families, Man and Battersby.

A.D. 1581   [Ibid. R. VII. A. 10, f. 136.]

It was ordered that 'bothe the stalles wherein they and their wiefes and families usuallie sit in the Churche shalbee at their commune charges equally devided in two partes by the said Man and that done the said Battersby to have the choyse of one parte of either of the stalles...to thende that either of theim their wieves children and servantes may sit severally in quiete from time to time'.

[Ibid. f. 146.]

The same Mr. Man confessed that 'he thrust one Marm. Kirkby furth of his stall in Kirkebymalserd churche in tyme of devyne service because he kept furth his wief Whereupon the Commissioners enjoyned him to repaire to the Vicar and to the churchwardens of the churche there and to protest before them quietnes in the churche henceforth with the which if they be contented he is dismissed or otherwise he is monished to aunswere in this suyte'.

Dispute between Robt. Kaye of Wetherby against Ric. Kay and Richard and Robert sons of Ric. Kay, for a stall or pew.

A.D. 1597   [Cause Papers (Miscellaneous), uncalendared.]

On one occasion Richard and Robert Kay found Thomas son of Robert Kay, aged xiiii yeres 'sittinge in tyme of divine prayers, whom they and every of them or one of them greatly abusyd in twitchinge of him and thrustinge pinnes into his armes and buttocks or into one of them and then and there Richard Kay son of Nicholas Kay deceased did give to Thomas Kay a blowe upon his head eare or face, not onely to the disturbance of the divine service then in hand and disquietinge of the Congregacion there assembled but also the evell example of others beinge there....'.

The trouble was by no means entirely Elizabethan.

A.D. 1553 [Cause Papers (Consistory), R. VII. G. 544.]

(i) Petition from Roberte Jacksonne of Ganthorpe and Dorathe his wif That wher as your Orators the xixth day of June instante beynge...in herynge of the holly and blessed Communyon and other service within his paroche churche of Tyrryngton...and then and there one Richarde Barton [and ten others named] with dyvers others riotouse mysdemeanyd persons and perturbors and breakers of [the peace and the laws] to the nomber of xvi persons...arayed with swords bucklers pykes staves ironforks and other weapons defensive with force and armes...and in most riotuouse maner dyd make one assaulte and affraye uppon your said Orators within the paroche churche of Terryngton And...dyd expulse and with violence ejecte and castefurth the said Dorothe...oute of her pewe or stall and the same did breake in pecs wherein she ever haith beyn accustomed to sytt and knele And her dyd sore hurte wounde and bayte...and hadde murdred and slayne [her] but that good men rescued....

Robert Jackson was a churchwarden of Terrington.

(ii) In the Attestations one witness attested that 'he hath seen [Dorothy] sitt in the said stall quyetlie by the space of iiii yeres before this sute beganne without contradiction of any man....He saw Robert Barton...at the begynnynge of the mattyns come into the church with a piche forke in his hande which he did leve in his owne stall and went to the stall articulate and called unto hyme one Henrie Prowde church warden of the church and demaunded of hyme who buylded the stall and he said Robert Jakson had sett it upe and then Robt. Burton pluckt it upe and cast it uppe in the north yle of the church then beinge in the church xx persons at the lest....He did se Robt. Barton assone as Dorothie was sett in the place wher the stall was come unto here and said Are ye sett ther ye shall not sitt ther and then she aunswered and said Yes Sir by youre licence, and then he plucke her owte of the stall and did swyng here so that he se her light againste the stowpe[1] of the stall which was sett harde in the grounde and then he harde Willm. Barton beinge in the stalle with Robt. Barton wif saye to Dorothie Gett the hence and thowe be well

---

[1] The main upright pillar of the stall-end.

for fere it be not ware [1] and then the prest beinge in the pulpitt at the Communion tyme commaunded the churche wardens to sett rewll in the church.'

The not very convincing defence that Robert 'did gentelie take Dorothie by the hande and bade here go sitt wher she shulde sitt for ther she shulde not sitt' probably failed.

A.D. 1555   [Cause Papers, R. As. 25/30.]

A dispute in Glaisdale Chapel. James Wynder 'dyd maliciously and violently pull Jayne Burton out of hir stall wher she was then knelynge'. The Articles allege that 'that Stall in whiche Jayne then dyd knell in, and out of whiche [she] was pulled by James Wynder dothe perteyne as it haythe of oulde tyme pertened and belonged as well by ould custome as by the appoyntement of the churche wardens of the Chapell of Glacedall unto the tenement or farmehould in whiche Myles Burton and Jayne his wyffe dothe now inhabet and dwell in...that althoughe the Churche or Chappell was about xx yeres syns taken downe and removed unto an other place wher it now standethe yet that notwithstandinge the stalles standethe... in the self same order as they dyd in the ould Chappell or Churche befor it wer removed'. The offence took place 'upon Lowsonday last past when the prest was redie to go to messe in Glacedale Chapell about ix of the cloke before none...'. The defendant was 'sitting in the quere', and according to one witness 'did come in a furie' and said 'he wold make here to knowe here better'—in this case, the defendant's wife, whose place he supposed Jane to have taken.

(e) *Absence from Church on Secular Occupation*

Besides those examples given elsewhere, e.g. for Scarborough on p. 77, the following may be quoted:

A.D. 1575   [Visitation Books, R. VI. A. 5, f. 3 v.]

York: 'All halowes parishe upon the Pavement. The people upon the Pavement do commonlie open ther shoppes on Sondaies and holiedaies if faires and marketts fall on suche daies.'

St. Maries in Castlegate: 'Robte. Sedgewicke cometh not to the churche, and kepeth evell companie in his howse tiplinge in service tyme.'

[1] For fear it may not be worse.

[Ibid. f. 30.]

Doncaster: 'Willm. Swaine and Roger Chase taken[1] drinkinge in service tyme at Thomas Wilbore his howse.'

[Ibid. f. 11 v.]

Otley parishe: 'Gilbert Dickson dyd plowe and sowe on our Ladyes day last past to the evell example of others.'

[Ibid. f. 92.]

Bridlinton: [Five men named] 'were founde at alehowse in service tyme and wold not paie the xiid. but ar obstinate and beggerlie.'

[Ibid. f. 85.]

Howden: 'Thomas Savage and Thomas Westabye and others not named being xx in nombre bowled in evenynge praier tyme at Whitsontide last.'

[Ibid. f. 62.]

Dighton: 'Robte. Fulbarn misused the Curate beinge but willed by him to leave of the unlawfull game of bowlinge in the churcheyearde the first of May last which Roberte did before hurt the Curate with his dagger and was never punished. Presented by the Vicar of Northallerton.'

'Chris. Hudson of Dighton beinge with Fulbarne at the said bowlinge laid violent hands upon the Curate at the said tyme and bett him grevowslie in the churcheyeard. Presented as before.'

18 Feb. 1582/3   [Ecclesiastical Commission, Act Books, R. VII. A. 10, f. 194 v.]

Robt. Browne one of the churchwardens of Bolton Percy confessed that 'on yesterday fourtnighte or three weekes beinge Sonday hee and other nyne [named] did bowle together in time of evening praier for two gallons of ale and came not then to divine service in Bolton parish, then and there standing by Joh. Robinson Edwde. Derwente and others'. The Commissioners ordered Browne to levy xiid. apiece from the other offenders, and to deliver the same 'with xiid. for himself to Mr. Buny to be destributed by him and the

---

[1] The 'taken' implies the house-to-house visits which the churchwardens were expected to make while divine service was in progress.

churchwardens according to their discretions And in case anie man shall refuse to pay the same then hee is to certify their names to Mr. Buny that furder order may be taken as shalbee conveniente. And Browne is furder enjoined to bee dutifull in repairinge to the churche and in presenting those that shalbe offendours in that behalf from time to time And hee is to certify the performance of this order on Monday in the fourthe weeke of this Lente at Yorke etc.'

(f) *Absence from Church for fear of Arrest, especially for Debt*

A.D. 1575   [Visitation Books, R. VI. A. 5, f. 13 v.]

Garforthe: 'Mr. Geo. Layton cometh not to the Churche It is thought to rather to be for feare of processe then for mislikinge of religion.'

[Ibid. f. 80.]

Wilberfosse: '...Edwd. Harlinge for feare of processe did absent him self vi or vii Sondaies from the Church....'

A.D. 1586   [Ibid. R. VI. A. 9, f. 148 v.]

Hesle: '...c. Chris. Leppington he dyd not communycate they thinke it be for feare of processe Quo die because it appeared by certificate that he received at Wetwang ideo respectuatur.'

The churchwardens of St Martin's Coneystreet, York, against John Stock:

No date (? c. 1570) Articles and answers only. [Cause Papers (Precedents), uncalendared.]

...Item they do put and article that the said John Stock nether having the fear of God before his eies...upon the Sonday next before the feast of the Natyvitie of St. John Baptist last past did coome into the parishe churche of St. Martyn in Conystrete in tyme of dyvine service that is to say abowt the reding of the latter end of the Epistell appointed to be red in the churche that day And then and there... did openlye lay violent handes upon one Willm. Owthwayte who was then in the churche quietlye hering of dyvine service, taking him by the bosome shoolders and armes togging and pulling him to have drawen him by force forthe of the churche In suche cruell manner and with suche lowde and highe woordes that all the parishoners there assembled whiche were to the noomber abowt twoo hundreth to here dyvine service were therebye greatlye amased troobled and disquieted so that there was suche a tumult and noyse in the same churche that nether the curate there celebrating the communyon or commemoracione therof coold any further procede in the same of a long tyme nor yet any of the parishoners here the same in case he had forther proceded....

The answer to this was:

...To the second article [he] aunswereth and beleveth that [he] beinge an officer or Serjant upon the Sonday articulate after the Service there was ended...did arreste Willm. Owthewaite by the vertewe of one precept to hym dyrected and delyvered And otherwise he beleveth the contents of this article not to be trewe in any parte therof. [No sentence is recorded.]

(g) *Examples of Disorder from Later Visitation Books*

A.D. 1590 [Visitation Books, R. VI. A. 12, f. 22 v.]

Aldbrough: [Two men] 'for behaving themselfs disorderlie in churche in service time, in piping dauncing and playing Mr. Hudesley ther vicar being then preaching.'

[Ibid. f. 60 v.]

Manchester: 'The wyfe of the Deanesgate called one of the churche-wardens pratinge Jacke and sayd she woulde talke and aske him no leave when he reproved her for talkinge in sermon tyme.'

[Ibid. f. 72.]

Warrington: [Ten men are named]. 'All these did go forth of the church in sermon tyme.'

[Ibid. f. 81 v.]

Lym: 'Rog. Bonde of Rawsterne parishe a sleper in the churche in service tyme.'

[Ibid. f. 87.]

Woodchurche: [Three men] 'laid upon the grasse in the churche yard upon Trinitie soonday in service tyme.'

[Ibid. f. 102.]

Stopport alias Stockporte: 'Willm. Coulsell of Stockporte usuallye goeth oute of the churche when the sermon begynneth.'

A.D. 1595   [Ibid. R. VI. A. 14, f. 82.]

Sutton upon Trent: 'Robt. Theaker...will not sitt in his owne appointed stall in the church but in other mens.'

[Ibid. f. 103.]

Bilton: 'Brian Abbay and two others "plaid at Tuts[1] on Low-soonday at evenyng prayer tyme".'

[Ibid. f. 107.]

Fuiston: 'Hugh Gryme did contende offensivelie at the chappell doore aboute caryinge in of rishes into the Chapell.'

[Ibid. f. 134.]

Topcliffe: [Three men] 'were lookinge upon strangers playinge at peniston[2] in the churche yarde in devine service tyme.' Compare the five men and their servants in R. VI. A. 10, 1590, f. 259 v., who 'go often tymes to Tanfelde churche upon Sondayes and hollydayes and ther committ dyvers disorders there as walkinge and talkinge in their churche and churcheyearde in servyce tyme and the churche-wardens of Tanfelde have presented'.

A.D. 1578   [Ibid. R. VI. A. 7, f. 39.]

Midleton ecclesia: [Two men named] 'of Oldam parish and four of Prestwiche parish beinge nigher theire churche then their owne will rather lye abrode under some hedge or some such like place after they have shewed themselfes once in the churche then abide in the churche the service tyme.'

[1] A game resembling stoolball, or a primitive form of baseball. The 'tuts' were the 'bases'.
[2] Not identified.

CHAPTER III

THE FIGHT AGAINST IGNORANCE

1. QUALIFICATIONS AND EXAMINATION OF THE CLERGY

A.D. 1594   [Visitation Books, R. VI. A. 9, f. 154.]

Mr. Gryffethe Rector of Rowthe Mr. Asheton Rector of Leven and Mr. Chynley Rector of Longe Ruston do not repaire to Mr. Whincoppe preacher att Beverleye with theyr exercyses accordinge to commaundemente.

A.D. 1595   [Ibid. R. VI. A. 14, f. 10 v.]

Wybunburye: 'The exercyse prescrybed to the clergie for thincrease of theyr learnynge dothe nowe cease and is neglected.'

(a) *Earlier Procedure*

Letter of Commission from the Archbishop's Commissary General 'Of the office of our Court in York', Mr. Tho. de Nassyngton, to ds. Willms. de Wirkesworth, the Archbishop's Receiver and Dean of the Christianty of York, previous to an Ordination. 10 Sept. 1344:

[Register Zouche, f. 286.]

...ad examinandos clericos nostre diocesis in instantibus ordinibus proxime celebrandis necnon admittendos clericos quos post diligentem examinacionem habiles et ydoneos scientia moribus et etate ac titulos sufficientes habentes reperieritis.

Letters Testimonial for Orders: a group of forty letters, ranging in date from 1554 to 1557, are the earliest of this class preserved in the Registry. [York, Diocesan Registry, not indexed.] Whether in Latin or in English, they show a marked adherence to a common form. They observe all the main requirements found in the Commission from Archbishop Zouche's Register, above. Typical quotations are:

(i) For Joh. Thomson of Foston in Holderness, 10 Dec. 1554:

...dictus Johannes Thomson fuit et est honeste conversacionis bone fame et opinionis illese, non conversans in locis aut cum personis

96

suspectis, tabernas non frequentans, lusu alearum cardarum trocharum
ve aut venacionibus ex consuetudine non utens nec contentionibus
sediciosus ve nec percussor neque ad pugnam defacili provocatus seu
erronia opinione maxime harisim infectus seu aliquo alio saltem
notabili crimine suspectus aut circumspersus sed talis qui ad sacros
ordines merito promoveri debeat et valeat....

(ii) Chris. Ampulforth of Kirkby Overblows, 6 Dec. 1556:
...grammatophorum hunc Chris. Ampulforth parochie de Kirkbie Overblawes scholasticum atque liberum legitimoque matrimonio
prognatum, etatisque viginti trium annorum et amplius, juvenem
honestum et probatissimis moribus preditum, nunquam conjugatum
nunquam excommunicatum neque suspensum neque heresibus schis-
matibus-ve coinquinatum aut conspurcatum vel aliquo alio crimine
saltem notorie defamatum, quo minus ad quoscumque sacros ordines
tam majores quam minores quos nondum est assecutus legitime per
sacrarum manuum vestrarum imposicionem promoveri non possit.
Habet quoque ipse Christoferus quandam annuitatem quinque
librarum de terris et tenementis...in parochia de Hunsingore...pro
termino vite sue naturalis....

(iii) Willm. Bache of Cheston, Salop, 12 Dec. 1556:
...[he] haithe ever been of good and honest conversacion and
borne in lawfull matrimonye allwaye applying lerning and vertue no
hawker nor hunter nor comonlye freqwentyng any common aile
house, nor using any evell and suspected places and companye nor no
comon carder nor dicer nor busie player at anye other unlawfull and
prohibite games, no brawler chider nor fighter never contensious nor
busye in erronious questions and opinions but ever of his nature
gentle curteouse and benigne in all his wordes workes and dedes
against all men....

(iv) R. Bell of Tadcaster, 4 March 1556/7:
...cum bonum habere testimonium ordinandos oporteat R. Bell
vestre paternitati presento, testificans eum esse virum ut grammatice
latine non ignarum ita moribus irreprehensibilem quantum intelligo
aut suspicor....

(v) Joh. Tyrrell scholaris of Wensley, with Letters Dimissory from Chester:

...[he] commeth to York at this tyme to be made subdeacon besuchyng your mastershep for your helpe and favor to admyt hym ther to tak orders he is a very honest young man, and had his grammer perfectly, but he hath ben this sex yeres last past frome the scoole, but he hath promessed me that he will apply his lernyng very diligently from hencforth And iff he be prest I shall fynd meanes to get hyme waiges at Wenslay to such tyme as he can be hable to serve one of my cures....

(b) *Examination of Clergy*

No record of any examination or of any course of instruction prescribed before Ordination has been found in the Elizabethan Registers, nor any document referring to a standard of proficiency in religious knowledge required of the clergy, but there are entries in Grindal's Act Book of Institutions which reveal an established practice:

Archbishop Grindal's Injunctions for the Clergy [Reg. Grindal, No. 22, f. 156 v.]

ITEM ye shall daylye reade at the leaste one chapter of the oulde Testament and an other of the New with good advisement, and suche of you as be under the degree of a maister of arte shall provide and have of your owne accordinge to the quenes majesties injunctions at the leaste the newe Testament both in latine and englishe, conferinge the one with the other everye daye one chapter thereof at the leaste, so that upon the examination of the Archdeacon commissary or their officers in synodes and visitations or at other appointed tymes it maye appeare, how ye profite in the studye of holye scripture.

There is, however, nothing to show definitely why nine only out of 195 clergy instituted were examined, unless these were all disputed presentations.

31 Aug. 1572 [York, Diocesan Registry, R. V. A. 2, f. 4.]
Before the Archbishop's Official. Willm. Taylor, asserting that he had Letters of Crown Presentation to the Vicarage of Hutton Bushell:

Et tunc idem Magister Joh. Gibson eidem Willelmo Tailor petenti respondendo dixit quod per examinationem ejus captam de mandato domini Archiepiscopi constat eidem Reverendissimo patri eundem

W. Tailor clericum hujusmodi Vicariam recipiendum minus esse idoneum precipue propter doctrinae ejus insufficientiam quocirca idem Reverendissimus pater duxit eum...non admittendum....

24 July 1572   [Ibid. f. 6.]

Tho. Asbroke clerk presenting Letters of Presentation from the patron of Hawton by Newark was rejected 'quia idem Tho. Asbroke per examinacionem suam inveniebatur minus sufficiens tam scientia quam doctrina ad hujusmodi beneficio gaudendum et habendum', and the patron was ordered 'ad presentandum alium personam idoneum infra tempus de jure sibi assignatum'.

Before the Archbishop personally in the Deanery at Westminster. [Ibid. f. 8.]

John Preston clerk presented Letters of Crown Presentation to the Vicarage of Brayton, but the Archbishop, finding him by examination 'ad acceptandum in se curam animarum parochianorum ibidem propter defectum doctrinae et scientiae sue aliasque causas canonicas minus idoneum et sufficientem fuisse', refused to admit him.

29 Aug. 1572   Before the Archbishop. [Ibid. f. 10.]

...comparuit personaliter Jacobus Stevenson clericus (ut asseruit) et exhibuit litteras...et petiit se virtute earundem ad Rectoriam de [Hawton] admitti...et tunc Reverendissimus pater quia ex responsionibus personalibus ejusdem J. Stevenson in presentia magistrorum Joh. Gibson LL.D. et Rad. Tunstall A.M. manifeste constabat et apparuit eundem Stevenson examinatum racionem fidei latino sermone nequaquam eidem Reverendissimo patri ordinario suo reddere potuisse nec sensum aliquem verborum Pauli ad Romanos viz. Qui sine lege peccaverunt etc., nec peccatum difinere aut differentia ulla inter legem et evangelium ponere immo nec grammaticarum regulas intellexisse longum sillabum corripiendo et brevem producendo (viz. legendo perībunt pro perĭbunt ac exprīmunt pro exprĭmunt) dictum J.S. ex causis predictis et aliis nonnullis...non admittendum ...sed tanquam minus idoneum ad curam animarum in se suscipiendum reiciendum fore decrevit et ipsum laicali habitu vel potius militari quam clericali judicialiter rejecit....

Ric. Helys clerk, exhibiting Letters of Presentation to the Rectory of Londesbrough:

19 Feb. 1572/3 [Ibid. f. 21.]

...Et tunc quia idem Helys alias examinatus in sacris scripturis satis peritus in eisdem...minime inveniebatur et sic ad curam dicte ecclesie suscipiendum haud idoneum.... [He was not admitted.]

Edwd. Trutbeck, B.A., having Letters of Presentation to the Rectory of Spofforth. The reference is to the Statute of 13 Eliz. ordering that the more lucrative benefices should be reserved for clergy who held the Degree of B.D. or were approved as Preachers. This entry gives the first reference to the Domestic Chaplain as Examining Chaplain, acting previously to examination by the Archbishop personally.

[Ibid. f. 23.]

...quoniam statuto hujus regni Anglie anno regni domine nostre Elizabethe...decimo tercio...nemo admittetur ad beneficium ecclesie curam animarum in se habens cujus valor in libris regie majestatis annuis summam triginta librarum excedat nisi qui baccalaureus theologie fuerit vel sacrosancti verbi Dei concionator legitime approbatus Et ipse Edwd. Trutbeck B.A. tantum examinatione debita prehabita tam per Magistrum Willm. Palmer capellanum Reverendissimi patris quam per seipsum dominum Archiepiscopum in sacris litteris inventus est ignarus nec pro concionatore sacrosancti verbi Dei approbandus sed inhabilis et ad tantam animarum curam in se suscipiendum inidoneus nec ejusdem Rectorie de Spowfurth secundum veram dicti statuti intencionem vere capax utpote qui sacras literas ignorat nec baccalaureus existat theologie aut pro predicatore approbandus sit.... [Therefore his application was rejected.]

28 May 1574 [Ibid. f. 46 v.]

The Archbishop deputed his function to Chris. Lyndleye clerk S.T.B. his Domestic Chaplain 'ad examinandum Willm. Ireland clericum manerio de Bishopthorpe accessum causa presentandi et exhibendi...literas presentacionis de persona sua ad Rectoriam de Harthill dioc. Ebor. factas.

Imprimis interrogatus fatebatur se exhibuisse presentacionem ad dictam Rectoriam per eosdem Geo. et Robt. Watterhowse, patronos....

Item interrogatus quomodo exponeret hec verba in presentacione sua, Vestri humiles et obedientes, respondet Your humbleness and obedience.

Item interrogatus quis eduxit populum Israelis ex Egipto respondet Rex Saul.

Item interrogatus quomodo probaret nos fidem habere ex verbo Dei respondet ex secundo capite Pauli ad Ephesios Gratia enim estis servati per fidem non ex vobis Dei dona est non ex operibus ne quis glorietur. Eodem die idem Wm. Ireland per...dominum Edmundum Ebor. Archiepiscopum...examinatus non potuit grammatices sensum reddere initii tercii capitis ad Romanos nec respondere quis fuit primus circumcisus. Unde idem Reverendissimus pater die et loco predictis...ob insufficientiam Willelmi Ireland doctrina et inscientia ejus sacris scripturis...decrevit eum non admittendum.'

The most lengthy of these entries is concerned with a case referred to the Archbishop from the Diocese of Chester. To give the history briefly: Peter Yate had been presented by Tho. Venables, the patron of Eccleston, to the Bishop of Chester as Ordinary for institution. The Bishop had refused to institute, on the ground that Yate was not 'sufficienter literatus'; Venables had taken the matter to the Queen's Justice at Chester, who had referred the matter to the Queen. The Queen, by brief dated 11 August 1574, had required the Archbishop to examine Yate and to take what action was necessary, and to inform the Justice at Chester of his proceedings. Copies of all the main documents are entered in the Act Book. The examination of Yate was brief. He appeared at Bishopthorpe on 26 July 1575:

...ac exhibuit Reverendissimo patri breve domine nostre regine clausum sibi prefato Reverendissimo patri directum pro examinatione dicti Petri an sufficienter literatus necne Quo quidem breve per eundem Reverendissimum patrem debita cum reverentia recepto ac aperto et perlecto Idem Reverendissimus pater virtute ejusdem brevis Petrum Yate super quatuor sententias decimi tercii capituli Epistoli Pauli ad Hebreos sic incipientes Horum corpora cremantur extra castra, debite sermone latino examinavit Ex quarum sententiarum verbis idem Petrus Yate sensum aliquem verum aut genuinum elicere non potuit nec reddere Unde idem Reverendissimus pater habuit eundem Yate pro non sufficienter literato et decrevit certificatorium inde fiendum juxta tenorem dicti brevis et certificavit.

(c) *Further Illustrations from the Visitation Records*

A.D. 1571   [Visitation Books, R. VI. A. 3a, f. 39.]

O.d.c. Rog. Menythorpe, a pluralist who 'serveth ii cures' at Holom and Old Malton: '...he shall not serve any cure before he be examyned by Mr. Palmer and that he shall have my L. grace his admission accordinglie.'

O.d.c. Ric. Bright, Rector of Whiston, who had also a Cure in Lichfield Diocese: '...he is to provide a sufficient Curate for Whiston and send him within thes vi wekes to my Lords grace or suche as shalbe assigned for thexamynacion of the said curate to thende yt maye be perfectlie knowen that [he] is sufficient to discharge the cure in all respects.'

(d) *Examination of Clergy by the Ecclesiastical Commissioners*

26 Oct. 1571   [Ecclesiastical Commission, Act Books, R. VII. A. 6, f. 115.]

The Commissioners received a report on the examination of Nich. Troughton, Rector of Bootle, as follows: 'Anglice distincte legit. Latinum sermonem utrumque intelligit. In sacris parum versatus. Examinatus per me Gul. Palmes.'

4 Nov. 1575   [Ibid. R. VII. A. 8, f. 155 v.]

O.d.c. Robt. Beverleye clerk, Rector of Bedall: 'The Commyssioners dyd assigne him to appeare again before the Quenes Majesties Commyssioners for cawses ecclesiasticall within the province of Yorke which then shalbe resiant at the Cittye of Yorke or three of them this tyme three yeres now next to come and then to offer himself to examination that his learninge and understandinge maye be knowen and how he is profited in the same, and appoynted him to go to his booke in the meane space And for asmuche as his benefice of Bedall is a good and an hable living for a preacher the Commissioners in respecte of the disabilitie of Robt. Beverleye did assigne and decree unto him a Coadjutor there to preache and to cathechise [but not to be any further charged with the cure there] for the space of thre yeres from the feast of the Nativitie of Our Lord next folowinge the date hereof, to be named and appointed by this honorable Courte And appointed unto him for his stipende yerelie for the tyme the somme of fortie marks of lawfull Englishe moneye to be paid at Easter and Michaelmas by even portyons in the parishe churche at Bedall, Robt. Beverleye consenting therto, and bond being entred by John Beverleye esquire his father so to paie the same furth of the fruits of the benefice if his son continew so long parson there.... And if Robert at his examination to be made be found not to have profited in learning and continew still ignorant the matter to be taken as it now standeth and the advantages therof to be re-streined and he further to be punished as the Commyssioners shall thinke mete either by contynewing or encreasing the stipende or by depriving him if he shall deserve it And if he be founde to have profyted Then the same stipende to ende and determyne if the Commyssioners shall so determyne, otherwise still to contynewe And so Robt. Beverleye is dismissed.'

22 Aug. 1580.   Examination in presence of the Commission.   [Ibid. R. VII. A. 10, f. 24.]

Tho. Brygges clerk Curate of Pateley Brygges '...beinge thought and reported to be him selfe backwarde in matters of religion and to seduce others by his synister whisperinge in ther eares And being wylled before thassemblie then and ther presente to yeilde his opynion upon these two textes of scripture viz. Tu es Petrus etc. and Hoc est corpus meum for ther satisfaction who stode in doubt of his zeale in Gods truthe he partely refused to do it publicquelie and shewed him selfe very unwillinge to do yt and at last spoke somethinge thereof verie absurdely Wherfore and for other causes the Com-missioners movinge the said Brygges was commytted to the Castell of Yorke ther to remayne donec etc.'

2. EXAMINATION OF SCHOOLMASTERS

The first of the Visitation Act Books in the Registry is a curious volume. Although it is headed 'Liber Actorum coram Commissariis Regiis Anno 1561', it is actually not so, but is the Archbishop's Act Book for his Court of Audience, yet as such it contains an unusually high proportion of business concerning the administration of wills. It differs from later Books of the Court of Audience after Visitation in being far more occupied with legal form; a presentment is rarely quoted, and in many cases it is necessary to read five or six successive records of complicated legal pro-cesses before coming to any statement of the matter alleged against the defendant. In this respect, the Book much more resembles the normal Consistory Court Book of Tudor times, and suggests that procedure in causes after Visitation was still in 1561 in a very experimental stage and had not yet been distinguished from that in Consistory or Prerogative business. On f. 38, without any preparation, the Book suddenly begins a record of the examination of schoolmasters, which is continued almost without any mixture of other business for the following sixty-nine folios, after which the testamentary causes again become the chief matters before the Court, to the end of the volume.[1]

[York, Diocesan Registry, R. VI. A. 1, f. 38.]

Die mercurii viz. xxvii die mensis Octobris A.D. 1563 infra ecclesiam Cathedralem et metropoliticam Ebor....coram venerabili viro Mag. Joh. Rokeby LL.D. et Waltero Jones LL.B.....

Officium dominorum contra Ludimagistros decanatus de Ponte-fract Ebor. dioc. Quibus die horis et loco preconizatis hujusmodi ludimagistris comparuerunt personaliter ut sequitur viz. Joh. Watson ludimagister apud Hallyfax Tho. Henley ludimagister apud Lud-dinden parochie de Hallyfax Joh. Shotwell ludimagister apud Wakefeld Robt. Hall ludimagister de Bradfurthe quos domini monuerunt (ad interessendum) crastino die hoc loco ad ulterius faciendum et recipiendum quod justicia in hac parte suadebit et ad subeundum examen Et preconizato Ricardo Laycock et judicialiter citato diutiusque expectato et nullo modo comparente dictus Joh. Rokeby...consentiente dicto Mag. Walt. Jones pronunciavit eum contumacem et in pena contumacie sue hujusmodi eundem Ricardum excommunicavit in scriptis....

[Ibid. f. 39.]

O.dd.c. Joh. Hall ludimagistrum apud Bradfurth. Monitus est ad interessendum istis die horis et loco ad ulterius faciendum et recipiendum quod justicia in hac parte suadebit etc. Quibus die

---

[1] The number of schoolmasters shown in this volume as examined in 1564 was fifty-seven, from all parts of the diocese. As usual, there is no indication why these were examined, and not others. Of the fifty-seven examined, nineteen, all clergy, were admitted to the highest qualification; thirteen described only as schoolmasters were admitted to teach, and six others to catechise also; six clergy and one school-master to catechise in English only. Two clergy and three schoolmasters were rejected altogether. The remaining seven were admitted to the highest category without indication whether they were clergy or not. The qualification in almost every case for the highest category was 'Latinum callere distincteque legere'.

horis et loco comparuit personaliter dictus Robt Hall et interrogatus per dominos fatetur et confessus est quod habet stipendium annuale octo librarum consistens in possessionibus temporalibus. Et domini monuerunt eundem Hall ad personaliter interessendum crastino die ad ulterius... [etc.].

[Ibid. f. 39 v.]

...c. Willm. Scott ludimagistrum apud Dewesburye...et domini examinaverunt eum et admiserunt eum ad docendum scholam grammaticalem in aliquo loco infra diocesim Ebor. durante beneplacito Reverendissimi patris seu ejus Vicarii in spiritualibus.

1 Dec. 1563   [Ibid. f. 46.]

...c. dnm. Hen. Cowston curatum de Agnes Burton ac ludimagistrum ibidem....quem dominus examinavit et inveniens eum idoneum admisit eundem dnm. Henricum ad catechisandum pueros et prime grammatices rudimenta docendum per diocesim Ebor. et etiam dictus Hen. Cowston subscripsit articulis.

2 Dec. 1563   [Ibid. f. 47.]

...c. dnm. Hen. Jackeson curatum de Norton...petiit beneficium absolucionis a sentencia excommunicacionis alias in eum latum sibi impendi Et dominus ad ejus peticionem eundem Jackeson absolvendum decrevit et postea examinacione habita dominus invenit eum minus idoneum ad docendum ut qui latina lingua ignarus... erat Et ideo interdixit predicto Henrico Jackeson officium docendi latinos autores at admisit eundem Jackeson ad catechisandum pueros lingua varnacula.

7 Dec. 1563   [Ibid. f. 49 v.]

...c. dnm. Joh. Thompson diaconum ludimagistrum apud Waykefeld...quem domini examinaverunt et invenientes eum latinum callere mediocriter et legere distincte tum anglice tum latine Admiserunt eum ad catechisandum pueros lingua materna et orthographiam docendum tantum Et interdicitur illi munus grammatices docendi. Examinatus super articulis...subscripsit eisdem.

Dec. 1563 [Ibid. f. 52.]

...c. dnm. Hen. Langdayle vicarium de Skardbroughe et ludimagistrum ibidem...comparuit...Hen. Langdayle educatus Canta-
brigiis in Collegio sancti Benedicti per quatuor annos continuos
bonis litteris operam locavit sub Magistro Waykefeld publico
Hebraices professore Quem domini examinaverunt et invenientes
habilem et idoneum et linguam hebraicam utrumque callere,
latinam autem bene, admiserunt ad publice docendum et catechisandum puerulos grammatices rudimenta tradendo per diocesim
Ebor ubilibet...(subscripsit)....

[Ibid. f. 53 v.]

xvii die mensis Decembris A.D. 1563 coram mag. Ric. Barnes
S.T.B. Cancellario Ecclesie...Ebor. Ric. Hurstus ludimagister apud
Almondbury distincte legit et latinum tum callet tum scribit ac
dictat mediocriter grammaticen ad unguem callet, unde examinatus
et inventus idoneus et habilis Mag. R. Barnes admisit eum ad
docendum et cathechisandum puerulos lingua materna et vulgari
ac etiam ad prima grammatices rudimenta tradenda et eundem
Ricardum decet super articulis synodi Londonensis[1] examinavit
quos omnes et singulos lubenti animo confessus est et subscripsit
eisdem.

6 Jan. 1563/4 [Ibid. f. 54.]

...c. Ric. Michill scolarem Oxoniensem ex contubernio aule
beate Marie ludimagistrum apud Heptonstall...inveniens eum
latinum callere, distincte legere, et in trivialibus artibus bene multum
versatum juvenem bone indolis admisit eum ad cathechisandum
pueros et ad docendum artem grammatices....

17 Jan. 1563/4 [Ibid. f. 55.]

...c. Tho. Standeven curatum de Cooley ac ludimagistrum
ibidem...inveniens eum anglice distincte legere, latinum nec bene
legere nec intellegere igitur admisit eum ad catechisandum pueros
lingua vernacula tantum et inhibuit eidem ne doceat omnino latine
donec licentia eidem fuerit concessa....

---

[1] The Thirty-nine Articles of the Convocation of 1562.

19 Jan. 1563/4 [Ibid. f. 55 v.]

...c. Chris. Henry ludimagistrum apud Huddersfeld...inveniens eum idoneum admisit eum ad catechisandum pueros lingua verna-cula And the Englysshe prymmer nowe allowyd and the Englyshe accedens and no further....

11 Feb. 1563/4 [Ibid. f. 60.]

...c. Joh. Hunte ludimagistrum apud Beverlacum...inveniens eum sufficienter eruditum linguis latina greca et ebraica aptumque et idoneum admisit ad docendum et publice profitendum artem grammatices ceterasque liberales facultates et scientias apud Bever-lacum....

[Ibid. f. 71 v.]

...c. Chris. Say lud. apud Retfourde...Christoferus Saius Cantabrigie in Collegio Jesu educatus et bonas litteras edoctus annorum xl latinam linguam adamussim callet sed et grecam bene intelligit ac interpretatur, latinos autores interpretari novit Exami-natus autem super articulos precipuos catholice fidei confessus est eosdem esse pios...et subscripsit lubens volensque unde domini eundem...admiserunt ad docendum publiceque profitendum gram-matices scientiarum studiose juventuti apud Retfourde....

[Ibid. f. 72.]

Eodem die...comparuit...Geo. Sanders ludimagister publice schole grammaticalis apud Newarke super Trent...adolescens viginti quinque annorum Cantabrigie per aliquod tempus bonis litteris operam dedit non sine fruge bona. latinam linguam callet et inter-pretari bene novit...admiserunt eundem G.S. ad grammatices scientiam publice profitendum bonosque authores studiose juventuti publice apud Newarke interpretandos et exponendos.

[Ibid. f. 84.]

Quarto die mensis Julii A.D. 1564...comparuit Fra. Hill de Byrd-lington...latinam linguam apprime callet bonosque authores latinosque bene interpretari novit, de vite autem probitate morumque honestate sufficienti virorum proborum testimonio nobis com-mendatus existit, zeli autem in deum pii ac in rebus Christiane synceritatis et religionis negocio judicii admodum synceri ac sani esse videtur....Unde domini prefato Fra. Hill ad catechisandum puerulos artemque gramatices docendum bonos autem authores quosque latinos exponendum et publice interpretandum sermone latino vel vulgari pro capacitate auditorum suorum apud Bridlington ac aliis in locis ad hoc congruis et honestis infra diocesim Ebor. quamdiu laudabiliter se gesserit in hac parte licentiam tenore presentium impartiti sunt....

Memorandum that lettres was directed to the balifs and churchwardens of Bridlington to inhibit Andro Olyvaunt a scotishman not to medle with any teaching any scole without license under seale etc. per Mag. Barnes.

[Ibid. f. 84 v.]

...Fra. Fletcher adolescens xvii annorum ludimagister apud Raskell...Oxonii per aliquod tempus bonis litteris operam navavit, latinum linguam callet utrumque sed non admodum, distincte legit, nec alicujus judicii est Unde interdictum est illi munus docendi infra diocesim Ebor.

Dictis die et anno domini Ric. Collie clericus Curatus de Bagby parochie de Kyrkeby Knoll ac ludimagister educatus apud Helmesley latinum mediocriter callet, distincte legit, judicii nullius neque omnino versatus est in sacra lectione Unde interdicitur illi munus instituendi juventutem grammaticamque docendi omnino etc.

The Commissioners also occasionally dealt with a schoolmaster.

16 Dec. 1570 [Ecclesiastical Commission, Act Books, R. VII. A. 5, ff. 177, 186.]

Forasmuche as by examination in that behalfe maide John Lacye was and is found unable and insuffyciente bothe for his learninge and otherwise to kepe the Grammer Schole at Bradforde [the Commissioners] did discharge [him] from the said office of scholemastershippe and commaunded and enjoyned him not onelye to surcease to kepe the said schole or teache children in the said towne of Bradforde But also to abstein from teaching in all places els where within the dyoces of Yorke and not to receive in any place a scolemasters stipende untill he be lycensed thereunto.

13 March 1570/1   [Ibid. f. 230.]

Joh. Nettleton, schoolmaster at Ripon, was 'discharged from his office of scolemastershippe at Rypon, yet they licenced him to kepe the same till a new Mr. be provyded lest the yowthe be neglected and untaughte and then warned him to departe and give place'.

3. RETURNS OF THE EXAMINATION OF CLERGY BY THE ARCHBISHOP'S CHAPLAINS

These returns were made by the Domestic Chaplains of the Archbishop going on special Visitation in areas roughly equivalent to the Rural Deaneries. The documents are not yet fully calendared, but will be found indexed under the Visitation group R. VI. B. in the Diocesan Registry.

i (a). A small paper attached to the larger return

Quot beneficia. Doctrina. Conciones. Catechismus. Registrum. Quos incontinentes presentatos per parochianos ad Arch. nec tamen prius.

Singula cap. Mathei ediscenda in proxima Visitatione Arch.

i (b). Charta examinationis Chris. Lindleii in Decanatu Bulmer
28 April 1575

Elvyngton.	Chris. Hustler Rector de Elvington baccalaureus artium sufficienter eruditus. conciones habuit at non iiii in anno secundum statutum. catechismum docet quem omnes...registrum habet et observat diligenter.
Thursce.	Michaell Jackson Curatus de Thurske per annum elapsum. Baccalaureus artium eruditus ac ut videtur zelosus. conciones habuit sufficientes, catechismum docet ac registrum habet etc.
Kneeby.	Joh. Rydsdale Curatus ibidem per 4 annos. zelosus. rationem fidei tenet. conciones habet plures quod...Thursc. registri ordinem observavit et similiter docet catechismum.

Miton.

Joh. Squyer Vicarius de Miton eruditus zelosus. conciones non habuerunt ibidem per 12 annos. catechismum docet diligenter. registrum habet.

Alne.

Lancelotus Person Vicarius per 10 annos. conjugatus. mediocriter versatus in sacris litteris. conciones habuit secundum statuta. catechizat etiam et registrum observat etc.

Newton.

Robertus Dande Curatus ibidem per annum et dimidium. mediocriter eruditus. juvenis ut videtur honestus, conciones nullas ibidem habuerunt hoc anno unam tamen superiore. catechismum docet. registrum nullum habuerunt ante ejus adventum, ille autem unum habet.

Overton.

Robertus Ridsdale Vicarius ibidem mediocriter institutus in scripturis. concionem ibidem nullam habuerunt hoc anno duos superiore. catechismum docet diligenter et registrum habet.

ii. Examinationes per me Georgium Slater Aprilis 28 1575.
Per Archidiaconatum de Cleveland

Thomas Rycherdson vicar de Sherif hutton.

Annos natus 27. Caelebs. sacram doctrinam quoad noticiam suam populo proponit. conciones tres in anno preterito habuit, unam per Magr. Colton Archidiaconum alteram per Geo. Slater tertiam per Magr. Smyth rectorem de Thirbasset. instruit juventutem in catechismo. registrum diligenter custodit etc.

Edwardus Otby rector de Tirrington.

habet annos 40. conjugatus. religiosus habetur. unam concionem habuit circiter annum preteritum per Geo. Slater. in doctrina catechismi parochianos instruit. registrum observat etc.

Anth. Myddleton V. de Sutton. Decanus.	religiosus et pius videtur. omnia cetera recte observat.
Chris. Englishe rector de Dalbye.	nullum beneficium preter hoc unum habet. 60 annos natus. pius videtur et religiosus. conciones non habuit quia nullos conciona- tores habere potuit qui facultatem predicandi habent. non instruit parochianos ac pueros in doctrina catechismi quia nulli ad eum veniunt, licet sepe ab eo prius moniti fuerunt. cetera omnia aguntur ordine et juxta statuta.
Edwd. Warde rector Wiginton.	satis notus est.
Edwd. Slater curatus de Wheldrike.	vicesimum quartum annum agens. nullam aliam curam habet. docet catechismum dili- genter. exercet se quotidie in sacris libris (ut ait).
Hugo Nixson curatus in capella de Farlington.	vicesimum sextum annum agens et celebs. nullas conciones habet tamen ipse pueros in doctrina catechismi docet. et cetera omnia observat quae requiruntur. videtur religiosus.

iii. [Heading torn away]

Craven...Gigleswicke.... Anno domini 15....

Jacobus Foster Curatus annos 66. Pontificius sacerdos. In sacris
literis mediocriter versatus et honesto testimonio Magistri Suti
non-nihil adjutus.

Boulton juxta Bollande.

Petrus Carter Rector ibidem annos 68 sacerdos pontificius.
hospitalis. coelebs. legit at mediocriter Latine. sua ipsius acquisi-
tione agrorum possessor (at in usus parvulorum quorundam).
conciones debitas gregi suo non persolvit.

Qui etiam fatetur viduam Henrici Pole et Magr. Pudson cum
uxore sua et tota familia se verbi et sacramenti usu semper privare.
nulla fatetur iodala aut quevis ejusmodi reliqua esse.

Arnecliffe.

Anth. Toppan Vicarius annos 60. sacerdos pontificius. conciones debitas hoc anno per alium persolvit. legit mediocriter atque intelligit. non fatetur se ullos habere qui se privant verbi aut signorum usu.

Scipton.

Ric. Heeles Vicarius annos 40. sacerdos pontificius. hospitalis. fatetur se nescire Comitissam de Cumberland plurimosque ex familia ejus unquam participes fuisse Coenae dominicae nec ulla monumenta papistica preter duo aut tria detrita vexilla in baculo reservata esse.

Capella de Gill in parochia de Barnoldeswicke.

Guilihelmus Cockson Curatus. annos 24. minister verbi. legit distincte. intelligit Latine mediocriter. nullas adhuc conciones habuit. reliqua omnia se bene habere apud suos contendit.

Ilkeley.

Constantinus Harrison ludimagister non admodum eruditus qui tamen juniores commode docere queat.

Braswell.

Joh. Catley Vicarius annos 66. sacerdos pontificius. legit et intelligit mediocriter. in sacris literis et praecipuis Religionis capitibus more pontificio satis infeliciter versatus est.

...on.

...Thorne Vicarius. annos 75. sacer[dos pont]ificius. intelligit mediocriter. ...indistincte. sanae doctrinae admodum expers. idola semper se abominatum esse vehementer contendit. conciones non persolvit.

Gargrave.

Chris. Procter curatus. annos 46. sacerdos pontificius. aliquantulum intelligit nec admodum distincte legit. [Three non-communicants.]

Tres conciones hoc superiore anno habuit.

iv. Gulielmus Palmes

Decanatus de Ridall apud Malton 16 die Maii A.D. 1575.

1. Joh. Bowthe curat of Newmalton. satis est cognitus. [A presentment for adultery.]

2. Cuth. Sheperde Parson of Nunnington. Minister est religionem...latinum satis intelligit. concionator ipse in sua parochia. ad chatechismum satis mittunt juniores parochiani ut doceantur, raro veniunt ad vesperas etc.

3. Peter Dale curatt of Kirkdale. presbiter fuit per 19 annos. zelosus est. Latinum sermonem intelligit. in sacris mediocriter versatus. conciones non habuit nisi...per Magr. Bunney. chathechismum docet sedulo.

4. Tho. Weddall curatt of Sinnington. minister fuit per biennium. conjugatus est. Latinum sermonem intelligit. pauper est. libros non habet et propterea non multum versatus sacris (literis) est. conciones non habuerunt in eo loco diu. catechismum docet. non habent in ecclesia tabulam ornamentorum nec libros paraphraseorum Erasmi.

5. Joh. Yeatson Viccar of Hutton Busshell. Satis est cognitus.

6. Roger Minithorpe curatt of Olde Malton. Minister fuit per 7 annos. zelosus est. Latinum intelligit. non est versatus sacris. profitetur religionem. conciones habuit per...Magr. Broke et me Gul. Palms et alios. registrum habet et custodit.

7. Willelmus Hammilton curate of Haram Chappell parochia de Hemislay. Minister per octo annos fuit. zelosus est. Latinum intelligit non tamen perfecte. in sacris aliquantulum versatus evangelicis. conciones v habuerunt in capella sua. catechismum...tenent. registrum custodiunt.

8. Joh. Mattison Viccar of Appleton. Satis cognitus est. conciones sex habuit intra biennium dictas per Mr. Slater et 4 per Mr. Bucke. superpelliceum...habent. registrum custodiunt.

9. Willm. Burnande parson of Slingesby. Presbiter fuit per 42 annos. zelosus est. Latinum non intelligit. in sacris (literis) parum aut nihil versatus. nullius est religionis (?). conciones habuit... quia Mr. Burnande in ea est parochia. catechismum sedulo docet et registrum habet.

10. Jhon Askwith parson of Hawenbye and Oswoldekirke. Satis cognitus est.

11. Tho. Stoorie parson of Scawton. Satis cognitus est. bachalaureus artium.

12. Willm. Crippelinges Vicar of Brunton. Sacerdos fuit per 51 annos. zelosus est. Latinum intelligit non tamen perfecte. parum versatus in sacris. in religione...est...-itetur religionem. conciones duas habuit per Mr. Watson. catechismum docet. registrum habet.

13. Jhon Cowper curat of Hovingham. Minister fuit per 8 annos. Latinum sermonem non intelligit. in sacris parum...versatus... evangelicis (?) nec profitetur. conciones multas habuit quia Mr. Burnande...est. catechismum docet. registrum custodit. fures... -furati sunt calicem....

14. Jhon Cowper curat capelle de Lockton parochia de Middleton. Diaconus est constitutus per dominum Archiepiscopum ante Pascham. Latinum intelligit. versatus aliquantulum sacris. cathechismum docet diligenter. registrum habet.

15. Geo. Simpson curat of Nesse parochia de Hovingeham. Sacerdos fuit per 26 annos. Latinum sermonem intelligit. in sacris bene versatus evangelicis. conciones quinque (?) habet. catechismum docet. registrum habet in parochiali ecclesia.

v. Examinatio ecclesiasticorum quorundam habita in Beverlaco
2 die Junii 1575 per me Henricum Wright

Ellerkar.

Tho. Brooke Curatus Capelle de Ellerkar percella de Brantingham. Hic avocatus non est reversus, itaque de eo significare non potui. sed non diu versatus in his partibus.

Skitbye.

Robt. Browne diaconus curatus de Skitby parcella de Cottingham. vir ut apparet industrius in evolvendis sacris scripturis et pietatis promovendo studiosus. legit articulate. Latine non intelligit. instituit juventutem in catechismo. natus est Colcestrie. annos numerat 35.

Leckingsfeld.	Jasper Boughan Scotus natione curatus aetatis vergentis in senium. videtur de religione recte sentire et non parum operis ponere in sanctis litteris. queritur de negligentia sui plebis in mittendis juniores ut catechizentur. notus alias ex actis superioris Visitationis.
Leven.	Willm. Gregges Rector senex. examinatus in Visitatione superiore ante annum quartum per Mr. Bunnye. pre se fert studiis pietatis.
Cottingham.	Jac. Steele Scotus natione assistens vicario in officio ecclesiastico. videtur pie sentire. doctus infra mediocritatem sive Latine lingue usum spectes sive scientiam religionis.
Scorbrook.	Hen. Lowghe Scotus natione natu grandior. utcumque exercitatus in sacris litteris. suos domi instituit ac juniores maxime in cate-chismo. pre se fert studium pietatis et super-stitionis odium.
Ryes.	Tho. Langdale Rector senex ut videtur pius. utcumque doctus. pollicetur industriam pro virili in promovenda cognitione Evangelii et in superstitione extirpanda.
Lockington.	Robt. Henrison curatus Scotus natione. Latine non intelligit. profitetur tamen pietatis studium homo vite inculpate et in erudiendis junioribus in catechismo aliisque sue vocationis officiis pro facultate diligens.
Rowlley.	Robt. Southerne curatus natu grandis. vir valde simplex sed qui pietatem animi pro-fitetur. non ignotus ex actis Visitationis 1571.
Sutton upon Darwin.	Joh. Williams Rector Latine parum intelligit. notus ex superiore Visitatione. vivit caelebs.
Hootham.	Tho. Coppeley Rector. notus item ex superiore Visitatione.

Cottingham.	Willm. Sawdon Vicarius. vir admodum pius et in officiis sue vocationis in primis diligens. alias etiam notus Reverendissimo.
Skearn.	Tho. Johnson curatus. vir penitus imperitus et ut videtur in veteres errores propulsior. docet tamen catechismum et alias apud suos bene audit.
North Cave.	Edwd. Browne Vicarius. juvenis pius et sacrarum litterarum studiosus, ac prorsus in omni officio diligens. alias etiam probe notus sacellanis Reverendissimi.
The minster chyrche of Beverlaye.	Joh. Fissher assistens. preterea etiam hypo-didascalus M. Richardsoni. juvenis probus et pius. Latine lingue et religionis utcumque peritus.
Burton Borealis alias Cherry Burton.	Tho. Davies curatus. juvenis item probus et studiosus. Latine intelligit. notus et ipse sacellanis Reverendissimi.

vi. Hulle et Holdernes. Examinatio tricesimo die Maii 1575 suscepta per me Geo. Slater

Fereby.	Egid. Barnes vicarius. Latine loquitur ac in sacris literis est utcumque versatus. bene audit de religione. conciones habet et pueros instruit in catechismo.
Beforth.	Tho. Bever in artibus magister. duo beneficia habet nempe rectoriam de Beforth et Rectoriam de Thornton in Lonsdale in comitatu Lancastrie. sacras literas bene novit et concionatur. Nich. Ashton curatus ibidem intelligit Latinum sermonem et ex parte loquitur. instruit pueros in catechismo.

Trinitye in Hull.	Symon Pynder Decanus de Hull et curatus Trinitatis. est zelosus. diligenter docet ac instruit in principiis religionis ignaros. conciones habet. licet in Latinis non sit peritus.
Frodingham.	Tho. Walker Vicarius. senex. Latinum sermonem bene intelligit ac loquitur (ut solent senes). instruit plebem diligenter et bene audit de religione.
Nunkelinge.	Joh. Barrowe curatus. principia religionis tenet et sensum scripturarum utcumque. conciones non habet. instruit pueros in catechismo.
Riston.	Geo. Claxton curatus. bene audit de religione. intelligit Latinum sermonem et loquitur. conciones habet. instruit ignaros.
Swine.	Chris. Mashlye Vicarius. sermonem Latinum intelligit ac loquitur ex parte. bene audit de religione. conciones non habet. pueros instruit in principiis religionis.
Homton.	Robt. Colingworth Rector. senex est et ut videtur bene de religione sentit, licet conciones non habet. tamen docet populum quantum possit.
Oram et Scipsy.	Tho. Jeffraye curatus de Oram. Latinum sermonem intelligit mediocriter. docet pueros in catechismo et pius videtur.
Oteringham.	Geo. Haygh curatus. parum Latinum intelligit quamvis in cognicione sacrarum litterarum meliores progressus fecit. concionem unam tantum habuit. pueros instruit diligenter.
Capella de Martin in parochia de Swin.	Willm. Carter tantum facultatem legendi habet. bene Anglice legit ac in catechismo pueros instruit. videtur religiosus.

Beverlye Junii 2.

South Dalton.

Robt. Ryngrose Rector vir honestus et sermonem Latinum bene et sensum scripturarum recte tenet, ac instruit. conciones habet.

Kyrk Burne.

Joh. Herdye sequestrationem habens ejusdem ecclesie Latinum intelligit licet mediocriter loquitur ac in scripturis versatur ac pueros instruit. conciones habet.

Rowlaye.

Hen. Browne rector, senex, et captus oculis. habet curatum qui instruit pueros. conciones habet ut articulatur.

vii. Examinatio Christoferi Lyndleii

Skipwithe.

Chris. Hervie vicarius de Skipwithe conjugatus. Latine non intelligit. parum versatus in scripturis.

Welwicke.

Hugo Gray sequestrator vicarie de Welwicke conjugatus. vir simplex. Latine nihil intelligit. in scripturis tamen non nihil versatus.

Bransburton.

Tho. Dixon curate at Bransburton honestus at parum doctus.

Scoolecots.

Willm. [? Paynter] curate at Scoolecotts conjugatus. ignarus et in sermone Latino et in sacris scripturis.

Pattrington.

Laur. [? Weyne] curate of Pattrington juvenis honestus zelosus doctus. catechizat diligenter etc.

Walkington.

Joh. Newcome rector de Walkington vir ut videtur [? honestus] et sacris scripturis racionem fidei sue racionem reddit Anglice.

Russton.

Ryc. Foxe curate of Russeton. juvenis bone indolis doctus et zelosus.

Bilton.	Ryc. Newsom Lector capelle de Bilton. Latine non intelligit.
Beverley.	Joh. Atkingson Vicaire of St. John's in Beverley. monachus olim Beverlacensis nunc honestus religioni sue.
Holtbye.	Edwd. Whitakers Mr. in artibus Rector de Holtbie.
Silston.	Ryc. Briggs curate de Silston rationem fidei sue reddit de scripturis Anglice.
Goodmadam.	Ric. Gill curatus of Goodmadam Latine intelligit honestus religiosus.
Foole Sutton.	Raffe Selby rector de Foolesutton senex honestus ut videtur. parum tamen potest propter etatem.
Watton.	Tho. Bollard curate de Watton honestus ut videtur mediocriter eruditus.
Wilberfosse.	Willm. Colson curate of Wilberfosse. Juvenis bone indolis doctus et zelosus.
Holme.	Tho. Sharowe curate of Holme catechizat at non diligenter propter negligenciam parochianorum. vir non indoctus.
Hayte.	Erbart Hayte curat of Wauter non examinatus quia notus.

viii. Examinatio...Slater [considerably torn]

Scarbrough.	Willm. Taylor curatus bene doctus in scripturis diligens in officio. catechizat et docet ignaros. religiosus est.
Semer.	Rad. Buckton curatus. mediocriter doctus. Latine loquitur. unam concionem non plures habuit. He saith the parishoners are negligent bothe in comyng to learne them selves and also will not send ther youthe to be instructed nether will the chirchwardens doo ther office therin.

Ganton.	Willm. Langdale bene doctus et religiosus est.
Ryton capella in Huningby.	Ryc. Leadbeter. Latine intelligit et loquitur. sensum scripturarum tenet. catechizat diligenter. est religiosus.
Hunmanbye.	Robt. [? Huld] vicarius est satis notus.
Burton Agnes.	Joh. Marshall curatus. Latinum non intelligit. est religiosus ut videtur et catechizat pueros.
Ibidem.	Joh. Grene Ludimagister in Latinis bene versatus. carmina reponere novit.
Auburne capella de Burlington.	Tho. Botterell curatus Latinum sermonem intelligit ut videtur.
Folton.	Willm. Crake vicarius Latine loquitur et intelligit. articulos fidei ex scripturis confirmare potest. catechizat diligenter.
Twhinge.	Joh. Bossall rector dimidietatis ejusdem ecclesie. Latinum sermonem bene intelligit ac loquitur. articulos fidei confirmare potest e scripturis. catechizat.
Se...[? Speeton].	Willm. Mase curatus Latine loquitur et intelligit. articulos fidei ex scripturis confirmare potest.
Benton.	Anth. Kynge vicarius satis notus. Decanus est ejusdem decanatus.
Byrlyngton.	Ryc. Rycherdson artium baccalaureus curatus. bene doctus.
Carnaby.	Joh. Ots vicarius Latine intelligit mediocriter. catchizat diligenter. est religiosus.
Foston (?).	Tho. Pacoke vicarius Latine intelligit parum... catechizat et videtur religiosus.

ix. Examinatio Christoferi Lyndley

Pro...um.	Religio doctrina status catechismus conciones. Hen. Grimstone rector de Callom approbatus quia notus.

. . .ingham.	Chris. Dales curatus de Lastingham religiosus. sufficienter doctus. approbatus.
. . .negrave.	Tho. Messinger curat de Stonegrave juvenis 24 annorum. zelosus mediocriter doctus at bone tamen indolis.
. . .urdsall.	Tho. Middleton curate of Burdsall senex valde. legit pessime. si per annum diutius vixerit aliter est providendus.
. . .iddleton.	Nicolas Robinson vicar of Middleton senex mediocriter legit quia laborat oculis. honestus ut videtur parum tamen doctus.
Levisham.	Joh. Watson rector de Levesham. 75 annorum. erat monachus abbatie Whitbaensis. legit anglice distincte. videtur zelosus. abjurat enim papismum. conciones habuit plures.
Helmesley.	James Lanton vicar of Helmesley annorum 68. legit Anglice distincte. mediocriter doctus. zelosus et honestus.
	Hen. Langhdale curate of Wickam within v myles of Scarborowe, Mr. Edwd. Hutchinson beinge the patrone a temporall man. he serveth for x li. huc diligentius examinandus.
Thornton.	Robart Stubbs of Thornton grandaevus 79 annorum. Anglice legit mediocriter et catechizat juventutem. vir ut videtur honestus. Joh. Bronsdale rector de Cropton catechizat pueros.
	Robart Emerse curate of St. Leonard in Newmalton senex 72 annorum. vir honestus zelosus.

x. Brodsworth

Robt. Scoley Vicarius ibidem. etatis 78. presbiter per annos 54. Latinum intelligit mediocriter. hospitalis. nunquam conjugatus. catechismum docet. registrum bene observat et ut asserit Evangelii verus professor.   Examinatus per Joh. Mey

Bramwith.

Ric. Grigory rector ibidem. etatis 34. nunquam graduatus. Latinum mediocriter intelligit. conjugatus per 14. Evangelium ex corde profitetur. hospitalis per triennium. catechismum docet. regestrum observavit ab institutione sua. presbiter per septiennium.

Exam. per Joh. Mey

Hickelton.

Charolus Stevenson curatus ibidem. etatis 29. presbiter per quinquennium. nunquam conjugatus. Latinum mediocriter intelligit. catechismum docet. professor Evangelii. regestrum observat diligenter ut asserit. neminem detegit. Exam. per Joh. Mey

Marre et Milton.

Joh. Mansfild curatus ibidem. etatis 30. presbiter per sexennium. Latinum mediocriter intelligit. nunquam conjugatus. Evangelium profitetur. catechismum diligenter docet et similiter regestrum observat. neminem detegit. Exam. per Johannem Mey

Wo... [Wortley].

Mich. Sherbroke rector ibidem...etatis 40 annorum. presbiter per duodecim annos Latinum mediocriter intelligit. non antea est conjugatus sed intendit esse breviter. Evangelium profitetur. docet catechismum diligenter et similiter regestrum observat et est hospitalis pro posse. neminem detegit. Ex. per Johannem Mey

Barneby super Dunne.

Wyllelmus Wylson curatus ibidem. etatis 34. presbiter per novem annos. clericus sed non Latinum intelligit. est conjugatus. veritatem Evangelii usque ad mortem defendet ut asserit. docet catechismum pro posse suo et similiter regestrum observavit hactenus. neminem detegit. Exa. per Johannem Mey

Maultbye.

Edm. Awkeland curatus et sequestrator ibidem. etatis 49. presbiter per duodecim annos. Latinum valde mediocriter intelligit. nunquam fuit conjugatus. videtur ex animo profiteri evangelium. catechismum diligenter docet et regestrum diligenter observat.

Exa. per me Johannem Mey

xi.

Byrkbye.	Fra. Grene rector de Birkbye. in scripturis bene versatus. conjugatus. honestus. zelosus. concionem nullam habuit per quinquennium. ipse tamen docet rudimenta fidei.
Cowsbye.	Geo. Mychell parson of Cowsbye. mediocriter versatus in scripturis. Latinum intelligit. zelosus. concionem nullam habuit per quinquennium. ipse tamen docet ignaros rudimenta fidei.
Dighton.	Tho. Masterman curate of Dighton parcell of Allerton. Latinum sermonem non intelligit. juvenis est...honestus et zelosus. catechismum docet diligenter. conciones favet a Marco Metcalfe rectore de Allerton.
Ollerton.	Joh. Turner curate of Ollerton senex parum doctus at zelosus ut videtur. conciones favet ibidem.
Osmotherlye.	Alex. Abe vycar of Osmotherley baccalaureus in artibus. conjugatus. 48 annorum. catechismum docet. conciones favet multas. He presenteth that his parisshioners kepith twoo handbells and other monuments of superstition as stoles and sutche lyke in the hands of Joh. Wighill of Osmotherley kept of him by this Alexandre his counsell to be reformed. [And he presents also various parishioners for minor offences, including a papist who 'comethe not to the churche but pipethe in service tyme; cannot say his beleve neither yeat learne'.]

123

Hinderwell.	Raynold Bridgehouse curate of Hinderwell. Latinum sermonem utrumque intelligit. parum doctus at catechismum docet, conciones nullas ibidem habuerunt per triennium preter unam.
Whitby.	Anth. Watson curate of Whitbye senex 70 annorum monachus abbathie de Kirkham. vir honestus ut videtur et zelosus. mediocriter doctus.
Northeottrington.	Bryanne Metcalfe vicar of Northottrington parum doctus at honestus ut dicit. concionem fere unam habuit singulis annis.
Ugglebarbe et Esdale.	Herbart Laverocke de Ugglebarbe et Esdale perteyninge to Whitby. senex 75 annorum monachus Maltoniensis. catechismum docet parum Latinus.
Danbye.	Simon Thirkleby curate of Danbye. Latine non intelligit. in scripturis parum aut nihil versatus. Anglice legit mediocriter. catechismum docet et conciones habuit v per biennium.
Egtonne.	Robt. Willemot curate of Egtonne chappal. juvenis honestus zelosus.
Hutton Ridbye.	Geo. Conyers vicarius de Hutonridbie. Latine intelligit mediocriter versatus in scripturis. honestus zelosus.
Seamer.	Joh. Conyers. curate of Seamer. Juvenis honestus doctus zelosus etc.
Westerdale.	Tho. Robson curate of Westerdale senex 85 annorum. legit Anglice mediocriter. sacerdos fuit per annos 60.
Scelton.	Rowland Erringhton curate of Scelton. Latine intelligit. honestus zelosus.

| Crathorne. | Joh. Starthe of Crathorne rector honestus juvenis doctus. |
| Kyldale. | Willm. Rogers parson of Kyldale licenciatus ad concionandum. |

Note. Robt. Emerse (St Leonard's, New Malton), Herbert Laverocke (Ugglebarnby), were Canons of Old Malton Priory at the Dissolution in 1539. Emerse [Emerson]. Herbert [or ? Robert].

4. MEASURES TO SECURE AUDIBILITY OF SERVICES

Archbishop Grindal's Injunctions for the Clergy [Reg. Grindal, f. 155.]

2. Item upon every Sondaye and hollydaye ye shall in your churche or chappell at convenient howers reverentlye and distinctelye saye or singe the Common prayer appointed by the lawes of this Realme both in the forenone and after none, standinge in a pulpitt or seate appointed for that purpose and so turninge your face towardes the people as they may beste heare the same and upon everye Wednesdaye and Frydaye in the forenone (not beinge holye daye) ye shall in like manner saye the letanye and other prayers appointed for the daye and likewise the eveninge prayer everye Saterdaye and holye even and shall also at all tymes requisite and conveniente duelye and reverentlye minister the two holye Sacramentes that is to saye baptisme and the Lordes supper commonlye called the holye Communion accordinge to suche order as is sett furthe in the booke of common prayer and administration of the Sacramentes.

Archbishop Grindal's Injunctions for the Laity [Reg. Grindal, No. 2, f. 157.]

ITEM to thintent that the people may the better heare the morninge and eveninge prayer when the same by the minister is sayde and be the more edifyed therebye, we do enjoyne that the churchewardons of everye parishe in places aswell exempt[1] as not exempt at the chardges of the parishe shall procure a decent low pulpitt to be erected and made in the bodye of the churche out of hande, wherein

[1] Places free from the control or jurisdiction of the Archbishop as Diocesan because they were 'peculiars' or places rightly having jurisdiction of their own affairs for Visitation, probate of wills, etc., their own officials, and a claim to complete independence.

the minister shall stande with his face towardes the people when he redeth morninge and eveninge prayer, provided alwayes that where the churches ar verye small, it shall suffice that the minister stande in his accustomed stall in the quere so that a convenient deske or letterne [1] with a rowme to turne his face towardes the people be there provided by the said churchewardons at the chardges of the parishe The judgement and order whereof and also all the forme and order of the pulpitt or seate afforesaid in greater churches we do referr unto the Archdeacon of the place or his officiall, provided also that the prayers and other service appointed for the ministracion of the hollye Communion be said and done at the Communion table, except the Epistle and Gospell whiche shalbe redd in the said pulpitt or stall and also the tenn commaundementes when there is no Communion.

A.D. 1567   [Visitation Books, R. VI. A. 2, f. 4.]

...c. Mr. Jo. Cresswell curatum de Bothomsall... 'that he dothe not audiblie and distinctelie reade and saie devine service unto his parishoners insomuche as therbie theye do not receive anye edificacion'.

[Ibid. f. 165.]

...c. Alex. Colsonne clericum Vicarium de Waldenewton. The said Vicar dothe not reade his Service on Sondaies and holiedaies him self distinctelie but settethe a boie of vi yeres of aige to read with him which boie so stutteth and stammerethe that he can not be understanded and the parishoners have oftentimes desired the vicar to reade it him self for ther edefienge but yet he will not Item he dothe not enstructe the yowthe of his parishe the Lordes praior the articles of the faiethe the tenne Commaundementes nor the Cathechisme as he ought to do...dicit that he in dede sufferethe a boie to reade with him the psalmes sometimes and that he can perfectlie reade the same that he maie be understanded and he deniethe that he was warned to reade it him self onelie....[Enjoined] that he do from-henceforthe him self onelie reade the morninge praior the Communion or Commemmoration and the eveninge praior distinctelie

[1] Lectern.

that his parishoners maie be edified And that he be on the holiedaies in the after none redye to enstructe the yowthe of his parishe the Lords praior the articles of the faithe the ten commaundements and the Cathechisme and give them warninge to repaire to the Churche to be enstructed et sic dimittitur.

[Ibid. f. 143.]
    ...c. Hen. Daill clericum Curatum de Coken in Bransedaill. The saide Curate dothe not celebrate and read the devine service plainlie and distinctlie that the hearers maie be edified.

[Ibid. f. 146.]
    ...c. Hen. Daill....Forsomuche as the Churchwardens and sworne men of Kirkbiemoreshed did presente the said Henrie Daill Clerk that he...dothe not celebrate and reade the devine service plainelie and distinctelie that the hearers maye therbie be edefied but mumblethe uppe the same and moreover this daie being tried in the Quere of this Cathedrall Churche wherebie the same evidentlie appearethe to be trewe, Therfore the judge did commaunde and inhibite the said Henrie Daill Clerk that he do not attempte or presume to serve as Curate or to minister the Sacraments or Sacramentalles in any Churche or Chapell within the dioces of York sub pena juris.

One entry gives the form of a penance to be done by Robt. Salven in the Church of Barneburgh where he was Vicar, 'at the Communion or Commemoration at suche time as the priest ther shall go into the pullpyt to reade the Gospell and assone as the Gospell is red'. The penance covered several charges, and included:

10 April 1567   [Ecclesiastical Commission, Act Books, R. VII. A. 3, f. 106.]
    Whereas I good people have many tymes in sayenge of dyvine service mumbled upp the same in suche sorte that fewe or none of my parishoners being then and ther assembled to heare divyne service coulde understande the same...by God his assistance I will endever my selve frome hencefurth to reade singe and say devine service distinctely and plainely so that you may understande the same....

127

5. INSTRUCTION IN THE FAITH

There is no matter to which all the records under consideration show closer and more consistent attention that that of the teaching of the Catechism; it was evidently regarded as an element in religious education for which there was absolutely no possible substitute. When Edward VI, in 1547, issued his first Royal Injunctions, there was of course no mention of Catechism, but the three main points of the Creed, the Lord's Prayer and the Commandments were already prominent, together with other provisions to be recognised in all later Injunctions, as those of Cranmer, of Ridley in 1550, in the Articles and Injunctions of Elizabeth in 1559, and also in the 'Advertisements' of 1564, the 'Liber quorumdam Canonum' of 1571, and the Canons of 1603. Special attention should be given to the fact that the Catechism was not only a standard body of instruction to be given to the young; it was also regularly and extensively used as a test of religious knowledge and even of religious conformity; it was used to guard the Sacraments of the Church against unqualified persons. Both clergy and laity, according to their respective duties, were subjected to a constant and scrupulous examination in their knowledge and use of the Catechism.

The earliest of the Visitation Books have not been used for evidence here. The Book for 1561–4 is too much occupied with the examination of schoolmasters, and this matter has received attention elsewhere (pp. 103 ff., and note on p. 104); the volume for 1567 is not particularly satisfactory, as it is not a 'Comperta' book but only quotes and makes a selection from that lost volume. The parishes represented, therefore, are an uncertain fraction of the whole number in the diocese, but even so the evidence has value. Four of the deaneries, Pontefract, Craven, Cleveland and Ryedale, reported nothing amiss in the teaching of the Catechism, and Holderness also was blank; this does not necessarily imply that there was in fact nothing amiss. The deaneries of Doncaster (a large and comparatively thickly populated area) and Dickering, which was rural, had one case each where there was neglect, and the whole archdeaconry of Nottingham had four. In each case, the offence is reported in almost exactly the same words.

The book for 1575, R. VI. A. 5, includes some of the most important references, and R. VI. A. 7 has some of the best references for Chester. The later volumes, as they show little difference in phrasing, are described in summary.

Archbishop Grindal's Injunctions are especially full and explicit in the matter of the Catechism. There perhaps remained still in Yorkshire some traces or tradition of the medieval instruction in the Creed, the Commandments and other fundamentals of the Faith which was ordered by successive Archbishops of York in the fourteenth and fifteenth centuries to be given to the laity in the vernacular, with some provision for examination in knowledge.

The Catechism   [Grindal's Injunctions.]

3. ITEM ye shall everye Sondaye and holye daye openlye in your Churche or Chappell call for, heare, and instructe the children and servauntes both menkynde and womenkynde that be of convenient aige within your parishe (at the leaste so manye of them at once by course as the tyme will serve and as you may well heare and instructe for an hower at the leaste) before eveninge prayer in the ten commandements the articles of the beleife and the Lordes prayer in Englishe and diligentlye examine and teache them the cathechisme sett forthe in the Booke of Common Prayer And to thintente this thinge may be more effectuallye executed ye shall take the names of all the children, yonge men, maydens and servantes in your parishe that be above sexe yeres of aige and under twentye whiche cannot say the catechisme, and shall call by course certaine of them by name everye Sondaye and everie holye daye, to come to the cathechisme, wherebye you maye easilye note and observe what parents or maisters be negligent in sendinge their children and servantes to be instructed and take occasion thereof both pryvatelye and openlye to exorte them to sende their youthe as they ar appointed, and shall present the refusers to the Ordinarye.

7. ITEM you shall not admitt to the holye Communion anye of your parishe men or women beinge above fower and twentye yeres of aige that can not saye by heart at the leaste the ten commaundements the articles of the faithe and the Lordes prayer in Englishe, nor anye beinge fouretene yeres and above, and under fower and twentye yeres of aige that cannott saye by harte the cathechisme that is sett furthe in the said booke of Common Prayer.

8. ITEM for that purpose you shall before Easter and all other tymes of the yeare when the holye Communion is to be by you ministred gyve warninge before unto your parishioners to come unto you eyther in the after noone of some Sondaye or holye daye, or the daye before they purpose to receyve or at some other tymes before, as necessitye shall cause you to appointe if there be anye multitude or if the number be but small, in the morninge at the farthest before they shall receyve so that it be before the beginninge of the morninge

prayer, so many of them as intende to receyve, and not onelye to
signifye unto you their names to the intente ye may kepe a register
or note of all suche persons as from tyme to tyme shall communicate
but also to be by you examined whether they can say by harte the
ten commandements the articles of the faithe the Lordes prayer and
the Cathechisme, accordinge as after the diversitye of their aiges is
above required, and suche of them as eyther can not, or will not
recyte the same by harte unto you, ye shall repell and putt backe
from the holye Communion untill they shalbe able and willinge to
learne, and can by harte recyte the same unto you: for your better
assistance wherein, ye shall call upon and require the churchewardens
and sworne men of your parishe to be presente (one of them at the
leaste) at everye suche examination, to thintente that they may helpe
to putt this good order in practise. . . .

9. ITEM ye shall not marrye anye persons, or aske the bannes of
matrimonye betwene any persons which before were single unles
they can say the Catechisme by hart, and will recyte the same to you
before the askinge of the bannes. . . .

10. ITEM. . . ye shall not admitt to aunswere as godfathers or god-
mothers at the christeninge of anye childe, anye person or persons
except he, she or they have before receyved the holye Communion
and can saye by harte the articles of the Christian faithe in Englishe,
and will recyte the same before you at the tyme of the ministration
of baptisme, or before the minister if he she or they be thereunto
required And beinge yonge folkes, excepte he she or they can saye
by harte the whole Catechisme and will recyte the same before you
as is afforesaide.

These are the Injunctions for the Clergy. Injunctions 10 and 11 for the
Laity repeat the substance of Injunctions 7 and 8 for the Clergy.

A.D. 1567 [Visitation Books, R. VI. A. 2, f. 15 v.]

Officium domini contra. . . Vicarium de Oxton. . . he hath not instructed the yowth of his paryshe according to his dewty. . . dicit
that. . . he hayth not bene so diligent in teaching of the yowthe the
Cathechisme but he promisethe to be more diligent in the premisses
frome hence furthe. . . .

Similar charges in this archdeaconry from Cromwell, Hockerton, Wink-
burne and Eaton.

[Ibid. f. 53.]

...contra Rectorem de Barneburgh...nor doethe or cause to be taught the children of his parishe the Cathichisme....

[Ibid. f. 163.]

...contra curatum capellanie de Harpham. He teacheth not the yowthe of that towne the Lords praior the articles of the Faithe nor yet the Cathechisme or ten Commaundments....

A.D. 1575 [Ibid. R. VI. A. 5, f. 10.]

Selbye: 'The yowthe do not repaire to the mynister to be taughte in the Cathechisme.'

[Ibid. f. 16.]

Broughtonne: 'Many ther be in ther parishe that can not saie the Cathechisme and they have named none.

Willm. Loftehowse the yonger about xv or xvi yeres olde Isabell Emott wyfe of Willm. Emott Isabell Symson and Isabell Singar do not receive the Communyon beinge of perfect age becawse they ar unconfirmed.'

[Ibid. f. 17.]

Skipton: 'The Vicar doth not generallie examyne the parishoners before they do communicate becawse of the multytude.'

At Brafferton (f. 40 v.), Buttercram Chapel (f. 44 v.), and Gillymoore Chapel (f. 48), the Vicar was at fault for not calling the children or teaching them the Catechism.

[Ibid. f. 54 v.]

Gysburne: 'Item Sir Willm. Allen their Curate doth not instructe the youth of their parishe everie Sondaie and holydaye.'

[Ibid. f. 61 v.]

Siggeston: 'Children ar not called to be taught the Catechisme but in Lente.'

[Ibid. f. 78.]

Cheryburton: '...their Curate doth not reade the threateninge against synners in their churche neither doth he teache the youthe of their parishe the Cathechisme.'

A.D. 1578 Including Chester. [Ibid. R. VI. A. 7, f. 6 v.]

Moberlye: 'Parentes and maysters do not sende ther chyldren to be instructed in the Cathechisme.'

[Ibid. f. 18 v.]

St. Oswald's, Chester: 'Ther is a faulte aswell in ther vycar in not instructinge as the parishoners in not sendinge ther chyldren to learne the cathechisme.'

Negligence in the minister was found also at Nether Pever, Newton, Choulerton (these three were chapelries), Ingleton, Staveley and Richmond.

[Ibid. f. 30 v.]

Witton: 'The masters and parents send not their children to be taughte in the cathechisme.'

[Ibid. f. 37.]

Manchester: 'The cathechisme is not taught nor the parentes and maysters monished to send ther chyldren and servauntes to be therin enstructed.'

[Ibid. f. 38 v.]

Eccles with Ellenburgh Chapel: 'The vicar doth not teach the Cathechisme but warneth the Parishioners to sende theire youth upon the weke daye but they do not for because they have schole-masters nigh them to instruct theire youth.'

At Sefton also and Richmond the parishioners were remiss.

[Ibid. f. 62.]

Preston in Amunderness. The entry is almost word for word the same as that for St Oswald's, Chester, above.

[Ibid. f. 98.]

Gilling: 'Jerome Wray ther curate refusethe to instructe the children in the cathechisme havinge wayges offered for yt and requested therunto.'

A.D. 1590 [Ibid. R. VI. A. 12.]

Nine entries referring to catechising; in eight of these the fault lay with the parishioners, the worst case being at Kyrkhame.

[Ibid. f. 49.]

Kyrkhame: '...none come nor sende to be cathechysed.'

One of the churchwardens in Bodon in Frodsham Deanery presented:

Ther vicar catechiseth not to his knowledge. He is parson of Warberton and vicar of Bodon....

The parishoners coom not to be cathechised and he haith not harde there vicar nor his curate give theme warnynge to coom.

A.D. 1595–6 [Ibid. R. VI. A. 14.]

Eight charges, seven of them against negligent clergy, at Dent, Pennyngton, Bothomsall, Southwell, Mansfeld, Firbecke Chapel, and Ashton-under-Lyne, where 'their preacher and curate is dyligente in preachinge but not in catechysinge'.

The only charge against laity was at Wereham alias Weverhame: 'The parentes and maysters are slacke in sendinge and the youthe in commynge, to be cathechysed.'

6. PREACHING: SERMONS AND HOMILIES

The preaching and exposition of the Scriptures was under control and supervision as careful as that exercised over any other matter concerned with instruction in the faith. The normal use was that none might preach unless he had the special preacher's licence granted by the Archbishop to persons suitably qualified. The complete figures for the total of such licences granted during the reign of Elizabeth are difficult to find with any approach to certainty. They may be ascertained easily and exactly for the not far distant period of the archiepiscopate of Tobie Matthew, 1606–27, since a list year by year is entered in his Act Book. In 1606 for the whole Province two licences only were issued to preachers. In 1607, the number was twelve; in 1608, ten; in 1609, seven; and in 1610, five. Some of these were valid for restricted areas only. The total for the whole period of twenty-one years over all areas was 245; there is reason to suppose that the number issued during the whole reign of Elizabeth was not so large as this. The incumbent who had no preacher's licence was required to procure, or to persuade his Rector or Rector's farmer to procure, a licenced preacher to deliver at least one sermon in each quarter of the year; when there was for any reason no sermon of this kind, the incumbent was bound by Injunction to read one of the authorised homilies and to instruct or to catechise in the Lord's Prayer, the Creed and the Ten Commandments. Any kind of glossing or exposition of either the Scriptures or the homilies was definitely forbidden. Sermons were occasionally but apparently not usually preached at the evening service. After the reading of the homily, it was regular to 'exhort the people to remember the poore', and to denounce the supremacy or usurped power of the Bishop of Rome.

Far outnumbering all other charges concerning the conduct of the services is that alleging that the required quarterly sermons were not preached. In the great majority of these cases, the fault lay either with the rector or farmer, in the former case usually because he was a pluralist. In the 1567 Visitation, thirty-two parishes lacked their due number of sermons; in 1575, no less than 142 parishes. In 1586, the number had fallen to thirty-nine, in 1590 to twenty-eight, and in 1594 to twelve. Of the thirty-two parishes in 1567, seventeen were definitely due to pluralism. In 1575, out of the deplorable total of 142, eight only are stated to be due to pluralists, sixteen to negligence by the rector, eleven to negligence by the farmer, six parishes were too poor to have sermons (preachers' fees are never mentioned, but evidently existed and were high), and two parishes were vacant; of all the rest, no details are given. Of the thirty-nine in 1586, six were by plurality, seven by the rector and nine by the farmer. In 1590, out of twenty-eight, four were by plurality, six by the rector and six by the farmer. Of the twelve in 1594, the numbers are one, two and three respectively. All other cases are unexplained.

Injunction 11 of Archbishop Grindal to the Clergy orders the preaching of sermons or reading of homilies:

...and when there is no sermon ye shall immediatelye after the Gospell playnelie and distinctelye recyte to your parishioners the lordes prayer the articles of the faithe and the ten commaundements in Englishe, and beinge not admitted by the ordinarye or other lawfull aucthoritye, ye shall not expounde anye scripture or matter of doctrine by the waye of exhortation or otherwise, and therebye omitte or leave of the readinge of the homelyes.

4 Nov. 1575   [Ecclesiastical Commission, Act Books, R. VII. A. 8, f. 157.]
...c. Nich. Troughton, Rectorem de Bootle....Preceperunt eidem sub pena privacionis seu deprivacionis sue a dicto beneficio quod tam honeste ac sobrie vita et conversatione vivat quam apparatu et moribus decenter inter parochianos suos se gerat et quod homilias diligenter et distincte legat juxta Injunctiones regie majestatis in ea parte editas Et quod quatuor anni temporibus seu singulis anni

quarteriis procuret aliquem discretum cruditum et approbatum ac
sufficienter licenciatum verbi Dei concionatorem qui in ecclesia sua
parochiali de Bootle eodem predicandi officio fungi posset et revera
predicet....

A.D. 1571   [Visitation Books, R. VI. A. 3 a, f. 93.]

...c. Joh. Boith clericum curatum S. Michaelis de Newe Malton.
'He expoundeth the Scriptures and doith not reade the homilies...
dicit that he haith not undertaken to preache or interprete any
Scripture sence my L. Grace his Visitacion et aliter negat.' He was
enjoined 'not to preache or interprete any Scriptures without speciall
warrant from my L. Grace'.

(a) *Disorder*

[Cause Papers (Precedents), uncalendared. High Commission.]

Ebor. [*Blank*] die Novembris 1577. A Confession appointed by
the L. Archbishop of Yorke his grace and the L. President of her
Majesties Counsell in the North Partes and other her Majesties Commissioners for cawses ecclesiasticall within the Province of Yorke to
be made and acknowledged by Ambrose Shawe Minister in the
parish Church of Penreth....Good people where as at a collation or
sermon by me made in this parish Church of Pereth upon Sondaye
the xxth daie of October laste paste at theveninge praier I forgetting
my duetye to almightie God and falling into great oversight did
inveigh against the right Reverende Father in God Richard nowe
Byshopp of Duresme and laitlie Byshopp of this Sea of Carlill and
did utter of and against his Lordshipp (although I do not at all knowe
him or of my owne knowledge understande anie falte in him) divers
false untrue and slaunderous woordes speaches and sentences and
called his honour unreverent uncharitable and unsemelie names
Especiallye in this manner That is to saye I called him a Cubbe
a Tyraunt a wolfe a Satanas and a moneymaister And further saied
that with him Pecunia omnia potest That is to saye With him money
maye do all thinges And in the same my Sermon or Collation in-
ferred theise wordes Miser est qui nummos admiratur Which is
Wretched is he that is in love with moneye, And likewise theise
wordes of the Vth Chapter of St. James Go to now ye rich men

wepe and howle for your miseries shall come upon yow and then applied them both to the saied Reverende father To the discredite of his good name so much as in me was wherebye I have greatlie offended almightie God and the saied Reverende father and abused yow being present at my saied Sermon in consuming the tyme so unprofitablie without edification. . . .

11 April 1581 Answers to articles only. [Ecclesiastical Commission, Act Books, R. VII. A. 10, f. 100.]

. . .c. Griffithum Briskin verbi dei predicatorem.

To the firste, credit esse verum usque ad hec verba And namely et ab illis verbis ad finem. . . verum in some respectes but not to thoffence of his Auditorye.

To the second. . .that hee did not preferre him self before the profites as the article purporteth, neither did speake the woordes conteined in the same article, nor had anie such sense.

To the 3rd. . .that he did in his sermon say and generally inveighe against all crueltie, and said that by the threshing articulate was condemned the crueltie of such as for gredines of their owne would arrest men without anie demaunde of the money and require the money of arrest when no arrest was.

To the 4th. . .that hee said in his sermon that as the prophetes were despised, so they be yet that preach the worde and so to this woorde [this] confesseth tharticle to bee true And for the rest of tharticle he beleveth it not to bee true.

To the 5th. . .that hee beleveth hee spake and uttred the woordes articulate so farre as they bee generall but did not touch anie particuler person nor did use these woordes [this man] nor anie other out-ragious woordes conteined in the same.

To the 6th. . .that unto this woorde [for my parte] the article is not true And as to the residue of tharticle hee saieth that hee hath though not upon occasion articulate reprehended Mr. Gregorie but not of anie evill will to him and otherwise beleveth tharticle not to bee true.

To 7, 8, 9, 10, 11. . .credit eosdem non esse veros.

To the 12th. . .credit non esse verum savinge that hee hath in generall woordes said that there is defecte in magistrats in punishinge poore men and bearinge with rich offendours.

136

16 Dec. 1570   [Ibid. R. VII. A. 5, f. 190.]

...c. Willm. Allen Alderman of York....upon Weddensdaye last past within the Cathedrall Churche of Yorke at the sermon then preached in the same when Mr. Rauffe Tunstall the preacher did speake of the mariage of thapostles, affirminge them to be maryed and to have accompanyed with ther wieffs, he to the discredite of the preacher and his doctryne said that he lied falselie in saying so. He confessed that 'after the sermon ended that daie and maid by the said Mr. Tunstall he walkinge after the Lord Mayor of the City of Yorke with thaldermen of the said Citie in the said Churche of Yorke said unto Sir John Myton clerke then being presente that if either he the said Sir John Myton or the preacher meaning Mr. Tunstall did saye that the apostles accompanied with their wieffs after they were called by Christe in so sayeng so farre as he had redd they lied'.

A.D. 1590   [Visitation Books, R. VI. A. 10, f. 141 v.]

Preston in Holderness: '...c. Hen. Sothicke He hath abused Mr. Byrche the preacher callinge him playne foole and sayd he woulde beleve no worde he spoke and beinge called in to prayers aunswered he woulde not come till he sawe his owne tyme.' [Enjoined to ask forgiveness publicly in the Church.]

A.D. 1594   [Ibid. R. VI. A. 13, f. 55 v.]

Gargrave: '...Joh. Readman disturbed the minister in the churche to the greate grefe of the preachar and audience.'

A.D. 1598   [Ibid. R. VI. D. 1, f. 26.]

Carleton: 'Willm. Hargraves for disturbinge of divine service and the minister forbidinge him he the said Willm. badd the minister come downe furth of the pullpit if he would the which he was forcyd to doe before he would stay himselfe.' [Not necessarily in sermon time.]

[Ibid. f. 43.]

Myrfeild: '...Fra. Howson for negligent comminge to the Churche Edm. Brooke for slepinge in the churche and beinge re-proved by the churchwardens did utter hard speeches sayinge he would mete with theim.'

A.D. 1590   [Ibid. R. VI. A. 12, f. 5 v.]

Wath: 'They present Mr. Stubs ther parson for hindering the preacher in the pulpitt and bidding him go to his text.'

(b) *Lack of Quarterly Sermons*

A.D. 1575   Out of twenty-six consecutive parishes. [Visitation Books, R. VI. A. 5, ff. 55 v.–58 v.]

Eastrongeton capella: 'They have no quarter sermons.'
Eastharlesay: 'They have no quarter sermons.'
Brotton: 'They had no sermons the last yere but one.'
Carleton capella: 'They have no quarter sermons.'
Eston capella: 'They want their quarter sermons.'
Middlesburghe: 'They want their sermons.'
Eshdaill capella: 'They want their quarter sermons.'
Whitbye: 'They lacke their quarter sermons.'
Stainton: 'They have not quarterlie sermons.'
Newton: 'They have not quarter sermons.'

[Ibid. f. 12 v.]

Thorparche: 'They have had no Sermon in their churche these xxty yeres.'

[Ibid. f. 81.]

Skerne: 'They had no Sermon this vii yere. The Q. Majesty is patrone ther. Edwarde Nettleton fermer ther he is also behinde with my L. procurations.'

No Sermons because of poverty of living.

A.D. 1575   [Ibid. f. 12 v.]

Walton: 'They have not their quarter sermons. the living is so small.'

[Ibid. f. 20 v.]

Gilkirke: 'They have no Sermons. the livinge is so small, ther is but a curate for it is but a donative.'

[Ibid. f. 79.]

Harswell: 'Theie lacke their quarter sermons. Pauper.'

[Ibid. f. 79 v.]

Wressell: 'They have had no sermons these x yeres. exile beneficium.'

[Ibid. f. 81 v.]

Ellerton: 'Theie have not their quarter Sermons by reason that
their quere is in great decaie. the Quenes Majestie standeth charged
to repaire the same.'

(c) Intruders

The Injunction of Archbishop Sandys which was briefly to the effect that
churchwardens were not to admit any minister without the sanction of
the ordinary points to a nuisance which apparently grew considerably
during the course of the reign, that of intruding unqualified ministers.
These appeared sometimes as preachers but occasionally were able to
settle themselves as incumbents, at any rate for a time. Many if not most
of them were Scots, and, from the fact that Bridlington suffered within
a short period from two of them, the invasion may have been not infrequently by sea. The first of these two attempted to settle as a schoolmaster, and was inhibited in July 1564 (R. VI. A. 1, f. 84 v.). The other
case was more serious and troublesome.

[York, Diocesan Registry, R. As. ff. 4–10.]

Salutem in Christo etc. 1589.

Mr. Archdeacon, the brynggars hearof churchwardens and sworne-
men of Byrdlington have earnestlye reqwested my lettre to entreate
your worship to take notice of an information by them concerninge
a certayne man which hath (and whether they will or no) preached
in theyr church, and that withoute any auctorytie or lycence Excepte
you take some good order shortlye the matter will growe to some
brawle in the churche; for the multitude are devided so that thes
men were forsed to departe from the doore and entrance to the
pulpitt and entraunce was made for hym contrarye to the Injunction
by certayne others as they can best signyfie unto you, whom I pray
you so to direct that they may be freed from daunger, her Majesties
lawes dewly regarded, and the parties qwyeted by his doing or
suffering as to your wysdome shall seme most mete....

Articles set forth that 'Laurence Wythers is his name, a meare
stranger here in the contry not knowne to be a minister, and not

139

licensed to preache within the dioces of York. He hath intruded hym selve into the pulpit and preached at Burdlington [up to] 10 last past Sondayes althoughe he hath bene often required and admonished by John Agars and Nicholes Bousded and other churchwardens of Burdlington not to presume to preache unles he were licensed by the Archb. of York. He hath answered the churchwardens that he had no licence and asked them what licence Peter and Paull had and said further that he wold preache ther who soever spoke against it. On St. James Day last in tyme of divine service he refused to come to heare publick prayers and went into the felds and ther catched doves with a nett.'

There is another paper in the same bundle (R. As. 4/13), undated but perhaps about the same date as the former, where a parishioner of Kirton objected to the person who had obtained the parsonage there. It is not stated on what conditions this minister had entered upon the living, although intrusion is strongly suggested; the parishioner's objections are at any rate quite clear: 'Roberte Blackwood clerke is a Scotchman and no free dinison.' Nor did he disguise his dislike; on one occasion he had remarked to the rector 'I was taken for yowe this daie, for one called me a hooreson dronken slave'; he had alluded to Mrs Blackwood as 'a Skottishe queane'; he had threatened to make the parson 'begge his meate with a paire of bones and his wiffe her breade in a wallette', where possibly there is a suggestion that they were really a pair of vagrants. He thought little of Mr Blackwood's preaching: 'the roaringe of an oxe in the toppe of an ashe tree is better than all the preachinge that he can preache.'

(d) Later References to Preaching and Sermons

A.D. 1595 [Visitation Books, R. VI. A. 14, f. 40.]

Manfeild (Richmond): [Two men] 'for talking in the church in sermon tyme to the great disturbance of ther preacher.'

[Ibid. f. 144 v.]

Oswouldchurche: 'Anthonie Thirlethorpe abused the parson in spechies sayinge these woords He were more mete to stande in a swyne stye then in a pulpitt.'

[Ibid. R. VI. A. 3 a, f. 89 v.]

...c. Robt. Pala Rectorem ecclesiarum de Stokesley et Kirkby in Cleveland...that fromehensforthe he shall not taike upon him to preach in any place within the dioces and province of Yorke untill further order be taken with him by the most reverend Father or his Vicars generall in that behalf Excepte in the churches of Stokesley and Kirkbye And when he shall chaunce to preache in either of [them] he shall not onelie use himself decentlie discretelie and comelie as becometh a man of his callinge But also use and declare in every of sermons the accustomed prayor for the Quenes Majestie as it is setfurthe in hir Majesties Injunctions....

CHAPTER IV

THE FIGHT
AGAINST SUPERSTITION

1. MONUMENTS

(a) *The Religious Changes* (1536–69)

Attachment to the 'old religion' showed itself mainly in two ways: preservation of the accessories of unreformed worship, as images, books, pictures, rood-lofts, vestments; and the preservation of old services and practices, as the Mass, praying or ringing for the dead, rush-bearings. Occasionally there is an allusion to an observance which evidently came from pagan times, as in the references to 'the flower of the well' on pp. 169 and 179. The policy of ecclesiastical authority was clear, firm and consistent; the accessories if objectionable must be destroyed or where possible converted to right uses, and the ceremonies must be discontinued.

For comparison with the account given by the Visitation records, my transcripts from the Churchwardens' Book of Sheriff Hutton, in the *Yorkshire Archaeol. Soc. Journ.* (1945), pt. 142, may be considered.

(b) *Forebodings of Elizabeth's Changes*

Will of Ric. Malthous of Roclyff, dated 6 Aug. 1558, buried in the Church of St Michael le Belfry, York. [York, Diocesan Registry, R. As. ff. 7–12.]

...to Belfrays one corporax case wrought with silke and gold and the corporax within it. Item I gyve one vestment of blew checkerde silke with stole and fannon with crosses of velvet to Sallay Chappell to be prayed for And if the uses of vestments do cease in churches or chappells or if the said Chappell of Sallay be pulled downe then I will the said vestment to remane to my wif and my childer....

(c) *Typical Survivals of Accessories*

A good example of these will be found in the presentments from Holderness in the Visitation of 1567, pp. 29–34.

(d) *Reaction and Opposition to Reform*

The rebellion of 1569 attempted to restore the 'old religion', but the effects of the attempt were only local and very superficial.

27 Feb. 1569/70 [Ecclesiastical Commission, Act Books, R. VII. A. 5, f. 33 v.]
The Commissioners contra Willm. Mattyson and Willm. Smyth, churchwardens of Thornton in Strata. They were admonished to 'provyde and get all suche bookes of Common service as in the late tyme of rebellyon by certeyne of the same rebells were taken frome them and burned and defaced', on pain of fine and imprisonment, and to certify of performance.

Similar orders to the churchwardens of Hoton on Wiske, Kyrkbie, Northallerton, Thormanby, South Ottrington, Alne, Myton, Thyrkilby, Husthwayte, Sand Hutton, Easingwold, Raskell, Stillington, Topclyf, Skelton, Bilsdale, Yarom, Ayton, and other parishes chiefly in Cleveland to a total number of fifty-five.

22 May 1570 [Ibid. f. 114.]
...c. Joh. Jackson, Robt. Foxe and Hugh Tomson of Ripon. Foxe confessed 'that he did beare the crosse in Rippon churche in the tyme of the late Rebellion at a procession song in Latine beinge thereunto forced by the Rebelles'. [He was assigned to do a penance by declaration.]

23 May 1570 [Ibid. f. 124 v.]
...c. Hen. Wiclif gen. and Ric. Hewar. It was objected against Hewar that 'in the tyme of the late Rebellyon he was present and hard the idolatrows masse said in the parish church of Kirkbie-fletham'. He confessed that he 'by chance came into the churche and hard some parte of the same for the which he is sory'. [Penance by declaration.]

2 Oct. [Ibid. ff. 137 v.–138 v.]
The churchwardens of all the fifty-five parishes appeared and certified that they had carried out the orders of the Commissioners, and were dismissed.

4 Oct. [Ibid. f. 144.]
...c. Ric. Perecye of Bedall: 'he was present at a masse done in Bedell churche in tyme of the late Rebellion.' [He confessed this, and was ordered to do penance in Bedale market and to certify.]

9 Oct.   [Ibid. f. 159 v.]

Chris. Symson clerk, Vicar of Kirkbye Fletham, confessed that 'he being forced did in the late Rebellion tyme saye the idolatrows Masse'. [He was ordered to do penance.]

? 9 Oct.   [Ibid. f. 169 v.]

James Bower of Ipswell confessed that 'he did beare the boks of servyce to Willm. Wrighte clerke curate of Ipswell to say Masse withall in the Rebellion tyme and was present at the said Masse'. [A penance was ordered.]

13 March 1570/1   [Ibid. f. 230.]

Tho. Blackburne of Ryppon clerk, and one of the Vicars there, 'for his offence aswell in hearinge masse in the Rebellion tyme as for his offence in hearing of other papisticall servyce', was fined 6li. 13s. 4d. and ordered to do penance in a white sheet over his accustomed apparel. Chris. Balderby clerk, also of Ripon, for the same offence was ordered to do the same penance but without the fine, 'intuitu paupertatis'.

15 March   [Ibid. f. 234 v.]

Chris. Huchenson clerk and Robt. Warde, both of Richmond, 'for the offences which they did committe in hearinge Masses and Latyne servyce in the Rebellyon tyme'. [They were fined and ordered to do penance.]

(e) *The Destruction of Images*

(i) *General Examples*

10 April 1567   [Ecclesiastical Commission, Act Books, R. VII. A. 3, ff. 104–105 v.]

...c. Ric. Bowes clericum Edm. Jake Rog. Hawmonde Chris. Hogge Joh. Metcalfe and Robt. Rogersonne.

...c. Joh. Deane. Ad audiendum finale decretum.

And then and ther the Commissioners upon long debating and deliberate hearinge and diligent considering of the thre severall matters have maid their finall order and decree therein as followeth viz. that Edm. Jake Rog. Hawmonde Chris. Hogge Joh. Metcalf Robt. Rogerson Chris. Tunstall Joh. Deane Tho. Blaykey and Joh. Taylior shall repayre to the dwelling house of Sir Chris. Metcalfe kt.

vhere the Images lately belonginge to the paryshe churche of
.yskarth doyth remaine and before Sonday next comynge shalbe
sevennighte beinge the xxtie day of this instant Aprill shall bringe
r cause to be broughte all the same Images to the Church stele of
.yskarth beinge at the West syde of the same Churche yearde and
.rthermore that they and every of theme shalbe redy in the paryshe
hurche of Ayskarth afforesaid upon the same Sonday beinge the
x day of this instante Aprill when the Curate ther shall begynne to
1y the Communyon or Commoracion bare headed bare foted and
are legged havinge every one of themme a sheyte abowte him
bove his other apparell and shall knele all together in the quere of
1e same churche untill suche time as the Curate shall go into the
·ulpytt to reade the Gospell at whiche time they and every of theme
hall followe the Curate downe into the body of the churche and ther
hall stande besydes the pulpitt with their faces towardes the people
ntill the Gospell be red the whiche beinge redd they and every of
heime shall say after the preyst with an audable voce as followeth
Whereas we good people forgyttinge and neclecting our dewtyes
swell to Almighty God as also to our soveraigne lady the Quenes
nd other hir highnes officers have throughe our negligence con-
eyled and kepte hyd certane Idoles and Images undefaced and lyke-
vise certaine olde papisticall bookes in the Latyn tonge which some
yme dyd belonge to this paryshe churche of Ayskarth to the high
·ffence of Almighty God the breache of the most godly lawes and
iolsome ordinances of this realme the great daunger of our owne
owles and the deceaving and snarring of the soules of the simple
or the whiche we ar now most hartely sory humbly confessinge
·ur negligences and offences and instantly desyringe allmighty God
or his deare sonne Jesus Christes sake to have mercy upon us and
orgive us for the same not myndinge heareafter to fall into the lyke
gaine and furthermore we do hartely desyre all you whome we have
1erein offended to forgive us lykewise and to take ensample at theis
·ur penaunce doinge to avoyde the lyke offences and also to assyste
is in our prayers to almighty God as he hayth taught us and to say
vith us Our Father whiche arte in heaven etc. The whiche beinge
lone they shall put on their accustomed parell and so sone as the
Communion or Commemoracion is done they shall go to the same

Churche stele and ther burne all the Images before so many of the paryshioners as shalbe ther assembled and furthermore the Commissioners dyd decre a lettre to be directed to Sir Chris. Metcalf kt and to Mr. Joh. Sare esquier or the one of theime to se the premisses executed as is above expressed in this order and to certify of their doinges therein upon the Monday nexte after Trynytie Sonday next. [See also p. 225.]

[Ibid. R. VII. A. 1.]
This, the earliest of the whole series of Act Books of the Commission, beginning in February 1561/2, starts with entries mainly concerned with the search for and destruction of images and books.

27 Feb. 1561/2   [Ibid. f. 5.]
'Officium dominorum contra Launcelot Whitlocke Robt. Hoper Ric. Wright Tho. Bell Tho. Williamson Joh. Lounde Joh. Barton Joh. Trotter Geo. Gramble and Chris. Barton.' These men were fined for non-appearance at first summons: '... Et deinde Domin injunxerunt eisdem gardianis et parochianis that they with al convenyent spede maike diligent searche throughe oute there parishe of Thirske aswell for ymags as abrogate bookes [of old service] and prepare the same to be all together in a redynes agains Monday come a sevennight that the Deane of Bulmer come to them for the burnynge of the ymags and defacyng of the books, and the money receivyd for the boks to be ymployed to the use of the poore of the parishe there at the disposycion of the churchwardens and oversight[1] of the poor And the Deane to certifye the nombre of the ymags burnte and boks broughte in and the somme of money taken the books etc. be sold for martis post dominicam in albis.'

Similar order for the churchwardens of [South] Kilvington.
8 April 1562   [Ibid. f. 13 v.]
Against the churchwardens of Crofton and Tho. Hart: '... A lettre is awarded to them and to Fra. Grene to search the late Chaple of Stapleton within the parishe what ymags be within the same and y any be found within the same to see them defaced and consumed by fyer. Retornable 3....'

<hr>

[1] Those who were 'Overseers'.

4 Aug. 1562 [Ibid. f. 27.]

A lettre is awarded to Ric. Smerthwat and the Constable of Bikerton to searche what ymags is within the manor house of Bykerton.

5 Aug. 1564 [Ibid. f. 160 v.]

...c. Withes of Wetherby, who appeared and 'did bringe in suche monuments as remayned in his custody at Bikerton. And the Courte decreed that the vestments and albis should be sold and the money given to the poore and the ymags and other supersticious monuments of idolatry to be burnt, and appoynted Mr. Bateman Deane of the Citie of Yorke to see the premisses done in open market upon the Pavement of the Citie, whiche saide Deane the said day did certefy that he had seen the premisses executed accordinglye'.

27 May 1562 [Ibid. f. 131.]

Copy of a bond or recognisance entered into by Robt. Symond of Kirkelevington clerk, in £40: '...that if he do make diligentlie enquerye for the searchinge furthe of the ymag of the Resurrection which he confessed of late to be in his chambre and yf he canne by any meanes fynde or here tell of the said ymage to bringe the same before the most reverende Father in God...to the Citie of Yorke the thirde daye of Auguste nexte, there to be defaced or otherwise used as by [the Archbishop] shalbe thoughte mete and conveniente, That then....' [The bond is to be void.]

? May 1562 [Ibid. f. 144.]

...c. Joh. Clesby and Hen. Kildell, churchwardens of Clesby. Because Joh. Clesby has not been diligent 'in seing the old alters pulled downe at Clesby as to his duetye being a parishoner and inhabitant there did apperteyn Therefore he was committed to warde quousque'.

2 Oct. 1564 [Ibid. f. 152 v.]

...c. gardianos de Hovingham et Alex. Smyth Willm. Harte nuper gardianos ibidem Tho. Dixe Matth. Hoope Ric. Peckett et Rad. Hardwicke nunc gardianos dicte ecclesie who were admonished to bring in such monuments of superstition as they have remayninge in there custody crastino, which day Mr. Bateman Decanus Civitatis Ebor. comparuit et certificavit vivo vocis oraculo that according to my L. Grace and the Courts commaundement he was presente and se the ymags brought in by the churchewardens of Hovingham according to the commaundement of this Courte and defaced and cutt in peces and burnt in open market, and herd the churchewardens declare suche things as they were enjoined, and see vestments brought in and sold to Richerd Heblethwate And further Mr. Tho. Lakyn being appointed for the examinacion of one brought in to be there clerke....

18 June 1565 [Ibid. R. VII. A. 2, f. 22.]

...c. Willm. Thompson of Burrowbrig, and Edwd. Wreakes of the same place, for 'keaping bookes Imags and other monuments of superstitious religion', were ordered to 'bring them hither'.

19 June [Ibid. f. 27.]

Willm. Thompson 'dyd confesse by the vertewe of his oythe that the Imags brought in by hym had bene in his house this thre yeres last past', and was committed to York Castle.

Same day [Ibid. f. 28.]

Edwd. Wreakes 'dyd confesse by vertewe of his oythe that the bookes and other vestments brought in by him this day were in a chiste within his house at suche tyme as he came to yt, which chist he knewe to be in his house at his commyng thyther yet he dyd [not] knowe what was in it'. He was committed to York Castle, but on 22 June appeared again and was ordered the following penance: that he 'shall tayke the bookes and carye the same to the Payvement within the Citie of Yorke and there to mayke a fyer and burne them aboute one of the clocke tomorrow at after none declayryng that he haythe offendyd in keaping the same contrary to the dewtie of a good Christian man desyering all others to tayke example by hym etc. In presence of Mr. Baiteman Deane of the Citie of Yorke, and lykewyse shall burne those bookes that he hayth at Borrowbrige upon Satterday next come a sennight in the market tyme there and that he shall carry away the vestments shewyd in this Court upon Satterday next to the said Payvement and there repp and sell the same and imploy the money to the churche of Borrowbrige'. [And to certify of performance.]

(ii) *Particular References to Books*

19 June 1565   [Ibid. R. VII. A. 2, f. 26 v.]

Willm. Hussey ar. was required 'to tayke an oythe upon the hoolly Evaungelystes to aunswere what bookes he hayth that was prynted beyond the seas...he confessyd he haithe a booke called Hardings booke[1] annother booke called Piggins[2] annother called Cocleus[3] and another called Archers[4] prynted beyond the seas'. He was commanded to bring in 'all suche bookes that towchith the hoolly Scriptures printyd sens the begynnyng of the Quenes highnes Regne'.

When he appeared on 8 August he was committed close prisoner to York Castle. After this date the matter of forbidden books disappears almost entirely from the proceedings of the Commission, except for:

7 Dec. 1568   [Ibid. R. VII. A. 4, f. 33.]

...c. Joh. Lawson, who was enjoined 'that he upon Sonday nexte shall bringe the booke mencioned in his awnsweres to the Churche of Rothwell and deliver the same to the Vicar of Rothwell and to Fra. Fletcher who shall cut furth of the booke so much as is superstitious and not allowed by the holsome lawes and ordinances of this realme the whiche beinge so cut furthe they shall deliver the same to the said Lawson who shall then and there in the said Churche before all the parishioners there assembled aske the saide Francis forgyvennes for callinge of hime heretyke and when the Communion or Commemoracion is done he shall prepare a fyre to be maid at the church dore and there before all the people as they come furthe of the Churche shall burne all the leaves cutt furth of the booke as is afforesaid'.

---

[1] Much controversial literature surrounds the name of Harding; see *The Epistle to Dr Juell, A Sparing Restraint, An Attack on Hardings many untruethes*, published in 1568.

[2] Albertus Pighius, or John Poynet, Bishop of Rochester and later of Winchester. *An Apologie fullie aunsweringe...a blasphemose Book gatherid by...S. Gardiner P. and other Papists...against the godly marriage of priests etc.* 1556.

[3] Johan Dobneck (Cochlaeus). *Apomaxis Calumniarum quibus Johannes Cocleus Henrici octavi...famam impetere studuit*, 1537. And see *The Paternoster Ave and Crede. The Paternoster the Ave Crede and X Commaundementes of God in Englishe with many other godly lessyons ryght necessary for youthe and all other to lerne etc.* R. Redman (London, 1539).

[4] Books not identified.

A.D. 1575 [Ibid. R. VII. A. 8, f. 149.]

This daie the Commissioners deputed and appointed Mr. Percye to resort to the Peters Pryson and take all unlawfull books from Tho. Williamson and Willm. Ustanson clerks and Joh. Fletcher late scolemaster prysoners in the same and to offer them to have the Bible and psalter the Communion booke and other allowed books and none other.

A.D. 1581 [Ibid. R. VII. A. 10, f. 131 v.]

Tho. Hunter of Flynton in Holderness, who was enjoined to make declaration in his parish church that he 'detesteth popery because he had a popishe booke called a Cathechisme for Catheliques taken with him which he used to pray upon', certified of the performance of his penance.

[Ibid. f. 134.]

Willm. Hilton alias Johnson 'had beades and suspicious bokes taken with him which he confessed he useth to pray of'. He was therefore sent to the Castle of York there to remain quousque.

[Ibid. f. 164.]

Chris. Smyth of Patleybrig, for selling a Testament of Tindall's translation for xs. to be paid 'whan masse shalbe said within this realme', was ordered to make a declaration penance and to certify of the performance of it.

(f) Evidence of the Resistance to Authority

30 April 1571 [Ecclesiastical Commission, Act Books, R. VII. A. 6, f. 8.]

...c. Rog. Wilberfosse and Edwd. Harlings of Wilberfosse, who were charged 'that they kepe undefaced the timber which was the rode lofte in Wilberfosse contrary to the order in that behalfe and that they have feald and putte into the grounde the crosse stones of the Church of Wilberfosse being unwilling to have them broken and defaced contrarie to the lawes...'. They denied the charge, 'savinge that they minded to make a bridge of the said crosse stones and cawsed it to be put by the way in the ground fearing it shall be defaced'. They were committed to York Castle, but released on recognisance on 9 May.

2 June 1571 [Ibid. f. 25.]

The churchwardens of Whorlton in Cleveland were asked 'whie they have not defaced the rode lofte at Whorleton, and answered and said that they were letted to deface all the same by one John Rychardson servaunt to Sir Valentyne Browne kt.'. The cause was postponed to 18 July, when the accused were dismissed without further action.

20 July 1571 [Ibid. f. 54 v.]

...c. Leon. Atkynson of Masham, who denied the articles objected against him [not specified], 'saving that he confessed that he maid printed breads and was unwilling that the imags should be burnt within vii yeards of his father's house. Mr. Ford examined said that by commission to him from this Court directed he appointed the imags found in Massam parishe to be burnte at the church wall in Massam. And John Walton and Willm. Askwith depose that Atkynson at the tyme appoynted for burning the imags came owt with a pike staff to resist the burning of them ther and Askewith saith he hard Atkynson say that he trusted to se them that plucked downe the rood lofts be as gladd to set them upp again and that the Archb. of Yorke had nothing to do[1] to cawse any rode lofte to be pulled down ther'. Atkynson was committed to York Castle, and it was decreed that 'before he be released he be bounde to bring his yrons for prynted caks to be defaced and to be of good bearing towards Mr. Ford and the curate of Massame and all other ministers', and to pay costs of case.

[Ibid. f. 55.]

...c. Evan Ryplye. Willm. Askwithe deposed that Ryplye said: 'My. L. Grace had none about him but raskelles about him to enforme him of suche idolatrous monuments as ar undefaced in churches and that he threatened the curate for the imags that were appointed to be in his custody till they were burnte and that he se him offer to draw his dagger at the Curate, also that the said Ryplye sayd that if he hadd an other man to sticke to him he wold put the Vicar Mr. Ford and the Curat and such as they were oute of the

---

[1] Had no business. It was no concern of his.

towne by the eares and that he wold get doggs to byte such ronna-
gates, and also that Joh. Walton sworne deposeth that if one or ii wold
take his parte he wold put the Vicar and Curate owte of the towne
by the eares.' Ryplye was committed to the Castle, bound over to
be of good bearing towards the vicar and the curate and all other
ministers, and to do penance and to pay the costs of the witnesses.

? 21 July   [Ibid. f. 55 v.]

...c. Percival Atkynson, Curate of Askrig, and the churchwardens there. 'Domini for that sence the pardon maid the imags
have bene reserved and the vestements kept in Askrig Church by
the negligens of the Curat and now churchwardens whos circum-
spection ought to have bene such as they should know what is in
ther church fyned the Curat to pay xiiis. iiiid., the churchwardens
to pay xs., each on 15 Oct. next. The Curate and churchwardens
shall make declaration of ther falte and cary the imags to the fyer
and put the fyer with their owne hands to them till the imags be
consumed and the imags must be burnte at such market dayes as
Mr. Forde shall appoint at Midleham and Richmond and the vestements and other trumpery must be defaced and solt to the use of the
parishe by the discretion of Mr. Ford and also the tymber of the rode
lofte is to be sold to the use of the church and bestowed at Mr. Ford's
discretion, and ther ar assigned ad certificandum de gestis xvi Oct.
Prox. under Mr. Ford's hand.'

18 Nov. 1577   Another method of disposal.   [Ibid. R. VII. A. 9, f. 122.]

'Whereas the pursivaunte by searche founde oute certein massinge
stuffe and monuments of superstition and idolatrie at Shereburne
The Commissioners dyd decree that the pursevaunt should have and
take the same to his owne use and behoofe first cawsinge the same
to be defaced in their presences in open Court, and this was decreed
by generall consente.'

Signed by the Archbishop, H. Huntyngdon, Matth. Hutton,
W. Fairfax, Tho. Boynton, Joh. Gibson, R. Lougher, and
Willm. Palmer, Commissioners.

(g) *Vestments*

(i) *General Policy and Practice*

27 July 1566 [Ecclesiastical Commission, Act Books, R. VII. A. 3, f. 21 v.]

O.dd.c. Melchior Smyth clericum vicarium ecclesie parochialis de Hesill et Hull ac Prebendarium prebende de Aplesthorpe. 'Cui Reverendissimus in Christo pater objecit that aswell by holsome lawes and statuts of this realme of England as also by the Quenes highnes Injunctions and lawdable customes of this realme every minister is bounde and oughte to were decent apparell aswell in tyme of administracion of the sacraments as also at other times owt of ministracion according as by the same lawes Injunctions and customes they are appointed to the which objection M. Smyth answering doyth confesse that ther is suche Lawes Injunctions and customes.... [Et domini objecerunt] that contrary to the same holsome lawes...he hayth worne other apparell then by the saide lawes...he is appointed aswell in the administracion of devine service as also many other sundry times aswell in the towne of Hull as also in other places....[Respondit]...he hayth ministred devine service viz. aswell the communion or comemeracion as also the mornyng and evening prayer in a surples onely without a cope howbeit he saythe they have not a cope in the churche of Hull to his knowledge but he sayth he never ministerd the same service without a surples and further sayth that he haythe diverse tymes worne a cornered capp not only in Hull but also here at this cytty and other diverse times he hayth worne a hatt. [He was enjoined that] frome hencefurthe he shall were suche apparell aswell in administracion of devyne service specially at the communyon and commemoracion as also at other times as by the lawes...is used and appointed and that he shall do this upon paine of deprivacion of his ecclesiasticall promocions.' [See also p. 209.]

Presumably on the same day as the cause against M. Smyth. Proceedings were by Articles; no copy of the Articles seems to have been preserved: [Ibid. f. 27.]

...c. Magr. Willm. Whittingham decanum ecclesie collegiate civitatis Dunelmensis.

Ad primum articulum respondendo dicit that he doyth not now well remember nor certainly know the lawes statutes ordinaunces and customes articulate.

[Similar replies to the next two Articles.]

Ad quartum...that he openly goeth abrode in the cyty of Duresme and also into the queare in the Cathedrall churche of Duresme doyth and hayth used to weare a rounde capp and some tymes abrode in the country.

Ad quintum...he cometh into the Cathedrall churche of Duresme and into the queare ther in a round capp and a gowne without a surples above the same, but not to the offence of any honest or grave personnes as he beleyvethe.

Ad sextum...he one tyme upon Chreismass day nexte comynge shalbe thre yeres he dyd minister the Communyon without eyther cope or surples howbeit he dyd not ministre the Communion sence that day and he receyveth the Communyon neyther syttinge nor standinge but bowing his kne towardes the grownde at the receyving therof.

It was enjoined to him by the Commissioners that '...frome hencefurth he shall were decent apparell aswell in the citty of Duresme as also in other places abrode in the country and especially in tyme of devyne service aswell in the Cathedrall churche ther as also in other churches accordinge to the lawes statutes...and usages of this realme of Englande and that upon payne of deprivacion frome his dignytie of the deanery of Duresme and that he shall thus conforme hime self onthisside the feast of All Sanctes next comynge and to appeare before the Commissioners or thre of theime at the cytty of Yorke upon Monday then next followinge to certyfy of his conformytie in this behalf and yf in the meane tyme he do not conforme hime self then to heare hime selfe depryved from his said dignytie Intymatinge hime that yf he do not appeare the said day and place then the Commissioners intendeth to procede to his deprivacion in paine of his disobedience and contumacy'.

? 7 Aug. 1566 [Ibid. f. 34.]

'Officium dominorum promotum per gardianos' of St John's Church, Beverley, against Joh. Atkinson clerk curate there. Atkinson was enjoined that 'he shall at all tymes frome hencefurthe when he comethe into the quere in Sancte John's Churche of Beverley aswell at mornyng prayer and commemoracion as also at evening prayer come into the same churche in a surples and so to minister in the same Churche upon payne of the lawe, and that he shall in his perambulacions lykewise go in his surples so that the paryshioners have no mynstrels in their said perambulacions'.

On Articles probably similar to those against Dean Whittingham:

14 Aug. [Ibid. f. 43.]

. . .c. Joh. Pilkington S.T.B. Archidiaconum Dunelm. et canoni-cum et prebendarium ecclesie Cathedralis Dunelm.

Ad primum. . .quartum articulum fatetur esse verum.

Ad quintum fatetur esse verum saving that he beleyveth that grave and honest persons were not offendyd with hys so doynge.

Ad sextum fatetur esse verum savinge that he beleyveth that grave and honest persons were not offendyd with his so doynge.

Ad septimum that he hayth ministryd often and sundrye tymes withowt ayther surples or cooppe in his parishe churche of Easington, and in suche apparell as is specifyed in this article and in no other churcheis.

He was enjoined from St Bartholomew's Day next to 'go in decent order of apparell as by the lawes. . .and to certify. . .upon paine of sequestracion of his fruictes'.

Similar proceedings against Robt. Swifte, LL.B., Canon and Prebendary of Durham, on apparently the same Articles. [He confessed Articles 1–6 to be true.]

[Ibid. f. 43 v.]

Ad septimum respondit that he never ministeryd the Communion and therefore he belevith the contents of this article not to be trewe And he never receyvyd the Communion sittinge but knelinge. [He received the same Injunctions as Canon Pilkington.]

An earlier and more full sentence is in the First Act Book of the Commission, R. VII. A. I. The original charge is not entered.

30 May 1564 [Ibid. f. 114.]

'Officium dominorum contra Robt. Dalton clericum:....and forasmuche as Robt. Dalton upon his apparaunce did utter no significacion of any conformitye on his behalf to be shewed, But rather of contumacye in his wilful obstinacye and stoberne contumacye And forasmuche as the hipocriticall pretence of simplicitie and conformitie in utter[1] gesture behaviour and apparell pretended by the said Dalton and divers others of his sorte, and his stubborne refusing in conformyng himself to the godlie order in the Churche of Englande administracion of the sacraments and other rites accordinge to the institution and doctryne of Christe and the usag of the primatyve Churche is, as by good experience is founde, an occasion of grete discorag to some good and religiouse in that there shulde be no differance in utterwarde gesture and apparell betwene the wicked supersticious hipocriticall and frowarde generacion and the well perswaded conformable Christians and to some other a Clooke of decept to thinke and judge well of suche hipocriticall persons as under the apparance of conformitie in there utwarde behavers do cloke there evill and cankerde hearts Yt is therefore decreed by the most Reverend Father in God and other his associats by the auctoritye of this Courte that frome the x th day of June nexte he shall not were any suche apparell as by the Ordinaunce of this Realme lawfullie established is appointed and prescribed to them that be placed in the office of the ministery or presthode, namelie square cappe tippet preste gowne and such lyke. And further that he shall not departe furthe of the dioces of Duresme and Yorke at any tyme hereafter withoute licence firste opteyned of [the Archbishop]', and to be ready to appear at any time on thirty days' warning. [He was bound in one recognisance of 100li. with two sureties of 10li. each.]

(ii) *The Use of the Surplice*

Archbishop Grindal's Injunctions for the Clergy [Reg. Grindal, f. 155.]

4. ITEM that at all tymes when ye minister the holye Sacramentes and upon Sondayes and other holye dayes when ye saye the Common

---

[1] Outer, outward.

Prayer and other dyvine service in your parishe Churches and Chappels (and like wise at all mariages and buryalls ye shall (when ye minister) weare a cleane and decent surples with large sleves....

A.D. 1578 [Visitation Books, R. VI. A. 7, f. 5.]
Gosworth: 'Their parson Mr. Rodgers and there Curate George Tailior do not were the surplesse, albeit there is one in the churche.'

[Ibid. f. 57.]
Burneley: 'The curate sometymes sayeth common prayer not wearynge a Surplesse.'

[Ibid. f. 57 v.]
Altome: 'Tho. Ryley and others are to restore agayne the Surplesse and that shortelye.'

[Ibid. f. 58.]
Eccleston: 'They want a surplesse which was lately stolen.'

[Ibid. f. 64.]
Hawkeshead: 'They want a Surplesse and the mynister weareth none.'

[Ibid. f. 99 v.]
Melsonby: 'Ther person sometymes sayeth devyne servyce not wearinge a surplesse.'
Forcett: 'Ther curate refuseth to were a surplesse.'

[The offence, but perhaps not the negligence by the parishioners to provide a surplice, increased somewhat as the century proceeded. A not uncommon feature is to find refusal or unwillingness to wear the surplice combined with refusal to make the sign of the cross in Baptism and negligence in going in perambulation.]

A.D. 1590 [Ibid. R. VI. A. 12, f. 8 v.]
Huddeswell: 'Ther Curat Willm. Dunnyng weareth no surples, but when he celebratith the Communion.'

[Ibid. f. 22.]
Kirkby super Moram: '...[Ther parson] will not wear the surples.'

[Ibid. f. 44 v.]

Michaelis super Wyer: 'Adam Wolfenden ther vicar useth not the perambulacion in the Rogacion weeke, nether weareth the surplesse.'

[Ibid. f. 49 v.]

Kyrkehame: 'Ther vicar doth not weare a surplesse, it is in contraversie betwene him and the parishioners who shall provyde one.'

[Ibid. f. 51 v.]

Blackburn: 'Mr. Walshe their vicar hath not worne a surplesse these six yeres last. they have no surplesse. Peter Irelande and Willm. Bolton are two of the Churchewardens.'

[Ibid. f. 52 v.]

Rossendale capella: 'James Kyrshawe ther minister doth not weare a surplesse they wante one. Wm. Shuter their late clerke toke it away. Edwarde Nutter and James Taylior there churchewardens are to be called to provyde one.'

[Ibid. f. 66 v.]

Ashton-under-Lyne: 'Tho. Sykes curate ther used not the perambulacions in the Rogacion weke neither weareth he a surplesse.'

[Ibid. f. 67.]

Ratclyffe: 'Mr. Leon. Shawe their parson nether useth to wear the surplesse nether denyeth to weare it.'

[Ibid. f. 67 v.]

[? Chorlton]: 'Edm. Shelmerdyne ther curate doth not use the perambulacions in the Rogacion weke nether weareth he the surplesse.'

Flixton: '...curate ther doth not were the surplesse.'

Sadleworth capella: 'They wante a communyon boke and their surplesse is not fytt to be worne.' [Churchwardens named.]

Denton capella: 'Otes Bradley Reder weareth not the surplesse for they have not any.' [Churchwardens named.]

[Ibid. f. 68.]

Ratchdale: 'Rycharde Mydgeley clerke vicar ther hath not worne a surplesse these twentie yeares. they have had none all that tyme. [Two churchwardens named.] Mr. Mydgeley doth not refuse to weare the surplesse but referreth him selfe to auctorytie sekinge the quyett of the churche.'

[Ibid. f. 68 v.]

Bolton in the Moores: 'Ther is a controversie emonges the parishoners who shall provyde a surplesse. [Churchwardens named.] Alex. Smythe vicar doth not weare the surplesse. they want one.'

[Ibid. f. 78 v.]

[From the generally deplorable parish of Weverham]: 'Edwarde Shawcros clarke there vicar is not painfull in studie. He dothe not service accordinge to the order set downe. he goethe muche to the ailehouse and is a common drunkarde. [he] weares no surples in service tyme. They further say that [he] is an extorcioner, and where his due is iiis. iiiid. for mortuaries he taikes vis. viiid. He also taikes brybes or summes of moonie for certefyinge false pennancies.'

[The complete absence of all references to the wearing of the surplice from R. VI. D. 1 is probably not to be taken as evidence of improvement or otherwise in this respect. Some of the Visitation Books clearly vary from deanery to deanery in the content of their reports.]

2. CEREMONIES

Archbishop Grindal's Injunctions for the Laity   [Reg. Grindal, f. 158.]

16. ITEM that no person or persons whatsoever shall weare beades or pray eyther in latine or englishe upon beades or knottes, or anye other like supersticiouse thinge, nor shall pray upon any popishe latine or englishe primer or other like booke, nor shall burne anye candels in the churche supersticiouslye upon the feaste of the purification of the virgin Marie commonlye called Candlemas Day, nor shall resorte to anye popishe preiste for shrifte or auriculer confession in Lent, or at anye other tyme, nor shall worshipp any crosse, or anye Image or picture upon the same, nor gyve anye reverence thereunto, nor supersticiouslye shall make upon themselves the signe

of the crosse, when they firste enter into anye churche to praye, nor
shall say de profundis for the deade, or reste at anye crosse in carienge
anye corps to buryinge nor shall leave anye little crosses of wood
there.

18. ITEM when anye man or woman dwellinge nere to the churche
in any cytye boroughe or great towne, is in passing out of this lyfe,
the parishe clerke or sextan shall knoll the bell to move the people to
praye for the sicke person. And after the tyme of the departinge of
anye Christian bodye out of this lyfe, the churchewardons shall se
that neyther therebe anye more ringinge, but one shorte peale before
the buriall and an other shorte peale after the buriall without ringinge
of anye handbels or other superfluous or supersticious ringinge,
eyther before or at the tyme of the buriall or at anye tyme after the
same, nor anye other forme of service said or songe, or other ceremonyes used at anye buriall than ar appointed by the booke of
Common Prayer And also that neyther on all Saintes Daye after
eveninge prayer, nor the daye next after of late called All Soules
Daye, there be anye ringinge at all then to common Prayer when
the same shall happen to fall upon the Sondaye And that no monethe
myndes or yearelye commemorations of the deade nor anye other
supersticious ceremonyes be observed or used whiche tende eyther
to the mayntenaunce of prayer for the deade or of the popishe
purgatorye.

19. ITEM that the minister and churchewardens shall not suffer
any lordes of misrule or somer lordes,[1] or ladyes, or any disguised

---

[1] References in any detail to these games are sufficiently uncommon to make
a description of them worth quotation here. The passage is found in one of the
fifteenth-century Cause Papers in the York Registry, where the attestations only
have survived in a suit which seems to have been matrimonial. The file is R. VII. F. 246,
the date 1469. Thomas Hird of Wistow deposed that 'juvenes ville de Wistow
adinvicem habebant prout mos patriae ibidem unum ludum estivalem vulgariter
vocatum Somergame....Die dominica tunc proxime precedente Margareta More
per juvenes electa fuit in Reginam in ludo supradicto erga dominicam diem de
quo articulatur qui ludus ipso die dominica in quodam orreo...prope et juxta
Cimiterium ecclesie situato tentus fuit, ad quem Margareta ante horam duo-
decimam viz. horam meridialem diei illuc aggrediens ab eadem hora usque post
solis occasum ejusdem diei ibidem continue expectabat regine solium tenens et
occupans. Et hoc dixit se scire...quia senescallus ipse fuit...et pincerna in ludo
Et cum Margareta ad orreum quo ludus tentus fuit vulgariter dictum Somerhouse
accessit ipse juratus et cum eadem usque post solis occasum...de hora in horam...

persone or others in Christmasse or at Maye games or anye minstrels
morice dauncers or others at Rishebearinges or at anye other tymes
to come unreverentlye into anye churche or chappell or churcheyeard and there daunce or playe anye unseemelye partes with scoffes
ieastes wanton gestures or rybaulde talke namelye in the tyme of
divine service or of anye sermon.

The Injunctions for the Clergy have:

4. ...also for the ministration of the communion breade ye shall
not deliver the communion breade unto the people into their
mouthes, but into their handes, nor shall use at the ministration of
the Communion anye gestures rites or ceremonyes not appointed
by the booke of Common Prayer, as crossinge or breathinge over
the sacramentall breade and wine, nor anye shewinge or liftinge upp
of the same to the people to be by them worshipped and adored,
nor anye suche like, nor shall use anye oyle or chrisme, tapers,
spattle or anye other popishe ceremonye in the ministration of the
sacramente of baptisme.

15. ITEM ye shall not proclaime byd or observe nor willinglie
suffer your parishioners to observe anye holye dayes or fastinge dayes
heretofore abrogated or not appointed by the new Kalender of the
booke of Common Prayer to be used or kepte as holye dayes or
fastinge dayes, nor gyve the people any knowledge thereof by anye
indirecte meanes.

(a) *Abrogate Days*

A.D. 1580   [Ecclesiastical Commission, Act Books, R. VII. A. 10, f. 18.]

To all Justices of the Peace within the Libertie and franchise and
to the gardians ministers and churchwardens of Ripon for the time
beinge and to all and everie of them.

continue permansit presentibus adtunc et ludo...perseverantibus Thoma Barker
de Wistow protunc Rege in eodem ludo Roberto Gafare de eadem et Willelmo
Dawson adtunc militibus nuncupatis in eodem ludo et pluribus aliis in multitudine
copiosa....' Other witnesses showed that Margaret was known as Regina
Estivalis, that both King and Queen must be unmarried, and that the game was
played on 'Dies dominica proxime ante festum Nativitatis S. Johannis Baptiste'.
In another file, R. VII. F. 307, of 1496, a witness referred to certain parishioners
who 'servabant lez Somergame in Capella de Kirkham...'.

Understandinge by verie credible reporte of sundrie honest persons inhabitinge within your parishe, that on Sondaies and other holie daies at times apointed by her majesties lawes for frequentinge the churche and divine service, manie undutifully and unchristianly absteine and refraine the churche, divine service and preachinge and receavinge of the sacraments to the great offence of almightie God, contempte of her majestie and evill example of others thinhabitants and neighbours: And that the omittinge of their dutie in this behalf ensueth and cometh of no one thinge more then that a greate number superstitiously geven do still contrarie to all good order solemnly keepe and observe by refraininge from their usuall and dailie worke olde superstitious holie daies and fastinge daies longe since abrogated and forbidden by the statuts of this realme: We have thought good in her majesties name and by vertue of her highnes commission for causes ecclesiasticall to us and others directed hereby to will and require you not onely to charge and commaunde all and singuler persons of the said parishe upon the Sundaies and holiedaies to repaire to the Churche and there quietly to heare divine service and sermons and to receave the holie Communion from time to time as by the lawes and statuts of this realme they ar bounde and as to the dutie of good Christians apperteineth: but also that you straightly commaunde theim upon paine of law to bee inflicted upon them that they and every of them utterly abstein from thobservacion of the said superstitious holie daies and fastinge daies And if it shall fall out that anie of the said parishioners notwithstandinge this our commaundement shall obstinately offende in the premisses That then yow or some of yow attache and apprehende the persons so offendinge, and take theim and everie of theim bounde with good and sufficiente suerties to her majesties use, or otherwise take such assured order with theim that they and everie of them maie bee furth cominge and personally appeare before us and others our associats in the said Commission or three of us at the Citie of Yorke upon such daies and times as you or anie three of you shall appointe theim, then and there to answeare for their contempts and disobedience in the premisses, and furder to do and receave as to justice and equitie shall apperteine and as the nature and qualities of their offences shall deserve And that against the daies of their severall appearances you returne unto us due certificates and advertisemente of your doings in the premisses togeather with such bondes as you or anie of you shall take in this behalf Wherof wee require you not to faile as you will answeare to the contrarie at your perills. Geven at Ripon under her majesties signet which wee use in this behalf the xith of Auguste 1580.

E. Ebor H. Huntingdon
Ro. Ramsden Ro. Lougher
Lawr. Meres.

(b) *Particular Ceremonies*

(i) *St Thomas's Herse at Seaton*

11 Aug. 1564 [Ecclesiastical Commission, Act Books, R. VII. A. 1, f. 162 v.]

Officium dominorum contra Joh. Lister, Joh. Westmorland, Joh. Wilkinson, Edm. Webster, Rad. Ellerton, and Joh. Hewetson of Seaton, who were enjoined to give 'the names of suche as were in the chaple of Seaton upon St. Thomas nyght last past mo then were named heretofore'. This was done on 2 October, when the men named 'brought in a bill of the names of suche as were in the Chapell of Seaton being called Catton wief Raife Steyll wief John Sawyer wief and Randell Buttell wief'. These submitted to correction, and all were ordered to do penance in Seaton Church on Sunday next before All Halowe Daye, when the preacher was to declare the cause of their penance. 'And the churche wardens are enjoined to pull downe the said St. Thomas chapell under payne of ymprisonment and fyne.'

...c. Geo. Mytchell, Joh. Catton and Willm Hesilwodde, who being 'bounde to appere this day and place and bring in the herse[1] which was called St. Thomas herse at Seaton with the names of suche as broughte in candells upon St. Thomas nighte last past into the Chaple of Seaton so farre as they canne learne', now brought in 'the herse before declarid'.

[1] A frame of metal bars and arches set over a tomb to support a pall on special days of commemoration and the like. The top and ends of the herse were provided with prickets for candles. The best known surviving example is perhaps that in the Beauchamp Chapel at Warwick, but there is another notable specimen over a Marmion tomb in West Tanfield Church in the North Riding of Yorkshire.

(ii) *St Wilfrid's Needle and Lady Loft, at Ripon*

12 Feb. 1567/8   [Ecclesiastical Commission, Act Books, R. VII. A. 3, f. 190.]

...c. Tho. Blackburne, one of the curates of the parish Church of Ripon. Immediately on his return to Ripon, he is to 'cause the place called Saincte Wilfrides Nedle[1] to be stopped up and an alter standinge in a lyttle chappell in the vawte where the same nedell is to be taken downe and defaced', and to do penance on Sunday next, saying from the pulpit at Ripon: 'Whereas I good...a most blinde guide of an olde and superst...custome have used private service... of women and suche ryts heretofore...comonly called the Lady... a perverse and disobediente purpose have refused the quere drawinge by my lewde example other frome that place to the said Lady Lofte where of old tyme Idolytry and damnable supersticious worshippings have been usually frequented to the perill and daunger not only of myne owne sowle but of those whome I have misled I am nowe hartelie sory.... And also for that I unto whome the chardge of the fabrick of this churche is committed have hitherto suffred the olde abhominable and supersticious vawte called the Wilfredes Nedle and the alter therein and certaine other altares also to remaine hitherto unto within this churche undefaced undestroyed and not tayken away contrary to the lawes of this realme and my dewty and to the great daunger of my soule. And I besiche you all to pray with me.'

It was further objected against him that he 'haythe used to say divine service in a lyttle Chappell or closett called the Lady Loft within the Church of Rippon which was sometime a chantry and there haythe used to purifye women and not in the open quere wher he shoulde have ministred the same'. This charge he admitted.

It was also objected that 'he hayth conveyed certaine Imags owt of the Churche of Ryppon'. This he denied, and was ordered to make compurgation with six of his fellows.

[Part of the text of the penance is mutilated.]

---

[1] A narrow passage in the Saxon crypt of Ripon Minster, ending in a small place through which only the chaste were popularly supposed to be able to pass.

(iii) *The Masindew, Tickhill*

7 June 1569 [Ecclesiastical Commission, Act Books, R. VII. A. 4, f. 89 v.]

...c. Geo. Aslaby, Vicar of Tickell, with the churchwardens of Tickhill: 'Ther is a Chappell or Masindew at Tickell wherein they have an alter standinge beinge covered with a whyte lynnynge clothe to the whiche Chappell many of the paryshoners do use dayly to resorte yea more comonly then to their parishe churche of allickly-hode[1] to heare some masses or other service contrary to the quenes highnes procedinges the whiche abuses he the said Aslaby being Vicar and they the said Reder and Wodrof beinge churchwardens of the same churche contrary to their dewty and office have permitted the said abuses, to whiche objeccions they awnsweringe said that in very dede they have suche a Chappell or masindew as is conteyned in the said objeccions wherein is an alter or els a tombe whether certainlie they cannot tell the whiche is covered with whyte lynnynge clothes and that the people do resorte diverse tymes to the said Chappel to pray ther as they have been accustomed but as for the sayeing or doing of any masse or other service contrary to the lawes of God or the lawes of this realme they have not seen or knowne any to be done in the said Chappell.' [They were committed to York Castle.]

8 June 1569 [Ibid. f. 92.]

A Commission was issued to John Hudsonne clerk the Deane of Doncaster and John Jeffourd clerk Vicar of Laughton in the Morning to repare to that place called the Masindew sytuate nighe unto the parishe Churche of Tickell...and ther to se pulled downe and utterly defaced and avoided the alter standing in the Chappell of the Masindew afforesaid and se the Chappell lykewyse purged of all other thinges perteyning to superstition And further they shall cause that all other personnes then the men and women contynuinge and dwellinge in the said Masindewe shall not pray in the said Chappell but when so ever they shall be disposed to pray they shall repaire to the trew parishe churche so to do And that the poore men and women of the Masindewe shall not ring or cause to be rounge

---

[1] I.e. all likelyhood, or a likelyhood.

any bell at all when they go to pray and that they pray accordinge to their olde order aswell the forenone as also the afternone each day And that the said Commissioners shall examine theme in what forme and manner they do pray and what prayers they do use and yf they finde theme owte of order or that they use any supersticion in their prayers then the Commissioners to reforme the same and appointe theme a dewe and comely order of prayer consonante to Gods worde and the comely order of this Churche of England appointed by publique auctoritie and further more that the said poore men and women shall repaire to the said parishe churche upon Sondayes and hollidaies ther to here divine service this order not-withstandinge.

(iv) *The Beginnings of Popular Canonisation*

Proceedings of 13 Nov. 1572 [Ecclesiastical Commission, Act Books, R. VII. A. 7, f. 40.]

Willm. Singelton esq. confessed 'that a Ryme or ballade made in commendation of the late executed earle of Northumbreland re-maininge penes dictos dominos Commissionarios is of his hand and of his owne compilinge Nevertheles he denied that either he hath redde the same or delivered any copy thereof to any man'. [Com-mitted again to the Castle.]

Willm. Tessymonde confessed 'that he had in his chest certein heires taken of the bearde of the late executed earle of Northumber-lande which he got after the execution by cutting it of him self when the head was in the Tolboothe on Owsebridge to be set upon the stake of the said earle and also he confesseth that he wrote the words upon the paper wherein it was enwrapped at the time of the finding of the said heire in his chest which words ar Thes (ar) the heire of the good erle of Northumbreland Lord Percy and within the paper The heare of the bearde of the good erle of Northumberland Also he confessed that he did not communicate nor come to the church to heare devine service this ii or iii yeres and that the cawse thereof was his misliking the order of the service for that it is not like unto the order of the service of the catholique Churche and for that sacrifice is not offered in the same for the synnes of the quick and the deade And hereupon and also for that being interrogate he yet denieth to communicate or to come to the Churche Therfore he is again committed to warde to the Kidcote yet being further interrogated before his dismission from judgement place wherefor he called and writte the said erle of Northumberlande the good erle of Northumbreland he answered that he so writte him for that he made so good an ende.'

(v) Rush-bearings

No date, perhaps 1581   [York, Diocesan Registry, Cause Papers, uncalendared.] Possibly a stray from the files of Court of Audience Causes:

1. In Dei nomine Amen. Coram vobis venerabili viro Mr. Robt. Lougher LL.D....domini Edwini archiepiscopi...vicario in spiritualibus generali...pars Joh. Standeven notarii publici officii vestri promotoris contra et adversus Tristr. Tildsley clericum vicarium sive curatum de Rufforth....

Inprimis ponit et articulatur That Tristr. Tildesley by the space of iiii v or vi yers last by past hath bene and yet is a prest or minister of Gods word and so comonlye reputed accepted and taken in the parishes of Rufford and Marstone and other places therabouts.

2. ...that the premisses notwithstanding [he] in the yeres of our Lord God 1577 1578 1579 1580 and 1581 or some one or other of the said yers not having the feare of God before his eyes very unmodestlye and to the great sclaunder of the ministerye once twice iii iiii v vi vii viii ix x xi or xii tymes everye of the said yeres upon Sondaies or hollidaies hath daunced emongest light and youthfull companie both men and women at weddings drynkings and rishbearings or wedding drinking or rishbearing in the parishe of Rufforth and the parishe of Marstone and other parishes therabouts and especiallie upon one Sonday or holidaie within one of the said yers in his dauncing or after wantonlye and dissolutelye he kissed a mayd or yong woman then a dauncer in his companie, wherat divers persons were offended and so sore greved that ther was wepons drawn and great dissention arose or was lyke to aryse therupon to the great disquietnes of Gods peace and the Quenes Majesties [and] to the great perill and daunger of his soull and to the greate sclaunder and offence of a multitude then present and to the pernicious and

wicked example especiallye of yong people then and ther assembled together....

3. ...that [he] by all the said tyme or some one yere of the said tyme hath bene and yet is vicar or curet of Rufforth wher upon a Sonday or holliday within the said tyme he did not onelye permit and suffer a Rishbearing within the churche and churcheyeard of Rufforth wherat was used much lewde light and unsemelye dauncing and gestures very unfit for thes placs but also he hym selve at the said Rishebearing very unsemelye did daunce skip leape and hoighe gallantlye as he thought in his owne folishe and lewde concepte in the churchyard emongest a great multitude of people wher he was deryded flowted and laughed at to the great sclaunder of the...in the dishoner of...and the damnable...soull and gret...sclaunder of the...example... [*Mutilated.*]

4. ...that he hath not had and used decent apparell and sware cap lyke a minister of his vocation and according to the lawes ecclesiasticall of this Realme, but hath worne and had most comonlye a long sword and round cloke to a Ruffyn or serving man And by all the said tyme hath bene and yet is a comon haunter and user of aylehouses and a comon player at unlawfull games in unlawfull tymes and places....

There were further articles alleging that he was a pluralist, and that on Sunday July 2 last he had played at bowls at Marston instead of saying divine service, and that 'he is greatlie and vehementlie suspected to be a papist or misliker of religion now established'. He denied most of the charges. The 'round cloke' which he wears 'when he rydeth or goeth abrode' is 'without sleves yet decent as he beleveth', and he wears a square cap 'on pryncypall feastes as Chrestenmas day and Easter day'. He admitted the plurality, but completely denied the bowling.

Date perhaps 1596 [Ecclesiastical Commission Papers, uncalendared.]

Contra Rodes alias Scotson ac diversos alios parochie de Aldburgh. Preceptum emanavit erga Martis in xlma.

Aldbroughe: May it please your worshipes to understand that the 14 day of July last the towneshipe of Roclife in the parishe of Aldbroughe bringing risshes to the churche and having strowed them, because the minister dyd reprove certayne disgised persons that were comed into the churche and wylled them to come in more humble and reverent manner to that place, Robert Rodes alias Scotson beyng in the alehouse and understandinge of it, hiered a gonne of Richard Scruton of Burrobridge and gave him ii d. to have a shott, and comyng into the churche, so sone as ever the minister had ended his sermond, and before he stirred his fote, the foresayd Robert Scotson discharged his gonne, amyng directly over the minister, eyther to hit him, as it was reported, or to afray him, and in deed the paper where with the gonne was ramed light very nighe him when he was comed out of the pulpit More over that the said Robert Rodes alias Scotson came not at the churche agayne tyll the 15 of September, and so hathe offended agaynst the statutes, bothe in discharging his gonne in that place, and in absentinge him selfe from the churche thre monethes.

Item the 6th day of January instant these [whose names are sub-scribed] havyng folowed theire vanitie althe night in sekynge there Mawmet commonly called the Floure of thwell would nedes bringe the same on a barrow into the churche in prayer times and althoughe they were admonished by one of the churche wardons bothe before and when they came to the churche stile, for to leave of theyre enterprise and not to trouble the congregation, yet they would not, but proceded forward with suche a noyse of pyping, blowyng of an horne, ringynge or strikinge of basons, and showtinge of people that the minister was constreyned to leave of readinge of prayer, yea it was suche disorder that Mr. Raufe Ellicar beyng a stranger merveled att it and spoke him selfe to the churche wardens that they should stay it, where upon the other churche wardon and the Cunstable went forthe, And althoughe by them they were stayed from commyng into the churche, yet they continewed the same tumult in the churche yeard for the space of a quarter of an hore to the great disquiettinge bothe of the minister and people.

The names of the principall of them which mayd this disorder and tumult. [Nine names 'and others'.]

Wytnesses Thomas Hundislay Vicar, John Scruton, John Allon Church-wardons.

Probably 1596   Articles only. [Ecclesiastical Commission Miscellaneous Papers, uncalendared.]

Articles of Information[1] exhibited unto the most reverende father in God Matthewe by the providence of God. L. Archbishope of Yorke... and others her Majesties Commissioners for Causes Ecclesiasticall within the dyoces and Province of Yorke, by Charles Barnebye gentleman against Willm. Skorer [and ten others] of the parishe or Chappellrye of Cawthorne within the dyoces of Yorke, joyntlye severallye and in articles as followeth:

Firste he dothe propounde and article that the Lordes Sabaothe is reverentlye to be kepte and Christians are that daye to geve themselves to prayer godlye meditation and exercyses and not to abuse or profane the same by ungodlye excercyses lighte or lascivious behavioures or uncomelye gestures. And he dothe propounde and article....

2. Item... that the churche or Chappell of Cawthorne was and is a place ordeyned for prayer and devyne service therein to be used and celebrated, and for the minystration of the Sacramentes, and not for anye profane use especiallye for playes interludes showes disguisementes rishbearinges or sommer games therein to be used. And he....

3. Item... that i ii iii iiii or v yere agoe or more, a godlye order was made and sett furthe in this honourable Courte by her Majesties

---

[1] The usual procedure in the Ecclesiastical Courts, especially the Court of Audience and the Consistory, when a case came actually to trial after often lengthy legal preliminaries, was for the 'proctor' or counsel for the prosecution or 'pars actrix' to open his case by putting in a 'libel' of 'articles' of allegation or points which he proposed to prove against the defendant or 'pars rea'. These articles of information must always necessarily be in writing. The original 'libel' might be strengthened at a later stage by putting in 'additional positions'. The case for the defence was also submitted in the form of articles, not 'articles of information', but technically described as 'exceptions'. Where, as not infrequently, information which might lead to the summons and trial of an offender was sent by any person to the Archbishop, to one of the Archbishop's Officials, or to the Ecclesiastical Commission, the information, which might come in the form of a petition or appeal, was generally cast into the form of articles before it was produced in Court.

The term 'promoter' is sometimes used as almost equivalent to 'prosecutor', and not seldom with a suggestion of the sense of 'informer'. The promoter-informer expected to receive for his services a part of the fines or penalties imposed.

Commissioners Ecclesiasticall in these Northe partes then beinge, that no rishbearinges sommer games,[1] morresse daunces, playes enterludes, disguisinges showes or abuses shoulde be used sett fourthe or practised in any churche or churcheyearde or upon the Sabaothe daye or other festivall dayes to the dishonor of God or to the evell example to others or to the hinderance of devyne service or profanation of the Sabbaothe or festivall dayes And he....

4. Item...that the premisses notwithstandinge the saide defendantes procured the Eveninge prayer upon Sondaye beinge the xxii th of Auguste 1596 to be sayde oute of due tyme and season that is to saye before the usuall and accustomed tyme wherein the same was and is used to be saide to the ende and purpose that they might have the more libertye and space to profane the residue of the saide daye in ungodlie exercyses and pastimes, and insolente and lascivious behavioures and had before purposed resolved and prepared to bestowe the residue of the saide Sabbaothe in suche profane and lewde sportes, and to dresse themselfes in the Churche or Chappell of Cawthorne And in very dede with the helpe counsell consente and presence of Marye Mountney the wife of Thomas Mountney gentleman did assemble themselves together in the said Churche or Chappell of Cawthorne the Sondaye aforesaide And there did arme and disguyse themselves, some of them puttinge on womens apparel, other some of them puttinge on longe haire and viserdes, and others arminge them with the furniture of souldiers, and beinge there thus armed and disguised did that daye goe from the Churche and so wente up and downe the towne showinge themselves drawinge the people to concourses with them and after them and shott of guns And when they had spent an houre ii or iii in goinge up and downe the towne, they returned againe into the said Churche or Chappell of Cawthorne And there putt of their apparrell and furniture and there also committed muche other disorder and abuse to the greefe of the godlye, the daunger of theire owne soules, the contempte of the lawes and goode orders aforeseide and to the moste pernicious example to others to offend in the lyke. And he....

[1] See footnote on pages 160–1.

5. Item...that in the monthe of Maye June and Julye 1596 the saide defendantes did procure make or was presente at or consentinge to a rishbearinge made and had within the said parishe or Chappellrye of Cawthorne upon a Sabbaothe daye and made towers and garlandes and other formes of thinges covered with flowers or procured suche to be made and carryed or procured to be carryed the same into the saide Churche or Chappell of Cawthorne and there sett them up or procured them to be sett up or consented thereunto beinge broughte into the said Churche or Chappell when the minister was readye to go to prayers, whereby he was forced to staye the prayers till they hadd sett up theire thinges to the hinderance of devyne service, the breache of the saide godlye orders, and to the evell example to others to offende in the lyke. And he....

6. Item...that the persons aforesaide and everye of them have beene and are negligente commers to the Churche upon the Sabaothe dayes and festivall dayes, and have withoute lawfull cause beene absente from devyne service, especiallye eveninge prayer upon dyverse Sundayes and holydayes this yeare of oure lorde God 1596 And also have not for these i or ii yeeres last paste receyved the holye Communyon at all at the leaste not three tymes in the yeere accordinge to the Lawes of this Realme And he....

7. The accused are of Cawthorne parish and of the jurisdiction of the Court.

8. There is a common voice and fame of the above in Cawthorne and the neighbourhood.

Wherefore he asks for condign punishment, on proof.

(vi) *Yule and Yule's Wife at York*

Decimo quinto Novembris A.D. 1572 [Ecclesiastical Commission, Act Books, R. VII. A. 7, f. 41.]

After our hartie commendacions whereas there hath bene heretofore a very rude and barbarouse custome mainteyned in this Citie and in no other citie or towne of this Realme to our knowledge, that yerelie upon St. Thomas Daie before Christmas two disguised persons called Yule and Yules wief should ryde thorow the citie verey undecentlie and uncomelie Drawinge great concurses of people after them to gaise often times committinge other enormities Forasmuche as the said Disguysed rydinge and concourse afforesaid besydes other enconvenients tendeth also to the prophanynge of that Daie appointed to holie uses and also withdrawethe great multitudes of people from devyne service and sermons We have thought good by thes presentes to will and require yow nevertheles in the Quenes Majesties name and by vertew of hir Highnes Commission for causes ecclesiasticall within the province of Yorke to us and others directed straitlie to charge and commaunde yow that ye take order that no such ryding of Yule and Yules wief be frome hencefurth attempted or used And that yow cause this our precepte and order to be registred of recorde and to be duelie observed not onelie for this yere but also for all other yeres ensuenge Requiring yow hereof not to fale as our truste is you will not And as ye will answere for the contrarie Fare you hartelie well At Yorke this xiii of November 1572. [Signed by 'your Lovinge Frendes' the Archbishop and five other Commissioners.]

(vii) *Wakefield Corpus Christi Play*

27 May 1576 [Ecclesiastical Commission, Act Books, R. VII. A. 9, f. 20.]

This daie upon intelligence geven to the Commissioners that it is meant and purposed that in the towne of Wakefeld shalbe plaied this yere in Whitsonweke next or therabouts a plaie commonlie called Corpus Christi Plaie which hath bene heretofore used there Wherein they ar done tunderstand[1] that there be many things used which tende to the derogation of the Majestie and glorie of God the prophanation of the Sacramentes and the maunteynaunce of superstition and idolatrie The Commissioners decred a lettre to be written and sent to the Balyffes Burgesses and other the inhabitants of the said towne of Wakefeld that in the said Plaie no Pageant be used or setfurthe wherein the Majestie of God the Father, God the Sonne, or God the Holie Ghoste or the administration of either the Sacraments of Baptisme or of the Lords Supper be counterfeited or represented or any thinge plaied which tende to the maintenaunce of superstition and idolatrie or which be contrary to the lawes of

[1] I.e. given to understand.

God or of the Realme which lettre was sent accordinglie and was
subscribed with the hands of Dr. Hutton and of others of the Counsell
and Commission.

(viii) *Bell-ringing for the Dead on All Souls' Eve*

See no. 18 of the Injunctions of Archbishop Grindal, p. 160. The Commission was much occupied with the correction of this offence; there
were cases from Hull in 1563/4, Kirkby Overblows, Nottingham,
Sneynton and Gedling in 1564, Ripon in 1568, Skipton in 1571, Middle-
wich in 1572, Burnsall in 1573, Bingley in 1577/8, Bulmer in 1585,
Bulmer, Birkin in 1586, and Hickling in 1587. The best-documented
cases are those from Kirkby Overblows and Ripon.

3 May 1564 [Ecclesiastical Commission, Act Books, R. VII. A. 1, f. 113.]
Kirkby Overblows: 'Lettres is awardyd to Roberte Stringefellowe
to appere xxix May for suspicious ringing of All Soules Day at night
last and to declare his felloes that rong with him that night.'

? 27 May 1564 [Ibid. f. 141 v.]
Robt. Stringefellow 'did confesse that he with Chris. Bramley and
Geo. Smythe did ringe upon All Soules night. Unde domini
decreverunt preceptum dictis Bramley and Smythe retornabile
[? 1] Augusti et monuerunt Stringefello ad tunc interessendum'.

? 14 Aug. [Ibid. f. 169.]
...c. Robt. Stringfellow and Geo. Smythe. Stringfellow appeared
and 'confessed that he ronge upon All Hallow daye at nighte And
begonne about half hour after iiii of the cloke, and ronge then half
an houre, and so seassed then, and begone then as he said by the
commaundement of the parson and contynued untill after x of the
cloke in the nighte. Whereupon the Commissioners did for his
offencs in that he ronge contrary to the quenes Majesties Injunctions
committed him to warde to the Castle'.

The entries for Nottingham (25 Jan. 1564/5, f. 208) and for Sneynton
(the same date, f. 208 v.) show that it was usual to make a collection of
money for the bell-ringing, and also that 10 o'clock at night was a usual
time for ending the ringing. At Nottingham the churchwardens admitted
that 'the belles within theyr parishe churche were ronge frome eight of

the clocke unto x of the clock'. They were committed to Nottingham
Castle and fined. Stringfellow escaped comparatively lightly, with
a declaration penance in Kirkby Overblows Church, ordered on 18 June
1565 (R. VII. A. 2, f. 24).

7 Dec. 1568 [Ibid. R. VII. A. 4, f. 33 v.]
    ...c. Tho. Buck of Ripon, who responding to objections said
'that he upon Alhallowes nighte last paste contrary to the most
godly and holsome lawes and ordinances of this realme dyd go with
one Thomas Shipperde undersextonne of Rippon to the moste parte
of the houses of Rippon and begged monay and candels for such
persones as did that night ringe the bels of Rippon and suche money
and candels and other things as they got they broughte then to the
said ryngers and there drunke ayle in the Churche with parte of the
monay they gott and the reaste they and the ringers dyd bestow
of good chere abrode in the towne the same nighte for the whiche
he submitteth himeself to the order of this honorable Court'.

10 Jan. 1568/9 [Ibid. f. 39 v.]
    John Arkendale of Ripon confessed 'that he helped to ring the
bells of Alhalowes nighte laste past'. Another offender, Willm.
Thompson, had fled.
There is apparently no record of the proceedings against these men.

(ix) *Burning Candles for the Dead*

24 April 1581 [Ecclesiastical Commission, Act Books, R. VII. A. 10, f. 105 v.]
    ...c. Willm. Barton clerk Vicar Choral of York Minster. 'There
war foure candles burning at the least over his wief being departed
this lief according to an old supersticiouse order and being sworne he
confessed the same howbeit he affirmed that yt was against his will.
And that fynding the same candles burning eyrly in this morning he
commaunded them to be put forth And himselfe being forwaked
lyeng downe to slepe this morning And awakinge (at some noise
made in the house) did ryse and fynding the candles burning and the
quenes pursivant and Tho. Sowthworth thapparitor there he ex-
clamed against the said woman and said Wo worth you that hath
brought me to this discredit by meanes of these candles, and hereupon the said Barton was dismissed.'

[*Blank*] Ellwick, [*blank*] Pereson, Eliz. Dales and Isab. Lockwood widow 'denyed that any of them caused the said candles to be lighted this morning And Lockwood wief affirmed that she moved the maydes of the said Barton to put furth the said lights'.

(c) *Survivals of Superstition and the Success of Authority*

The extracts given elsewhere, pp. 29 ff., from the Visitation Book for 1567, particularly those showing the presentments for the Deanery of Holderness, will serve to show the extent to which 'monuments of superstition' in the form of images, vestments, books and church furniture had survived and were found at the beginning of Elizabeth's reign. Elsewhere also, on pp. 160 ff., will be found examples of the policy of authority towards ceremonies and observances which were regarded as conducing to the perpetuation of 'superstition' or to the fostering of disorder. The succeeding Visitation Books should show how far the attempt to remove 'superstition' and all the adjuncts of it was or was not successful.

The Book for 1568 (R. VI. A. 3), a Court and not a 'Comperta' book, is perhaps the least satisfactory of the whole series, but it shows clearly a marked change in the Deanery of Holderness. In 1567 parish after parish had to record the presence of images, banners, crosses, or the like; in 1568, two parishes only in the deanery show anything of the kind.

[Visitation Books, R. VI. A. 3, f. 108.]

... (gardiani) parochie de Hombleton... contumaces in non certificando sub manu decani de Holdernes of the defacinge of certeyne Images in the Rude lofte.... [Sent in the certificate that the defacing had been carried out.]

[Ibid. f. 178.]

The churchwardens of Swine: 'They were monished to amende their bible to mayke dew collection for the poore and to levie xii d. of suche as did absente theme selves frome the churche to deface a crosse and a scutchion having the figure of v woundes upon it and to repaire the bodie of the church and to certifie. They now certified.'

R. VI. A. 7, for the Diocese of Chester in 1578, shows a remarkable decline; the survivals are usually objects which were too large to be either easily hidden or quickly moved, as churchyard crosses.

CEREMONIES

[Ibid. R. VI. A. 7, f. 29.]

Grapenhall: 'They have a crosse standinge in their churchyearde.
Tho. Satton hath in his hands a cope of read velvet imbrodered with gold a cope of white satten a vestment of satten bridges[1] blacke and grene a vestment of counterfeyte clothe of golde a vestment of sackclothe an other of sackclothe a banner of grene sarcenet iii cansticke and ii crosses latelie belonging to the churche the which they presented to my L. of Chester who appointed it to be sold to the churches use but yet it is not.'

[Ibid. f. 30.]

Warberton: 'They have a Stumpe of a crosse in their churchyeard, the head beinge smitten of.'

[Ibid. f. 31.]

Church Lawton: 'There standeth a crosse in the churchyeard but onelie to sitt upon.'

[Ibid. f. 47 v.]

Prescott: 'Sir Rauf Hunt curate at Saynt Elens in ther parishe useth to make holly water by reporte goyinge about with the same to blesse people and beastes.'

[Ibid. f. 62 v.]

Lancaster: 'Geo. Covell of Seale a suspected hinderer of her Majesties procedynges bought of one Fra. Oteson a grayle and other bokes of poperye and styll kepeth them.'

[Ibid. f. 64.]

Hawkeshead: 'Willm. Walker hath certayne Latyn bokes in his custody.'

[Ibid. f. 72.]

Bryndehill: '. . . ther is two crosses standinge in ther church yearde.' Enjoined to 'pull downe and deface the same utterlie before saynt Barth. day next and to certyfye at Manchester'.

[1] Satin of Bruges.

[Ibid. f. 92 v.]

Kyrkebye Kendall: 'The altare in Skellsmer chappell is defaced but not clerely pulled downe, the altare at Selfeild is not pulled downe.'

[Ibid. f. 108 v.]

Leonarde Burton: 'Margaret Wade wyef of Chris. Wade doth or is vehemently suspected to brynge beades to the churche and to pray of them.'

This is not a very serious total for a district so strongly disposed to the 'old religion'. But the decline in later books is even more marked. In 1586 (R. VI. A. 9), in 1594 (R. VI. A. 13) and in 1595 (R. VI. A. 14), there is no reference at all to any survival of any kind of 'monuments of superstition' in the whole Deanery of Holderness. In 1586, the only entry of this kind is at St Saviour's, York, where a woman 'is suspectid to have masse in hir house', and generally in that year there is a great decline in all serious offences except neglect of chancels and 'fornication'. In 1590 even the Diocese of Chester could produce only two entries:

[Ibid. R. VI. A. 12, f. 48.]

Stalmyn capella: 'The church is in decay and the Rowde lofte is standing.'

[Ibid. f. 65.]

Burye: 'Nich. Babington had a superstitious boke taken upon him.'

In 1594, even the Deanery of Cleveland, although it was riddled with recusancy, had no 'superstition', and the same is found in 1595. In this latter year (R. VI. A. 14) Chester provided three notices:

[Ibid. R. VI. A. 14, f. 2 v.]

St Brygettes (Chester): 'Edwd. Davye and his wyfe Jane presented for kepinge of popishe reliques as a super altare and popishe bokes.'

[Ibid. f. 14.]

Lawton: 'There was a Maypole sett uppe upon Lawton Grene upon a Sabbothe or holly daye, where a pyper and dyvers youthe were playinge and dauncinge the pypers name is Hen. Dowse.'

[Ibid. f. 93.]

Goteham: '[Two men] behaved themselfes unreverentlye at church tempore divinorum in striving for places. They had also a Maypole painted on the Saboth by one Willm. Longley of Bunny.'

In the same year Topcliffe provided an unusually interesting entry:

[Ibid. f. 134.]

Isabell Stangar broughte in the flowre of the well into the churche in devine service tyme upon twelfe day laste.

In this year again the general run of offences is obviously petty although the only suggestion of any slackness in presenting is found at Mellinge Chapel (f. 28 v.): 'They presente nothinge. Vocentur curatus et gardiani quia non presentarunt recusants non communicantes et adulterers.' The Deanery of Buckrose, where fifteen out of twenty-nine parishes said 'They presente nothinge amisse' and evidently were not accused of slackness, was by no means alone or unusual in this. Superstition, and the furniture, the apparatus and memorials of superstition, had indeed disappeared, even though recusancy was increasing. In this field of conflict, clearly, a great measure of victory rested with authority.

CHAPTER V

RECTORY AND PARISH

1. Neglect by the Rector or Farmer of the Rectory

The darkest area of all the ecclesiastical picture is that concerning the failure of rectors and especially farmers of rectories to fulfil their obligations. The two main matters with which the parson or rector, and the farmer of the rectory, were concerned were the upkeep and repair of the chancel of the church, and the provision of the quarterly sermons; in both there was shocking neglect. It must be emphasised here that these evils were not the product of anything in Elizabethan ecclesiastical legislation, but were inherited from earlier times and conditions. An analysis of the Cause Papers relating to tithe, from the records of the Consistory Court, is instructive. Papers have survived in the Registry from 259 causes heard in the fourteenth century, from 323 in the fifteenth century, and from 283 in the sixteenth century previous to the year 1540 and from 520 after that year to the year 1560. Of the 259 in the fourteenth century, forty-five are tithe causes, divided as follows: between rector and parishioner or tenant, thirty-one; between rector and rector or vicar, eleven; between vicar and tenant for the lesser tithes, one; uncertain, two. In the fifteenth century forty-two causes out of 323 are for tithe; twenty-eight of them between rector and parishioner, the remainder between rector and rector or vicar. Of the 283 between 1500 and 1540, forty-four are tithe causes; twenty-five between rector and parishioner, five between rector and vicar, four between the farmer and the rectory and the vicar, three between farmer and parishioner, and seven between vicar and parishioner. But in the much shorter period from 1540 to 1560, roughly from the Dissolution of the Monasteries to the accession of Elizabeth, there is a sudden and startling change. The number of tithe causes shoots up to 180 out of 520, and of these 180, twenty-nine are between rector and parishioner, sixteen between vicar and parishioner, and no less than 135 between lay farmers and parishioners. The extent to which these new farmers were moved to the repair of chancels in the churches of which they took so large a part of the revenue is revealed uncompromisingly enough by the record of the Visitation Books. Yet this was their especial charge and responsibility.

For brevity, the examples given are derived all from one Book, the 'Detecta' volume for 1575, one of the most detailed in all the series.

[Visitation Books, R. VI. A. 5, f. 27.]

Huddersfield: 'The chauncell is oute of reparations and the rayne raineth into the churche, and it fell downe vii yeres sence and slewe the parishe clarke, and thoughe it have bene verie often presented yet the sworne men saie they can never gett any amends any waie.'

[Ibid. f. 28.]

Sandall magna: 'The Sowthside of ther chauncell is in decaie and Mr. Tho. Watterton ought to repaire it.'

Frieston bywater: 'Their Chauncell is in great decaie so as the parishoners can not sitt drie in it.'

Almonburie: 'Their Chauncell is not in good reparations but in whose defalt it is theie know not. Citetur Vicarius et firmarius. vocatur Jo. Ramsden.'

[Ibid. f. 32 v.]

Adwicke by the strete: 'Their Chauncell and highe quere is in ruyne and decaie (the Queenes Majestie beinge patrone) so that devine service cannot be said in it; nor the Communion ther minis- tred for daunger of fallinge downe upon their heads. One syde of an other quere is in decaie which can not well be amended till the highe quere be also amended.'

[Ibid. f. 35 v.]

Barnebye upon Donne: 'The Chauncell is in decaie in the timber therof like to fall in the defalt of Mr. Richarde Whalleye fermor or proprietarie ther.'

Melton: 'The Chauncell is in decaie so greatlie that in raynie wether the mynister can not well saie service in it in the defalte of the Q. Majestie.'

Marre: 'Ther Chauncell is in decaie which is through the defalte of one John Gifford gen. who ought to repaire the same.'

[Ibid. f. 47.]

Kirkbyemoresyde: 'The Chauncell is in great ruyne and decaye (and hath bene so these vii yeres) both in the walles glasse wyndowes and leads therof And it hath bene often compleyned upon and no redresse had. They thinke that Sir Roberte Constable knight fermor of the parsonage ther ought to repaire the same.'

The record for the whole of Holderness Deanery (ff. 70–74 v.) is as follows:

Skeflinge parishe: 'All is well. Donington capella. The Chappell is in decaie. Beeforde, Nil. Barmeston, Nil. Northfrodingham, Sutton, Marflete [no reference to chancels]. Atwicke, Their chauncell is oute of reparations in defalt of Mr. Draxe. Horneseye, Their Chauncell is out of reparatyons and hath continewed the space of ten yeres in defalt of John Armitage who ought to repaire the same. Swine [no reference]. Ryston, Omnia bene. Pawle with Thorne, The Chauncell is out of reparations the Quene beinge patrone. Nonkelinge [no reference]. Owthorne, The Chauncell is almost fallen downe and the Quene ought to repaire it. Kilneseye, Ther Chauncell is in decaie and almost downe and the Q. Majestie ought to repaire it, and many tymes it hath bene presented but no reformation had. Esington, Rosse, Skipsee, Sprotley, Aldburghe, Skecklinge, Lisset capella [no reference]. Catwicke, The chauncell is in some decaie but the parson is in amendinge it. Goxhill, Rowthe [no reference], Winesteade, Nil. Drypoole [no reference]. Withernsee, The chauncell is in decaie in the windowes the Q. beinge patrone. Kaingham, Their quere is fallen into great decaie My L. Grace beinge their parson. Ottringham, nothing. Hollim, omnia bene. Humbleton, Their quere is fallen into great decaie. Marton, Holmepton, Southskirley capella [no reference]. Hilston, Elstanwicke, Ryall in Holdernes [no reference]. Garton, omnia bene.'

The total of chancels in decay, in this year 1575, is sixty-six, of which the Queen was responsible for eleven. In 1594, a year which for fullness of record corresponds well to 1575, there were forty-nine chancels in decay, about half of them being of those presented in 1575.

2. The Officers of the Parish

(a) *The Churchwardens*

The best general view of the position, duties and responsibilities of the churchwardens is given by Archbishop Grindal's Injunctions for the Laity, Injunction 3.

ITEM that the churchewardons according to the custome of everye parishe shalbe chosen by the consent aswell of the parson vicar or curate as of the parishioners, otherwise they shall not be churche-

wardons neyther shall they continue anye longer than one yere in
that office, except perhapps they shall be chosen againe: They shall
not sell or alyenate anye bells or other churche goodes without the
consent of the ordinarye in writinge first had, nor shall putt the
money that shall come of anye suche sale to anye other uses than to
the reparations of their churches or chappells: And all churchewardons at the ende of everye yere shall gyve up to the parson vicar
or curate and their parishioners a iuste accompte written in a booke
to be provided at the chardges of the parishe for that purpose of all
suche money ornamentes stocke rentes or other churche goodes, as
they have receyved duringe the tyme they were in office and also
shall particulerlye shew what coste they have bestowed in reparacions
and other thinges for the use of the churche And goinge out of their
office they shall truelye deliver upp in the sight of the parishioners
to the nexte churchewardons and note in the said churche booke
what so ever money ornamentes stocke or other churche goodes shall
remayne and be in ther handes at the tyme of givinge upp of their
accomptes.

4. Item that the churchewardons in everye parishe shall at the
costes and chardges of the parishe provide (if the same be not alreadye
provided) all thinges necessarye and requisite for Common Prayer
and administracion of the holye sacramentes on this syde the xx daye
of [blank] next ensewinge, speciallye the booke of common prayer
with the new kalender and a psalter to the same, the Englishe Bible
in the largiest volume, the two tomes of the homelies, with the
homelies latelye written against rebellion, the table of the ten com-
mandementes a convenient pulpitt well placed, a comelye and
decent table standinge on frame for the holie Communion with
a faire linnen clothe to laye upon the same and some coveringe of
silke buckram or other suche like, for the clene kepinge thereof,
a faire and comelye Communion cupp of silver and a cover of silver
for the same whiche may serve also for the ministracion of the
Communion breade, a decent lardge surples with sleves, a sure
coffer with two lockes and keyes for kepinge of the Register booke,
and a stronge chiste or boxe for the almose of the poore with thre
lockes and keyes to the same and all other thinges necessarye in and
to the premisses And shall also provide before the said daye the

paraphrases of Erasmus in Englishe upon the Gospels, and the same sett upp in some convenient place within ther churche or chappel, the chardges whereof the parson or proprietarye and parishioners shall by equal porcions beare accordinge to the Quenes Majesties Iniunctions, all whiche bokes must be whole and not torne or unperfitt in anye wise, and...provide breade and wine for the Communion, and...shall take some order amonge the parishioners that everye one may paye suche a reasonable somme towardes the same as maye suffice to the findinge of bread and wine for the Communion throughout the whole yeare so as no Communion at any tyme be disapointed for want of breade and wine.

5. ...To take down altars...and rood lofts....

6. ...To repair their churches...and to keep them clean...'so that they be not lothesome to anye eyther by duste sande gravell or anye filthe, and that there be no feastes, dinners or common drinkinge kept in the churche, and that the churchyeard be well fenced and clenlye kept and that no folkes be suffered to daunce in the same'.

7. ...No antiphoners, mass books...vestments...pixes paxes... images and all other reliques and monumentes of superstition and idolatrye....

12. ...to suffer no pedlers to set out wares in church porches or churchyards in service time....

13. ...to present inn-keepers etc who allow drinking or games in their houses during service time....

14. ...to note and present absentees from services....

15. ...to note and present those who walk or talk in service time...to note present and fine all absentees and late comers....

16. ...to assist the incumbent in the choice of two collectors for the poor...and to present those who refuse to pay their poor rate....

22. ...to make half-yearly presentments of all blasphemers, swearers...drunkards...scolds...usurers....

23. ...similarly of all married within the degrees of affinity...or without banns...who have forsaken wives or husbands...or are living apart....

24. ....similarly of all favourers of 'the Romishe and forreyne power, letters of true religion hearers or sayers of masse or of anye latine service preachers or setters forthe of corrupte and popishe doctrine, maynteyners of sectaryes, disturbers of divine service, kepers of anye secrete conventicles preachinges or lecture, receyvers of anye vacabonde popishe preistes or other notorious mislikers of true religion or maynteyners of the unlearned people in ignorance and errour encouraginge and movinge them rather to praye in an unknowne tonge than in Englishe or that stubbornelye refuse to conforme themselves to unitye and godly religion now established by publicke aucthoritye'.

25. ...similarly whether the Injunctions be duly observed and published.

The Visitation Books and records themselves are the best evidence of the conscientious and even over-scrupulous manner in which the church-wardens all over the Diocese discharged the duties laid upon them. Charges against churchwardens of neglect of their duties, brought by incumbents or by succeeding churchwardens, are of striking rarity. Two cases only are found, both in 1590, where wardens elected refused to undertake the office; one only, in 1594, where wardens 'wittinglie and willinglie omitted notorious offenders'. Indeed, any suggestion of slackness, still less of collusion, in presenting offences, is of the utmost rarity, and one instance only has been found of deliberate making of a false return.

A.D. 1590 [Visitation Books, R. VI. A. 10.]

Helmesley: 'Willm. Knott a churchwarden the last yere gave wronge evidence at Malton touchinge the xxiiith article sayinge a crosse was defaced which indeed was not and hath concealed the said crosse undefaced and also one pax and censors with other popishe ornaments of the churche....'

A.D. 1575 [Ibid. R. VI. A. 5, f. 24.]

Dewesburye: '[Six men] churchwardens for the last yeare have not made their accompts.' [Similar entries at Wakefield, Armthorpe and Thwing in this year. Otherwise an infrequent charge.]

In making presentments churchwardens were careful to show that they had not been negligent, although they were not always able to give complete information.

A.D. 1578   [Ibid. R. VI. A. 7, f. 5 v.]

Wilmesleye: 'Ther is a crosse in the parishe undefaced not presented with whome it remaineth.'

[Ibid. f. 4 v.]

Alderleighe: 'No forfeiture taken for such as absent them selfs from the churche for that they have no offenders.'

[Ibid. f. 17.]

Nelson: 'They have no sermons nor have had in their churche these iii yeres in the defalt of the Deane and Chapter of Chester, and if they have no reformatyon theye will no more present it again.'

[Ibid. f. 80.]

Brygham: 'Ther chauncell is falled downe and hath bene these twenty yeres and never reformed eyther her Majestie or John Hudson and Peter Hudson her fermors ought to repayre yt, whereof they humbly crave reformacion.'

Saynt Johns: 'The chauncell is fallen downe to the grounde and so hath bene these seven yeres the Quenes Majestie ought to procure the reperacion thereof and dyvers meanes they have made for yt But cannot get redresse they do humbly crave assistaunce in the premisses.'

[Ibid. f. 109.]

Staveley: '[Two men] refused to make an assessment at the request of the churchwardens for the dischardge of thinges necessarye.'

As might be expected, the wardens bring presentments most frequently for offences in church and for absence from church. Examples of both are given elsewhere, but the following may be added:

A.D. 1590   [Ibid. R. VI. A. 10, f. 222.]

Kirksmeaton: 'Contra Tho. Scoley did unreverently abuse him self in taking of his neighbors wiffs hat in the church violently to the disturbance of service.'

[Ibid. f. 224 v.]

Thirnscogh: 'They present Tho. Spark ther parson for want of bread and ale usually had at his charges on Easter day at after evening prayers.' The parson was dismissed with an admonition 'that he some way satisfy the demaunde of the churchewardens'.

[Ibid. f. 242.]

Heptonstall capella: '[Eight men named.] All these have kept men in service time drincking and talking in service time. They wold not suffer the churchwardens to serch ther howses in service time.'

[Ibid. f. 244 v.]

Ealand: '[Two men] drinking in the house of Tho. Wilkinson in service time die dominica. The said Wilkinson and his wief chid with the churchwardenes 13 Novembris for seing what disorder was in his house.'

[Ibid. f. 258.]

Wakefeild: '[Three men] bowlers on the Sabbothe day in tyme of prayer and beinge required by Hen. Yowle a churchwarden to leave there play and go to churche Chris. Feeld did beate him and would not leave his sporte.'

A.D. 1571 [Ibid. R. VI. A. 3 a, f. 47 v.]

Bishophill Senior, York: Against the churchwardens '...that they have neglected ther dewtie in presentinge the decay of ther Chauncell beinge in greate decay, that they have no decent Communion table and that ther alter stone is not defaced, and that they suffered a table of ymages in ther churche undefaced and that they have no pulpit in ther churche and that they have no sufficient bookes for devyne servyce...dicunt that they have provided a decent table to minister the Communion, a decent cupp of silver for the Communion, and a decent pulpit, and that further they will provyde suche books as they want in their churche...'. They were assigned 'that they shall provide all suche books as they want in their churche and further to make all things in good order belonging the churche', and to certify.

[Ibid. f. 112.]

Mytton (in Craven): Giles Taylor 'he denyeth to be a churche-warden and to serve God and the Churche and wold not aunswer when he was called in my L. Grace Visitacion being a churche-warden'. He pleaded that 'there is an order in the parishe that none shall be churchwarden but that payeth above a mark rent and he payeth under that somme'. [Order to the Rural Dean of Craven to deal with the matter.]

(b) *Maintenance of Church Fabric*

The contrast here between the assiduity of the churchwardens and the neglect of the farmers of rectories is very marked. The money required for repairs and maintenance was obtained by rates assessed on the parishioners. There was often difficulty in collecting these.

A.D. 1575 [Visitation Books, R. VI. A. 5, f. 45.]

Sherifhoton: 'Mr. James Westroppes tennants, Mr. Withams tennants Mr. Neviles Tennants, Rafe Hirste servant to Sir Valentine Browne, and Mr. Willm. Swale Swaill holdinge of Sir Robt. Stapleton of the Northe Ings and the Tennaunts of Farlington all parishoners of Sherifhoton do refuse to contribute to the reparations of Sherifhoton churche being latelie repaired as theie ar cessed.'

[Ibid. f. 36 v.]

Wathe: 'The churche roofe is in ruyne and decaie the inhabitants of the chapelrie of Wintworthe being in greatest defalte.'

[Ibid. f. 86.]

Skarburghe: 'They have not a comelie surplesse and their parishe churche is not good in reparations throughe the defalte of the whole parishe.'

[The chief reference to church repairs comes from the Ecclesiastical Commission, Act Books.]

A.D. 1575 [Ecclesiastical Commission, Act Books, R. VII. A. 8, f. 103 v.]

Gardiani de Cattericke contra gardianos de Bolton.

Domini...statuerunt et ordinarunt that forsomuche as the churche of Cattericke is presentlie in decaie and greatlie nedeth reparations that reparations of the ruynes and decaies of the same be made with all possible spede and cessements made throughe the whole parishe for moneye the inhabitants of Cattericke Towne and of suche as usuallie resort thither to devine service and the inhabitants of the chapelries of Hipswell and Hudswell (amongest them) everie man being indifferently rated shall beare two parts and the inhabitants of Bolton and of the townes resortinge thither to devine service shall beare the third parte everie inhabitant being indifferentlie rated, the rate for Cattericke and the townes of that side resorting thither and of the inhabitants of the chapleries of Hipswell and Hudswell to be rated amongest them selfs and likewise the rate for Bolton and the inhabitants of the Townes resorting thither to service to be made amongs them selfs, so that estimation be first made bye the knowledge and consent of certein honest men of everie of the said places...what the whole reparations will growe unto And if one cessement and collection will not serve mo to be made after the maner abovesaid till the decaies be repaired...[arrangements for the repayment of any surplus money collected]....And moreover it is ordered that this order be published at Cattericke Bolton Hudswell and Hipswell on some holie daies in service tyme, the publishing whereof shall stande in place of an injunction unto the inhabitants that some of the substantiallest inhabitants of everie of the said places shall assemble them selfs, and with advyse of indifferent workemen estimate what money will suffise to make the reparations or els the same estimation to be made by the inhabitants and churchwardens of Cattericke and workemen to be elected by them, in pain of the absences of suche of the inhabitants of the other places as will not come....

(c) *The Parish Clerk*

Archbishop Grindal's Injunctions for the Laity, No. 21.

ITEM that no parishe clerke be appointed against the good will or without the consent of the parson vicar or curate in anye parishe and that he be obedient to the parson vicar or curate especiallye in the tyme of celebration of divine service, or of the sacramentes or of anye preparation thereunto And that he be able also to rede the firste lesson the epistle and the psalmes, with aunsweares to the suffrages as is used, and that he kepe the bookes and ornamentes of the church faire and cleane and cause the churche and quiere, the communion table, the pulpitt and the fonte to be kepte decent and made cleane againste service tyme the Communion sermon and baptisme, and also that he endevour himselfe to teache yonge children to rede if he be able to do so.

2 Oct. 1564   [Ecclesiastical Commission, Act Books, R. VII. A. 1, f. 152 v.]

Officium dominorum promotum per Jac. Carlell contra gardianos de Hovingham et...nuper gardianos ibidem. [The Rural Dean of York certified that he had seen the defacement of certain images brought in from Hovingham.] ...And further Mr. Tho. Lakyn being appointed for examinacion of one brought in to be there clerke did reporte that he was not met for that purpose Whereupon the Commissioners by the consent of the churchewardens did enjoyne them to prepare them with as much spede as they may to provide them suche a clerke as shalbe hable to do the office of a parishe clerke and besids...teache children Grammer and to write yf ned be....

3 Oct. 1570   [Ibid. R. VII. A. 5, f. 143.]
The churchwardens of Kirkburn were ordered to allow peaceable posses-sion to Joh. Marshall, parish clerk, and to restore to him the church door keys. They had ejected him for laying information against them for the keeping of a tabernacle and other monuments of superstition. This case was long protracted. On 19 October 1571 some of the churchwardens were prisoners in the Castle 'becawse they have displaced Joh. Marshall enformer against them from the clarkshipp of Kirkburne', when an order was made by the Commissioners that Marshall was to exercise his office and receive his wages and arrears, and a letter was sent to Kirkburn authorising the gathering of 'the sheiffes' due to him.

In the same year 1571 (f. 70 v.) the parish clerk of Askrig was fined 5s. and ordered to do public penance for negligence in allowing images to be restored in his church.

19 June 1581   [Ibid. R. VII. A. 10, f. 109 v.]

After an order for the sale of certain 'reliques of supersticion' at Bolton-by-Bowland, it was 'also ordered that the churchwardens and parishioners there shold mete togither upon Sonday next and there agree and conclude upon some mete man well affected in religion to place him as parishe clerke there and to displace the parishe clerke who lately executed there thoffice of a parishe clerke'.

6 Oct. 1584 [Ibid. f. 279.]

An order to the parson and all the parishioners of Bolton Percy 'to electe and chose with spede a parishe clerke (that office as they were given tunderstand being voide) such as should make his abode within the church town for the better and more redy service of the parson and curate of the same churche'.

A.D. 1567 [Visitation Books, R. VI. A. 2, f. 4.]

...c. Tho. Stafford alias Lawe Clericum parochialem ecclesie parochialis de Warsop...he is a greate swearer and a disobedient person unto his masters the parishoners ther. [He entered a total denial, protested that he was 'diligent and willing and obedient in exequuting his office', and was ordered to make compurgation.]

A.D. 1575 [Ibid. R. VI. A. 5, f. 9 v.]

Saxtonne: 'Some of the parishoners ar contented with the Clarke and other some not, and so the Clarke is not aunswered his wages.'

[Ibid. f. 29.]

Hallifaxxe: 'Robte. Otes his habilitie to be clarke is doubted of and he doth not kepe cleane the churche.'

[Ibid. f. 44 v.]

Buttercram capella: 'The Clarke doth not read the first Lesson as he should do.'

[Ibid. f. 71 v.]

Swyne: 'Ric. Halome the parishe clarke is presented to be a defender and mainteyner of the Romish religion and saieth it will never from his harte. Item [he] doth not his duetie in kepinge cleane the Churche nor any thinge in the same that he is commaunded neither doth resort to the churche at tymes appointed for service neither wilbe obedyent to the vicar at any tyme.'

[Ibid. f. 89.]

Carnabye: 'Peter Otes sonne of John Ots vicar of Carnabye clarke of the churche being appointed against the consent of the whole parishoners of the age of xi yeres did on Thursdaie in Easter weke last past burye a child of Peter Marwicks of Carnabye aforesaid (being but clarke) contrarye to all lawes as they thinke.'

In the 1586 Visitation there were six 'insufficient' parish clerks, in 1590, three. 1594 produced probably the worst of them all, at Skirlaughe, 'insufficient in knowledge and negligente in the exequcion of his office (infirmus et impotens)'.

The greater number of entries refer to the payment or non-payment of dues to the parish clerk. At Fenton in 1590 (R. VI. A. 10) one parishioner had not paid his share of the clerk's wages 'for these xxiiii yeres last viz. viii d. yerelie in all xvi s'. But payment was more usually in kind, evidently by a regular assessment rated proportionably according to each parishioner's holding of arable or other land, and probably house property.

A.D. 1590   [Ibid. R. VI. A. 10.]

Preston in Holderness: '[A man] Behind with the clerke for viii yeres lxiv sheves of wheate and for ii oxganges more for foure yeres xxxii sheves, and for peny wage for foure yeres.' Another for $2\frac{1}{2}$ oxgangs for one year 10 sheaves; a third for $2\frac{1}{2}$ oxgangs for one year 10 sheaves and for penny wages for two years; a fourth was behind for 3 oxgangs for five years, 60 sheaves and 'for two oxgangs two yeres before that'; and two others at the same place owed respectively for penny wages for nine years 2 s. 3 d. and for half an oxgang for one year 2 sheaves, but both these two had paid since the charge was brought.

Archdeaconry of York, 1598   A common offence. Eleven instances. [Ibid. R. VI. D. 1, f. 7.]

All Hallowes in the Pavement: 'Tho. Weare for not payinge Clerke waigs for two yeares and other dutyes iii s.'

St. Mary Castlegate: 'Mast. Anth. Teale gen. and his wife executors of Anne Wiseman for not payinge Clerke waigs viii d. and Laur. Waide executor of Willm. Wollar for the same ii s.'

[Ibid. f. 25.]

Long Preston: 'Hen. Pele alias Clerke for not payinge his Clerke waigs for one yere a pecke and a halfe of ote meell and xviii ote sheaves.' [Ordered to pay before Midsummer and on promise to do so, dismissed. And four other men in the same place, for up to three years, to a total of $2\frac{1}{2}$ bushels and a peck of oatmeal and about 75 oat sheaves.]

Ibid. f. 25.]

Bracewell: 'Tho. Goodricke for not payinge his Clerke waigs
for two yeares a stroke of otes in the yeare.'

(d) *Further notes on the Parish Officers*

A.D. 1578 [Visitation Books, R. VI. A. 7, f. 20 v.]

St Olave's, Chester: 'They want a communion Cuppe by reason
of the povertye of the parishe.

They are enjoyned to buy one before Shrovetyde next sub pena
uris.'

Ibid. f. 39 v.]

Gorton capella: 'They have a Communyon cuppe of tynne and
sometyme Communyon is celebrated in a glasse.

They have no surplesse nor boxe for the poore.'

A.D. 1586 [Ibid. R. VI. A. 9, f. 11.]

St Margaret's, York: '...c. Pet. Jackson clericum parochialem
an obstinate fellow prout patet etc. Pendet hec causa in Curia
Cancellaria.'

A.D. 1590 [Ibid. R. VI. A. 12, f. 101 v.]

Stopporte alias Stockporte: 'The clarke is over muche gevin to
gammynge and is negligente in his dutie.'

A.D. 1595 [Ibid. R. VI. A. 14, f. 84 v.]

Norwell: 'Nich. Holman must be sent for to expound the residue
of this parish presentment.'

Ibid. f. 134 v.]

Sherifhuton: 'Willm. Broughe there parishe clerke is not sufficiente for he can not write nor scarce rede. He is poore. the wages
and all duties not being worth forty shillings yearly.'

Ibid. f. 137.]

Brafferton: 'The churche is not repayred. thay say Mris. Eliz.
Thin is the cause thereof for that she refusethe to pay her cesmente
thereunto/ no not all that which she promised to Mr. Doctor Gibson.

By her slacknes the churchwardens havinge laid oute monie and cannot gett the same againe others ar unwillinge to enter into that office.

The clarke wagies ar decayed in Mris. Thins defalte because she haithe dispeopled halfe the towne.

And lykewise the moonie to be collected for provision of breade and wyne for the Communion vide presentamentum.'

[Ibid. f. 138.]
Escrige: 'Geo. Weddall used unreverente spechies to the churche-wardens in the streete callinge theme vyle raskalls and darde bothe theme and the person to fetche theme into the churche.'

[Ibid. f. 154 v.]
Yarome: 'The surples is verie ould and badd.' [The church-wardens were named to appear.]

[Ibid. f. 159 v.]
Fyley: 'Tho. Rychardson theyr parishe clerke teachethe chyldren not knowne to be lycensed. infirmus et pauperrimus leprosus unde dimittitur.'

[Ibid. f. 163.]
Huggett: 'They presente nothinge amisse savinge that Mr. Kay theyr Parson dothe not weare a surplesse not for any dyslyke but for that it is not a decent one/he went not the perambulacion this yere for that the auncyente men of the parishe dyd not offer them selfs.'

[Ibid. f. 164 v.]
St John's Beverley: 'Mr. Willm. Moxon Mayor of Beverley is sayd to be in default for two homely bokes awantinge and for not causinge ther surplesse to be wasshed accordinge to theyr old custome.'

3. SOME SMALLER MATTERS

(a) *Alehouse kept in the Vicarage*

The charge of keeping an alehouse in a vicarage is not altogether easy to explain; the use as an alehouse may have been due to a desire to supplement an inadequate stipend, or it may have been prompted by the need to provide refreshment for those attending church from outlying parts of the parish who did not wish or were not conveniently able to return home between services, when the vicarage would be in a suitable position near the church and would also be under better supervision than other places of entertainment in the town or village. The attitude of authority was generally, but not absolutely, one of disapproval.[1]

A.D. 1571   Archbishop Grindal's Injunctions to the Clergy.

23. ITEM ye shall not kepe or suffer to be kepte in your parsonage or vicaredge howses anye ailehowses tiplinge howses or tavernes, nor shall sell aile beere or wine....

A.D. 1571   [Visitation Books, R. VI. A. 3 a, f. 64 v.]

...c. Geo. Chester cler. vicarium de Killome. He suffreth an ayle house to be kept in his Vicaridge...[admitted the charge]... monuerunt that hereafter he shall not permite any ayle house to be kepte in the vicaridge sub pena juris.

[Ibid. f. 65.]

...c. Joh. Cockerell cler. Vicarium de Burton Flemyng. He suffreth a vittaling house to be kept in his vicarage...monuerunt to certifie istum in tres that ther shall not hereafter be any aylehouse kepte in the said vicarag house sub pena juris.

[Ibid. f. 78.]

...c. Joh. Lake parochie de Warter. He kepeth an ayle house in the vicaridge.

[1] It should be remembered that ale was then the drink in almost universal use, to many the only drink. Tea and coffee were unknown, and water often undrinkable.

[Ibid. f. 143.]

The Vicar of Darfield 'permitteth an ayle house in his vicaridge'. Similarly at Skipton, Dewsbury and Kirkby Malhamdale.

In 1575 (R. VI. A. 7) vicarage alehouses are found at Adel, Whitkirk, Ilkley and Kettlewell; at the last it is noted that 'ther is an Inne kepte in the vicaredge howse for honeste resorte'. At Skipton also the alehouse was still in existence: 'the vicars brother doth dwell with him in the vicaredge howse and sometymes breweth ale and selleth to his frends'.

In later years the charge is found less and less frequently.

A.D. 1578   [Ibid. R. VI. A. 7, f. 70.]

Hyton: 'Officium dominorum contra Wm. Warde vicarium ibidem. They have no sermons and ther is an alehous in the vycaryage hous....And for thalehouse he is to certyfye at Manchester at the next sessyons ther that he kepeth no alehous in his vycaryage.'

(b) *The Hunting Parson*

Here the attitude of authority was not altogether inclined to disapproval; a justifiable distinction was evidently recognised between the cases of the parson of Coddington and of the Curate of Kirkby Chapel.

A.D. 1595   [Visitation Books, R. VI. A. 14, f. 8 v.]

Chester [Codding-]ton: 'Evan Rycrofte theyr parson sometymes hunteth for whiche the churchewardens presente him it semeth they hold it offensive.'

[Ibid. R. VI. A. 15, f. 63.]

[Evan Rycroft] fatetur that he kepeth a dog and sometymes hunteth but not offensively Unde domini injunxerunt eum that he shold not hereafter to the offence of his parishioners hunt et sic dimittitur.

[Ibid. R. VI. A. 14, f. 47.]

Bedall: '[The Vicar] doth use hunting at convenient tymes.' And a similar case at Patrington, f. 173 v.

A.D. 1571   [Ecclesiastical Commission, Act Books, R. VII. A. 6.]

Robt. Cloughe, curate of Kirkby Chapel, 'a sorcerer a hawker and a hunter', was referred for correction to the Bishop of Chester.

(c) *Stipends. The Large Parsonage House*

The information found on the subject of stipends is insufficient for a satis-factory general view. In the few cases where payments are mentioned, it is not clearly stated whether each was the whole payment to the in-cumbent or curate, and in any case the evidence is difficult to interpret. Any calculation is complicated by the fact that the money payment was certainly not the whole or even the main part of the income; evidence from the Clergy Wills in the Registers shows decisively that many parishes which paid small stipends yet enabled the incumbent to run quite a large farm and to maintain several servants. Thus the effect of such statements as those in R. VI. A. 5, 1575, that the value of the vicarage of Gargrave was twenty marks in the tithe-books, or that the patron of Kirksmeaton paid twenty nobles as the stipend is of uncertain value.

There is, however, some evidence that even then the over-large parsonage house was a problem.

A.D. 1567 [Visitation Books, R. VI. A. 2, f. 55.]

Officium dominorum contra Geo. Aslabie vicarium de Tickhill. He doethe suffer his vicarage to fall into extreme ruyne and decay... cui objeccioni respondendo dicit that he hayth bestowed asmuche of his vicaredge as he is able and as the lyvinge will beare notwith-standing the same is in decay because yt is suche a greate house Et tunc domini decreverunt commissionem fieri decano Doncastrie to vew the same vicared [and] to appoint suche house of the same vicaredge as shalbe sufficient for the lyvinge and that suche other howses therof as ar superfluous may be pulled downe wherwith the other may be sufficiently repayred et ad certificandum de gestis per decanum....

Possibly also R. VI. A. 5, 1575, at Leven, the parson was found to have 'let his parsonage to one Mr. Fenwicke and dwelleth in the towne him self and serveth the cure'; more than possibly, in the same year 1575 at Arksey, the vicar lived with his father and 'kepes no howse becawse the livinge is so small'.

(d) *Witchcraft and Magic*

Presentments for witchcraft and like offences are perhaps less numerous than might be expected. In the Visitation of 1567 four cases were returned; in 1571, none; in 1575, two; in 1586, ten; in 1590, sixteen; in 1598, thirteen for the Archdeaconry of York only. The offence appeared rarely

before the Commissioners, and then always apparently as a result of
pseudo-scientific study by the clergy. For the laity it ranks as one of the
major offences, not comparable with immorality or Sabbath breaking or
failure to pay assessments, but about on a level with scolding and more
frequent than drunkenness. About half the cases were on suspicion only
and were dismissed with or even without compurgation. Many of the
charges were for activities which were not considered malevolent but
rather the reverse, since they were for the purpose of healing or 'un-
bewitching', but the charge was always taken seriously, although there
is no trace of that barbarous and stupid cruelty which seems to have been
the introduction of James I.

Feb. 1563/4 [Ecclesiastical Commission, Act Books, R. VII. A. 1, ff. 98, 104.]

'Md. quod quarto Februarii Sir Joh. Betson was enjoined upon
payne of forfatynge his recognisaunce to appere personallie xiii
Martii prox. and to bringe in suche books as he hath concernynge
the practises of conjuracions and speciallie Plato Spere [1] and Pithacoras
Spere and such lyk.' On his second appearance, he confessed 'that
he had Pithagoras Spere which he delivered in to this Courte and
usethe the same as he saieth for thinges lost and that he had Platos
Spere etc.'. [He was ordered to do public penance by declaration in
the markets of Yarm, Richmond and Northallerton.]

A.D. 1571 [Ibid. R. VII. A. 6, f. 64 v.]

...c. Ric. Deane clerk...to behave him self in religion as a conformable subject in all respects and that he shall not accompany
harbor nor relieve any popishe preists nor use any predictions
divinations sorceries charmings or inchantements....

[Ibid. f. 67 v.]

...c. Pet. Carter, schoolmaster of Whalleye, 'supposed to be
a papist and to be pryvy with the roving preists. An open professor
of astrologye and necromancy....Bound over not to intermeddle
hereafter with any predictyons or with sorceryes charmings or the
vayne art of astrology...'.

[1] Uncertain in this context, but known elsewhere as a chart or figure used in
divination by numbers. An early reference to the use of the Sphere of Pythagoras
in astrology is found in *Dives et Pauper*, 1493.

A.D. 1567   [Visitation Books, R. VI. A. 2, f. 22.]

...c. Margaretam Harper parochie S. Nicholai Nottingham...
tayketh upon hir to tell where thinges ar that be gone or loste and to
heale sick folke and sayth she healeth theme by helpe of the fayries.

[Ibid. f. 25 v.]

...c. Robt. Garmann parochie de Lowdame...is comonly reputed
to be a wiseman or a sorcerer and great repair is maid unto hime...
dicit that he hayth healed beastes beinge forspoken[1] and that by
sayenge of these wordes yf any come and aske hime for gods sake
and sanct charitie[2] to heale their beastes being forspoken then he
saythe God and sancte charytie blysse the beast they come for....

[Ibid. f. 26.]

...c. Aliciam More alias Shadlock parochie de Arnall...tayketh
upon hir to amende things that be spoken[1] and is tayken to be
a soothesayer....

A.D. 1575   [Ibid. R. VI. A. 5, f. 8.]

Draxe: 'Alison Welles suspected to use witchecrafte and can for-
speake thinges as horse, cowe, milke, drinke etc.'

[Ibid. f. 47 v.]

John Skelton a maried man of Marton in Synnyngton parishe is
a southsayer or inchanter and suche as telleth men of their goods
when they ar stollen awaye, and where they ar become.[3]

A.D. 1590   [Ibid. R. VI. A. 10.]

Guyeslay...Jas. Sykes he hangs wrytinges in horse maines to cure
diseasies.

...Hen. Mathewe he useth lyke woords for curinge beasts.

A.D. 1594   [Ibid. R. VI. A. 13, f. 28.]

York City. St Michael le Belfry: '...c. Cuth. Williamson. He
can tell if one be forespoken and helpe them...beinge asked how

---

[1] Bewitched by the 'speaking' of words, charms, or formulae powerful for evil.
[2] Charity canonised.   [3] Where they have gone.

he knoweth when one is forspoken he saith that so sone as his help is craved in that case his eies will furthwith run with water in case the parties be forspoken.'

A.D. 1598   [Ibid. R. VI. D. 1, f. 60 v.]

Doncaster: Three women named for 'sorcery with sive and sheares'.

[Ibid. f. 64.]

Darton: 'Willm. Taylior younger for that he sent to one Haigh widdowe or widdowe Carre of Darfield reputed wise women to knowe a remedy for his sicknes and her resolucion was that he was bewitched.' [The charge was denied.]

A.D. 1595   [Ibid. R. VI. A. 14, f. 46 v.]

Scruton in Catterick Deanery: 'Dorothy Jenkinson alias Taite for a slandering that there dwelleth a witch within thre houses on one tyme and fyve houses at an other, and upon further examination she confessed herselfe to be ridden with a wiche thre tymes of one night, being thereby greatly astonished, and upon her astonishment awaked her husband.'

(e) *Usury*

The offence of usury is found hardly at all before 1580; the Ecclesiastical Commission Books show a marked increase in the offence, or a marked increase of attention to it, in the last twenty years of the century. This is borne out by the Visitation Books, except that most of their instances are concentrated in the year 1586. Of twenty-one or perhaps twenty-two offenders in this year more than half denied the charge, and nearly half appeared as definitely cleared by compurgation. There was great variation in the seriousness of the offence, and evidently some practical difficulty in defining it exactly.

A.D. 1586   [Visitation Books, R. VI. A. 9, f. 3 v.]

York, St Martin's, Coney Street: 'Anth. Geldart a dealer in usurie and hath answered it before my L. Grace. Non citatus.'

[Ibid. f. 72.]

Three men at Slaidburne accused of usury were dismissed on compurgation.

[Ibid. f. 88].

Slyngesby: 'Tho. Pereson de Swinton he solde a quarter of barley to John Pratt for xxiiis., which was so muche above the pryce in the markett that it is thought to be usury.'

[Ibid. f. 30.]

Drax: '...Fra. Riccard an cruell usurer.'

[Ibid. f. 130.]

Walkinton: 'Chris. Champney, usurer. "He lent money at vli. for an hundreth and yet never received either the principall or the interest."' [Dismissed with admonition.]

[Ibid. f. 131.]

St John's Beverley: '...Ric. Reade usurer takethe after the rate of vis. viiid. att the pound within the yeare.'

[Ibid. f. 185.]

Huddersfield: 'A usurer took "xvs. for the lone of xxli. and more for thre quarters of a yere and that in mortgage".'

In several of these cases no proceedings or sentence are entered, only the heading showing the charge.

CHAPTER VI
LONGER DOCUMENTS FOR GENERAL ILLUSTRATION

❧

1. INSTRUCTIONS TO RURAL DEANS

A quotation from some book of Acts at present unidentified, possibly a Court Book; it is inserted without note or heading amongst entries of Institutions and Subscriptions, in a volume of three parts bound in one. From the context, the date of this entry should be 5 October 1571.

York, Diocesan Registry, Act Book 2. [Institutions 1553–71, f. 146.]

Quibus die horis et loco comparentibus coram Mr. Joh. Gibson legum doctore antedicto Decanis respective de Bulmar, Rydall, Harthill et Hull, Holdernes, Dickering, Pontefracte et Cleveland Dominus monuit eos et eorum quemlibet to visit all there churches in there severall Deanryes ecclesiatim, and to se all rode lofts taken downe and all ornaments thereof defaced, and to se that every churche be provided of a Communyon table with a frame and a decent cover and a convenyent low pulpit for service to be said in, the minister turnynge to the people or in litle churches a deske or convenyent pulpit with communyon cuppes, and to se that no reliques of crosses remayne in any churche or chaple yard within there severall Deanryes and to make due certificat of all the premisses affore the next synode And further the said Mr. Gibson did generally inhibit all the saide Deanes not to commute penance by any meanes to any maner of person whatsoever theie be.

2. CASE AGAINST FUGALL, THE VICAR OF HESSLE

(a) *Certified Copy of Articles*[1] *of Information*

A.D. 1561   [Cause Papers, R. VII. G. 1041.]

To the moast reverende father in God the Archbushop of York his grace.

Artycles mynystryd on the behalf of Christofer Legeard of Anlaby in the countie of Kingeston uppon Hull esquier against Thomas Fewgale clerk parson of Lowthropp and vycar of Hasill and Hull concerning his lewde and evill lif and wicked conversacion wheruppon the said Christofer prayeth that the said Thomas Fewgell may be sworne and examyned in dewe fourme and order of lawe.

Inprimis whether you Thomas Fugell abovenaimed in the fyrst yere of the raign of our soveraign Ladie Quene Elizabeth after that the act of parlyament for the usage of common prayer to be hadd and donne in the Englishe tong past was desired and praied to saie the service in Englishe according to the booke auctoryzid by parlyament by the maior of Hull called Alexander Stokdale and his Brethern or not, and whether you being so required did obstynatlie refuse to doe the same saing that the quenes majesties proclamacion in that behalf proclaymid was rather an Inhibicion unto you not to saie the same then a warrant, and whether you said if any other did saye Englishe service in your church you wold accuse him of sacryledg, yea or not.

2. Item whether you have byn resident in your benefices in suche sorte as the Lawe doth require you or not and what facultie is graunted unto you wherbie you may possesse more benefices then one and whose chapleyne you be at this presente tyme and whether you have warnyd openlie in the church of Hasell your parishners of Hasell to use no beads according to the quenes majesties Injunctions yea or naye.

3. Item whether you being in an alehowse situate in Hull in the time of the raign of quene Marye said openlie to those that were there present with you God be praysed the time is come that

---

[1] See footnote on p. 170.

St. George shall goe afoote and St. Nicholas shall ride on hors back or not, and what you ment by that saing.

4. Item whether you beinge by the quenes majesties vysiters appointed for Yorckshier enjoyned to recant your wilful errours and obstinacies did according to ther commaundement recant the same in such fourme and maner as ye wer warnyd to do or not.

5. Item whether you have kept howse uppon any your benefices sithens the tyme that you had them or not and whether you have byn bourded at an alehowse in Hasell by the space of twoo or thre yeres or not, and how you spent your tyme at the same ale howse betwixt meales all those yeres.

6. Item whether you did trowble one Willm. Harland of Hull in the tyme of Quene Marye[1] for that he was a maried priest or not, and whether you trowbled one Rowland Wilkinson and his wif of

---

[1] Proceedings against this man, a Canon Regular, who had married in the reign of Edward VI, are to be found in the Diocesan Registry Books. R. VII. A. 19 contains only the record of the original summons on 9 April 1554 (f. 18), when Harland was declared contumacious by non-appearance and ordered to appear on the following Friday, when (f. 29 v, 13 April) again he did not appear. In R. VII. A. 34, f. 13, on 21 May 1554, he appeared and was charged by the judges 'quod religionem canonicorum regularium est professus et postea quandam Agnetem in uxorem duxerit'. This he confessed, and was assigned to hear 'sentenciam divorcii' on Thursday after St Magdalene, when he was to appear and to bring with him Agnes 'uxorem suam'. The next entry is on f. 104 for 12 Jan. 1554/5, when neither Harland nor Agnes appeared. There is no further reference to them, and the probability is that the judges proceeded as in other cases to declare sentence of divorce. As Harland was not beneficed, they could not add the usual sentence of deprivation. In view of the charge against Fugall in the text above (p. 204) it is interesting to note that R. VII. A. 34 shows that the Vicar of Hessyll in 1554 was active against married clergy in his area; on 13 June he was present in Court to bring in a certificate of penance done by another Canon Regular, Ric. Wager, who had married, and it is to be noted that of eight unbeneficed clergy punished by this Court three were from Hull, and that in addition the judges had before them the Curate of Hull, Willm. Otlay or Utley. The course of the evidence against Harland suggests that he had gone into hiding, which is borne out by the later evidence against Fugall for his persecution of married clergy. Proceedings against eighty beneficed clergy are found in these Court Books, including chantry priests, and against only eight unbeneficed, at least half of whom were old religious, although it has not been possible in all cases to trace the house to which they formerly belonged. Of course, the clergy who had taken advantage of Edward VI's permission to marry had never supposed that the King would die so soon.

Hull for religion so as they durst not tarie at Hull by the space of a yere together or not, and whether you refusyd to burye one Richard Allen at Hull because he had favored the word of God in his time and whether the maior and his brethren did warne and commaunde you to burye him before you wold burie him And howe longe he did lie above the ground unburied and for what cause.

7. Item whether Christofer Legeard abovenamyd suspecting his wif and you to live incontinentlie to gether did before Christenmas last past forbid you his howse and his companie, and whether you after suche warning gevon unto you by him was at his howse privelie twise And for what purpose thowe didst resort to his howse after thowe wast forbydden by him to comme thither.

8. Item whether thow haddist ever carnallie to do with the wif of the said Christofer Legeard at his howse or elliswhere and how oft.

9. Item whether the vycar of Brantingham being asked by his patron whie he used to saie the Latin service dailie the last yere said he did saie the same by the counsell of the vycar of Hasell and Hull which was a lernid man and whether you did gyve him such counsell or not.

10. Item whether the said Chris. Legeard for the causes aboverehearsed hath put awaie his wif and whether you have at any time since that [he] put his wife from him spoken with her or byn in her cumpanye where and when.

11. Item whether ye did ever gyve any drincks to the wyf of the said Legeard to thentent that she shuld therbie conceive child by you or her husband or whether ye did ever counsell her to take any drincks for that purpose yea or nay.

[Articles 14, 15 and 16 give other charges concerned with Legeard's wife.]

17. Item whether you leaning uppon the Communion table in the churche of Hull did wryte this posee Redde votum Lebase sainge that it was a good posee to be put in a ringe, and whether you put a ringe to makinge shortelie after or not, and whether ye have anie ring wherein is written Redde votum or not or hath had.

18. Item whether you did write or make a ballet to the maner of a farewell from your mestres or anie parte or parcell therof and uppon what cause or respect ye dyd make the same or anye parte of it or causid it to be made.

[Articles 19, 20 and 21 refer to other charges of misbehaviour with women.]

22. Item whether in the tyme of Quene Marie you did cutt with your knif in the howse of Willm. Wedall of Hull the Bible in English which a man of Yermowth did reade uppon or had redd uppon and for what cause ye did cut the Bible.

23. Item whether you in the last yere of the raign of Quene Marie did openlie declare affirme and bragg in the towne of Hull at any time that if you lyved till the next Lent then to comme that you wold mak all England to wonder of the towne of Hull, and whether you have said at any time since that time that if the world shuld evyr turne you wold not beare with them of Hull as ye had done before time.

24. Item whether the last daie of Marche last past you did saie evening praier in the church of Hull or not and howe [you] wer occupied all that after none that daie.

25. [Suggested offences against married women at his other benefice of Lowthorpe.]

Concordat cum originalibus et registro.
Will. Bedell notarius publicus.

(b) *The Answers on Oath of the Accused to the Articles*

Die Sabbati xviii Aprilis 1561 coram Ric. Goodericke ar. in presentia mei Will. Bedell.

Responsiones personales Thome Fugell facte quibusdam articulis ex officio dominorum contra eum ministratis.

To the fyrst he aunsweryth that he was required by the Mayor to sey the procession in Englishe bringing a proclamacion with him for that purpose, which this respondent denied to doe as he saithe for that bycause the ordinary there [was] not his frende, if he shuld do any thing before a lawe he wold do him displesure, and the rest of the contents herof he deniethe.

To the seconde he saithe that he hath byn alwais resydent uppon his benefice of Heasill and Hull and that he hath no more benefices but that, and that according to thinjunctions he gave openlie admonicion to his parishners that they shuld ley away ther beads.

To the thirde he deniethe, saving that he said that nowe Saint Nicholas shuld ride aswell as Saint George.

To the iiii th he saith he was commaunded by the commyssyoners to make no suche declaracion and the rest he deniethe.

To the v th he saithe at his first cumming to Hasell he bordid one yere in an ale howse untill he was able to kepe howse him self.

To the vi th he denieth in every of them, saving at the fyrst he denied to burye the man articulated but afterwards he voluntarilie buried him.

[To the charges concerning Mr Legeard and his wife he entered a general denial, except that on Article 10 he admitted 'that as the common reporte is in the cuntreye Mr. Legearde put away his wif for this examinants cause and company'. He denied altogether Articles 8, 9, 11, 12, 13, 14 and 16 but admitted Article 15 in part.]

To the xvii th he saithe that he went to a Goldsmith in Hull to have a ring made and so the Goldsmith delivered this respondent his [stone?] wheruppon he departed and tooke the same within to churche and there invented and wrote divers posies to be sett in it emongest the which was Redde votum etc. and cam againe to the goldesmithe, and shewid it unto him who said that he could not well put that posie in the said ring, and so put his name uppon it and otherwise he denieth.

To the xviii he saithe he made a pec of a song for a young man that went to the sea the forme wherof he remembrith not....

To the xxi th he saith that he buried a man of Lambehithe at lowewater marck there, which he did bycause he refusid to receve the sacraments in quene Maries time and otherwise he deniethe.

[He denied the 22nd, but witnesses showed that there had been some such incident.]

To the xxiii he denieth saving he saith that he said if they wold not pay ther tithes and dueties better then they have done he wold make more speake of hit.

To the xxiiii th he saithe that he went the last of Marche to a bowling alley at Hull to fetche one of his suerties to the maior who was then bowling, who seid to this respondent he wold not cum yet, and willed this examinant to bowle a game or twoe with him and then he wold goe and so he was absent from evening praier that daie.

[There follows a copy of Fewgill's bond in £100, dated 30 May 1561, to appear before the Archbishop on or before 13 June.]

(c) *Attestations*

The attestations which have survived on this file generally support the Articles, and occasionally amplify them.

John Hardcastle, confirming the first Article as to the 'inhibition rather than a warrant' remark, proceeded:

And then the maior declared unto the vicar that yf he wolde not do service himselfe...he wolde appoynte Sir Thomas Turner thereunto, And the vicar aunswered sayng, That yf any enterprised to execute and do any thinge within his Cure without his licence, he wolde accuse them of sacrileg, notwithstanding he saieth that service was done according to the tenor of the proclamation in the body of the churche the said vicar sitting in the quere the first daye of the execucion thereof, with his cappe on his heide and wolde not come downe to here the same as others dyd, but obstinately refused so to do.

Super secundo articulo...he this examinate having occasion to be at Hesill to christen a childe upon St. Stephens daye in Christenmas last did see a grete nombre of women were beeds, And thereupon asked the Curet there being a Scotishe man why they used so much to were beadds, and marveyled much they were not warned to leave the same And the Curet aunswered saying I founde it thus And I may say noghte, and further he saieth that he is well assured that the vicar did never prohibit beads nor rede the quenes majesties Injunctions in the Trinitie church of Hull being within his parishing....

Super sexto... the vicar of Hesill in quene Maryes tyme did dryve the said Wilkinson mencioned in this article uppe and downe the countrey so as he durst not for feare of the said vicar remayne and contynue in any certeyn place And over this... he herde certeyn wymen of Hull move the vicar to burye Richerd Allen named in this article, to whome the vicar aunswered and sayd that he was a beest, and dyed more lyke a beest then a Christen man, and therefore he wolde not bury him But badde them bury him at the lowe water marke for that was a place mete for a beest And afterwards the wymen seynge that he wolde not bury him broughte him to the churche yerd and there did lay him who was afterwarde buryed by commaunde of Mr. Maior and his bretherne, but by whome he cannot tell, albeit he saieth that before he was buryed he laye one daye and on nighte in the house and almost a day and an other nighte in the churche yerde.

3. CASE AGAINST SMYTH, THE VICAR OF HESSLE

Articles and answers in a cause, the Ecclesiastical Commissioners of York against Melchior Smith, Vicar of Hessle and Hull. A.D. 1563/4 [Cause Papers, R. VII. G. 1396.]

It is not clear when or where this cause was heard in 1564. Smith had appeared before the Commission, as is shown by their Act Book, R. VII. A. 1, in February 1564, when he was ordered to 'use himself soberlie and discretelie aswell in his sermons and exhortacions and ministracions accordinge to the lawes of God as also in wearinge of decente apparell, accordinge to the lawes, Injunctions and settled order of this Realme, as becometh a man of his callinge, upon payne of deprivacion etc.', which must surely be connected in some way with the articles and answers below; he appeared again in July 1566, when the proceedings were more full and detailed and much concerned with vestments, and again he was threatened with deprivation. In February 1567 he was cited for contumacy, and 'for that he hayth not proved to have conformed hime self in this behalf' was summoned to appear on 17 March, and 'ther to heare hime self depryved frome all his spirituall promocions intimating him that whether he come or no the most reverend Father and other his associats intendeth to procede to the deprivation of hime his absence or contumacie in any wise notwithstandinge'; he was bound over in £100 with 100 marks surety for appearance. Yet he did not appear until 7 April 1567, when he 'exhibuit quasdam litteras certificatorias de conformitate sua in hac parte sub sigillo majoris ville regie super Hull ut apparuit sigillatas'; he was then after a delay of one or two days allowed to depart, and did not appear again.

In this cause the influence of the Mayor of Hull on the affairs of the parish church is notable.

In all the Cause Papers no document has been found hitherto which can be compared with these Articles and answers for the copiousness and variety of the information which they give about many aspects of parochial life and ecclesiastical usage.

[Ibid. R. VII. G. 1396.]

Artycles of informacione exhibyted to the most reverend father in God the Lorde Archebusshopp of York his grace and others his associates the Quenes majesties Commissioners for causes Ecclesiasticall within the dioces and province of York by Edmund Roberts against Melchyor Smyth clerk.

i. Imprimis ponit et articulatur that the said Melchyor Smyth hayth bene vicar of Hessell and Hull sins Lammas was twoo yeres or there abowts, and hayth bene continuallie resident there duryng the said terme And the foresaid Edmound during the said tyme heyth bene parishoner there....

ii. Item ponit that Melchior is noo prest nor minister ordered after the Ecclesiasticall lawes as may be well supposed by the artycles next folowing. [A marginal note: 'PROBATUR per partem Smyth per exhibitionem literarum ordinum suorum sub sigillo Nicholai episcopi Lincoln.']

iii. Item ponit that at any tyme during his residens he haith not ministred any sacraments or sacramentals within his cure nor haith doone or said any communyon there within the said tyme at the eest wais so farr as his parishoners or more parte of them have knowen seene or hard tell of Or at the leest if he have ministred doone or said any of the premisses it haith bene so seldom tymes, that his necligence in that behalf is boothe marvaled and grudged at by his parishoners or moost parte of theim.

iv. ...that during the said tyme he hayth not receaved nor used to receave the hoolye Communion, except at one tyme and then muche unreverentlye, standing upon his feet, or at the leest he hayth receaved thoolye communyon so seldome during the said tyme that the parishoners or moore parte of theim have and doo boothe mervale and grudge at it.

v. ...that in tyme of dyvine service and Common Prayer and also when by order of the quens majestie booke of common praour the parishoners have bene on their knees at their praers The said Melchior hayth dyvers tymes and in maner of custoome used to walk in the said Trynitie churche with his hatt upon his heed; yea and some tymes talking with one or other to the great offence and evill example of the parishoners there.

vi. ...that M.S. hayth and doothe kepe a woman in his house at Hull as his wife boothe at bedd and at boord during all the tyme of his residens there....

vii. ...that he did take the said woman first to his companye to lyve with hir as his wife sins the first yere of the Reagn of our soveraign ladye the Quene that now is And did not in his taking of hir observe and kepe the manor and facone in that behalf provided nether yet did solemnize matrimonye with hir in the face of any churche and so is the common voyce rumour and fame in Hull and other places there abowtes.

viii. ...that the said woman whom he reteneth as wife [he] doth handle divers tymes verey uncharitablye In so muche that by his crueltye and unientle handling of hir She haithe bene forced what with feare and sorow to rone from him toward the great water of Hull and to lepe over the stayth there into the water or els into the oses dirt or myre to the great offence of all his neighbours.

ix. ...that Melchior haith bene a great occasyon of contentyon and great strif emonges thinhabitauntes of Hull And a great sower of discorde emonges theim in tyme of his being there And this is the common opinion of all thinhabitauntes of Hull or the moore part of theim.

x. ...that Melchior in other places where he haith dwelt before tyme haythe bene occasyon of great discentyon and debate and a great sower of discord viz. in Boston where he dwelt abowt thre yeres last by past and in Burton upon Trent where he dwelt abowt four yeres by past.

xi. ...that Melchior making many sermons in the Trynitie churche of Hull in tyme of his first being resident there did always omytt and neclect to pray for the Quenes majestie that now is In so muche that dyvers of thinhabitauntes were offended with him and some of theim did challenge him for yt and yet that notwithstanding he did omitt and neclect the same untill he was dyvers and many tymes challenged and threatened to be complened upon for that his dewtye neclected So that yt may well be supposed that he now doth pray for hir grace not with good stomake and good will but rather for dowt and feere to be complened on....

xii. ...that in his sermons he hayth dyvers tymes to the estymacione of his herers inveyhed against the ruleres and nobylitie and difference of blood and perswaded all men to be equall and lyke.

xiii. ...that Melchior sins the tyme of his being Vicarr there hayth not used to weer a prest capp nor yet a Surpless in the churche in tyme of dyvine service, but openlye in his sermons hayth called prest capps and surpleses vile clowtes and ragges and hayth said that preestes capps ar knaves capps.

xiiii. ...that the said Melchior sens his tyme of being vicar at Hull in his open sermons in the sayd churche he hayth said that the mares offycers of the towne which daly beere the swoord before the said mair and the maces having on them the quenes majestie armes are but bondes and staves.

xv. ...that [he] in his sermons made in the place and tyme aforesaid muche unreverentlye hayth lykened the Bisshops to doome dogges and theves whiche woold not travale throughe their dioces and preche and hayth said if thei woold gyve over their lyvinges there were men moore meter and woorthyer then they to supplye their roomes.

xvi. ...that [he] upon All Saintes day at night last within the churche aforesaid did take and pull one Nicholes Laborn maryner by the beerd And also gave him suche a strooke upon the face with his fist that Laborn brast owt of blood boothe at the mouthe and at the noose All which Melchior haythe confessed to be trew.

xvii. ... [he] in his sermons muche unreverently and raling against the Busshopps haith said that he was not a thefe onelye whiche stood at a woode end edge nooke or corner, but the busshopp that wold not preeche was the great thefe and robber.

xviii. ...upon XII Day last or there abowtes when the said Melchior had an inkeling that he shoold be complened on for this his said lewd misdemeanours he said oponlye in the churche in his sermon That there were certein men in Hull to be compared to Herod for thei went abowt to put down Christ and his gospell as muche as in theim lay and did go abowte to take away other mens lyvinges And therefore that they were to be compared to Herod and his companye, for thereupone dependeth salvatione and dampnacion And that they were accursed to the third and fourthe generacione And that thei shuld have as shamefull an end as Herod had Whiche woordes he did speke so ernestlye and bytterlye that in maner everye man hering him did and might judge that he meaned of theim whiche went abowt to promote him for his reformacione and amendement of his misdemeanours aforesaid.

xix. ...that upon all and singuler the premisses there is common voyce and fame wythin the towne of Hull and other places there abowtes....Wherefore the premisses or so muche therof as is re-quisyte being proved the said promotour desireth justice...with his resonable costs...[etc.].

The personall aunswers of Melchior Smythe clerke....

i. To the first article he aunswerethe that he belevith that he this Respondent was presented to the vicaredge of Hessill and Hull abowte Mychaelmes whiche was in the yeare of our Lord God a thowsand fyve hundrethe three score and one And was admitted and instituted to the same vicaredge the iiii th daie of November then next following And ever sence for the moste parte haithe beyne continuallie resident at Hessill and Hull. And further [he] belevith that by the tyme articulate the said Edmound Robertes haithe had a chamber in Hull whereunto he commith and goithe And so haithe the tyme aforesaid at his pleasure as a stranger, but not as a townsman or parishoner there.

ii. To the second he belevith this not to be true in any parte
therof For he before the tyme articulate was and yeate is a preiste
or Minister sufficientlie ordered and auctorised by the right reverend
father in God Nicholas...Busshope of Lincoln according to the
Ecclesiastical lawes of this realme. [Marginal note: 'Proved by
the Respondent per exhibitionem literarum autenticarum Episcopi
Lincoln.']

iii. To the third [he] saiethe that sence this suete beganne he hathe
ministred the sacramentes and done or saide the hollye Communyon
him self within the parishe articulate And during the residew of the
tyme articulate he haithe dulie at all tymes ministred the sacraments
and sacramentalls by his sufficient and able curate and minister whome
he haithe hiered to do the inferior thinges as towching ministracion,
because [he] might have more tyme and leisure to applie the worde
of God and exercise the office of a preiste or minister in his owne
person as preacher (being the highest and most excellent function
of a preiste or minister) in his owne person the better and more
worthelie; whiche thing [he] belevithe is agreable to the worde of
God and the doinges of the Apostles who rather then to hynder the
worde the full course rase and perfyte knowledge therof did elect
and chose certeyne bothe learned and godlie to serve at the tables,
that is to minister the sacramentes, thapostles onelie applying thoffice
of preaching Wherefore [he] belevith that the most parte of the
parishoners do not grudge nor yeate marvell for that he haithe not so
often ministred the sacramentes and sacramentalls in his owne person
And further he belevith that not one of the parishoners haithe any
juste cawse at all to be offended therat But rather with there
hartes to allowe and wishe the same as a thing tending to there
gostlie profett and the discharging of the conscience of this
respondent.

iv. To the iiiith he belevith that during the tyme articulate he
haithe communycated x or xii tymes at the leaste And further [he]
belevethe that one tyme and no oftner he did receyve the blissed
communyon standing upon his fete upon this occasion [he] at the
communyon tyme did se the people holde uppe there handes, knocke
upon there breistes worshippe and commytt Idolitrie, and then he

stode uppe upon his fete, thinking to reprove there offences And evyn
so came the minister to [him] so standing (before he could speake)
with the Blessed Sacrament And not knowing what wold have
commed on yt or how it wold be taken emonges suche a rude
compenye if then he should have spoken he kept silence and receyved
the sacrament and so kneled downe againe Wherefore he belevithe
that the circumstance before rehersed dewlie considered yt was
no cause of offence so to receyve it standing for one tyme onelie,
especiallie because perfection dothe consist in the onelie worthie
receyving and in no ceremony or gesture.

v. ...[he] aunswerithe that oneles upon just occasion he be
letted [he] haithe by the tyme articulate and yeat dothe come in to
the Quere bothe to the mornyng and evenyng praier withowte
departing frome thence unto thending therof Sometymes loking
upon his booke, and sometymes reading the lessons, And further
this is his order Betwix the morning praier and the communyon he
usithe either to go home to loke on his booke and call thinges to
remembrance or elles to go in to some other secret place in the churche
commonlie in to a walking place at the upper ende of the quere
behind where the high alter stood, where no man dothe ether here
or se him oneles they purposlie comme unto him, there calling to
remembrance suche matter in Godes worde, as that daie he is abowte
to preache and open to the people And this he haith done and dothe
sometymes bareheaded and sometymes having his heide covered
And so remayneth to the Sermon tyme And then goeth to the place
of preaching, Whiche thing [he] belevithe that no good man haithe
beyne nor yeate is offended withall.

vi. ...he belevith this article not to be true in any parte thereof,
For [he] was maried with the said woman the xviii daie of Maye
1560 before magistrates bothe of the spiritualtie and temporaltie in
the congregacion of men women and children in Leycester Towne
in the parishe of Sanct Martyns by one Fra. Daynsworthe minister
there after the order sett furthe in the communyon booke. [Marginal
note: 'Nota he name the persons present and wheddir it were in
parishe churche or house.' A further note: 'Married in the ministers
house.']

vii. ...[he] belevithe that he haith kept a woman being his lawfull wif as is conteyned in the article and not otherwise.

viii. ...[he] belevith that he and his said wif at there furst commyng to Hull did not at all tymes agree so perfytelie as they aught to do, Nevertheles what so ever was betwene theme yt haithe beyne done so secretelie and quietlie that no honest or true person is able justlie to burthing either of theime with yt.

ix. ...he belevithe this article not to be true in any parte therof, for he wittinglie or willinglie haithe never beyne occasion of any offence in Hull, oneles it be for preaching against papistrie and heresye or for beating downe of wicked vices reyning in theis evill daies emonges theis synfull and adulterous generacion. Yf thorow suche preaching dissention comme emonges the people what is he to be blamed therefor No other thing haithe chaunced unto him then did unto the prophetts thapostles and disciples, yea unto Christ him self at whose preachinges there was as muche dissention as at any mans.

x. ...he belevith that as towching Boston [he] was so hated emonge the people there That he wold wishe suche hatred to followe him in everye place, for some of theime offred unto him to be taken of there landes during the lif natural of this respondent v li. yerelie, somme iii li. some iiii li. vis. viii d. Somme xls. And somme more and some lesse according to there abilities Yea they did offer him at Boston besides the premisses a paten of there Scole, there love was suche towardes him that willinglie they wold here none preache but [him] And that [he] had not commed from thence yeate had yt not beyne for the earnest and importunate suete of theme of Hull who sent for him once twise or thryse by one Mr. Parker then Chamberlaine of Hull. But as for Burton upon Trent he never dwelt there Saving that being borne within vii or viii myles of yt and having Freindes dwelling there [he] haith lyne there one tyme iii monethes to geither or there abowtes, abowte v yeres ago last past, during whiche iii monethes he haithe taught the children of his freindes Calvyns Cathechisme and David Psalmes in verses in the common Scoles whereat he belevith certayne papistes were offended but contention was there none.

xi. ....he belevithe that at his first commyng to Hull he did use to make a generall praier for the churche the Quene and all other estates, after, for brevitie onelie and to avoyde tediousnes he appoynted the hympne to be song called Come Holie Spiritt, at the begynnyng of everie sermon, Wherein the Quene hir Counsell the Nobilitie the States bothe of the spiritualtie and temporaltie were praied for, And therefore dothe he beleve this article not to be true in any parte thereof. He affirmeth also that two yeres last or there abowtes so far as he remembrith he hathe prayed for the Quene in the prescribed manner.

xii. ...he belevith that in his sermons frome tyme to tyme in Hull he haithe exhorted the people to obedience and feare, he haithe also in all his sermones praied for the Magistrates and officers declaring that they are allowed by Godes worde confirmed and established by the same, Nevertheles he belevithe as towching the kingdom of God Godes free grace and merecie he haithe saide, that there is no respect of persones, nether is it of valew before God, whether a man be a King prynce Duke, Earle, or Lorde, Jewe, or Gentill, learned or unlearned, wyse, or unwyse, magistrate or subjecte, man woman or child, Soo that he comme, when he is called of God and contynew to his power in his vocacion after the infallible and most rightuose rule of Godes worde. He haithe also invaide againste prowde bosters of there blode, and haithe compared theyme to the wilfull and wicked ignorant Jewes, whiche had also in there mouthes the Sede of Abraham the blode of there forfathers And so by example he haithe admonished theime, That as all men ar one fleshe and one blode, Soo ought all men to become one misticall bodie, in the whiche everie member is in order and office as God haithe appoynted yt, And yeate the bodie all of one substaunce, the order degree and office therefore appoynted and instituted by God is to be reverenced, No man therefore because of his blode but rather that he is accepted as good, for Christes sake is allowed before God. And otherwise he belevith this article not to be true.

xiii. ...he belevithe that he haithe worne the surplesse dyvers tymes, And so often that he cannot well nombre the tymes, no nor none other except they have noted the tymes in writing, And further he belevithe that he haithe preached That if any man had estimacion or supersticion in theime thinking the minister his office or Godes worde, or the Sacramentes, to be better therefor, or would not be withowte theme, In that respect he haithe said That it was to be wisshed that all men wold take theme, but for clowtes and ragges and rather worse then better, And this notwithstanding he haithe said also That to wyn the people he wold not onelie were theime but also a freares cote. Moreover he belevith that speaking in a sermon upon John Boughes degradacion, he haithe said That after they had invested him they putt a knaves cappe on his heade, whether it was a Busshoppes cappe or his Chapleynes capp For there was no difference betwix theime, not one of theime being honest....

xiiii. ...he belevithe That he haithe said in his sermons at Hull That if there were any sergeant that went abowte to abuse the Maior to hinder him to do justice, to putt lyes in to his head, to make him do any poore man woman or child any wrong, he haithe wished that sergeant to remember that he was nether of Counsell nor in the Commission with the Maior But rather in that respecte his servant and his slave to go and comme at his commandement.

xv. ...he belevith that as towching the old Bushoppes deprived, he haithe tolde to the shame and confucion of the papistes, how they were offered to be disputed with all in nomber daie and place appoynted in the presence of the Quenes Counsell, But when the tyme came they were rather given to brawling and rayling then to reasoning or disputing, Then said [he] that they shewed theime selfs as they did afore, all dombe dogges that could not barke, But as concerning our Bushoppes, he willed all men to be thankfull for we had never so many learned men at one tyme, nor never earnester or oftner preachers, nor perfiter followers, Moreover he willed all men to be thankfull For emongest the papistes there were not three in England that were able to rede the Byble in the Ebrew tonge, muche lesse to translate and expound it, But emonges the protestantes there were an hundrethe at the least, that could exactlie and absolutelie do all three That is rede, translate, and interprete, the Holie Scriptures owte of the Ebrew....

xvi. ...he belevith that he haithe preached that he was not a theif onelie that brake open mens houses, Robbed in the highe waies, did stand at a wodd syde, or hedge corner, But he also that satt in his chaire at home by the fier syde and studied to deceyve his neighbour with false waires false measures and false weightes, decetfull yron and flax etc. And who so ever walkethe not truelie and justlie in his vocacion according to Godes worde.

xvii. ...he belevith that the tyme articulate viz. upon All Sanctes daie at night last past there was certeyne disordered persons in the Trenytie churche or chapell of Hull, emonges whiche Nich. Labourne was one, Rynging the belles for all Christen soules This respondent then being with the Maior of Hull whiche Maior iii severall tymes did send unto theme, commanding theme to cease of there rynging And nevertheles the said disordered persones contynued still rynging and wold not cease, So that the Maior in his owne person accompaned with his officers, this respondent and dyvers other did go in to the churche or chapell, And at his and there commyng thither, the disordered persones began to rune awaie And then the Maior did command his officers, this respondent and all other accompeyned with him to lye handes upon theme and bring theme unto him, the churche or chapell at that tyme being verey dark because there was no light but one lynke that came in before the Maior, whiche lynke did cast but a small light in that churche or chapell being so greate as it is, And so this respondent with others runnyng abrode in the darke to apprehende the disordered persons, one runnyng against another, emonges whiche Nich. Labourne was hurte and bledd at the nose onelie, But whether he was hurte on the nose by this respondent or some other, he knowethe not certenlie, but he belevith it was not by [him] Nevertheles if it can be proved that Nich. Labourne was hurt by this respondent on the nose which he belevith cannot be proved, then he aunswerithe that nether he did it wittinglie nor willinglie but by chaunce in the darke.

xviii. ...he belevith that he haithe preached in his sermons how King Herode under a godlie pretence to comme and worshippe Christ wold have putt away and slaine Christ, And he saide in like maner that the wicked in this world wold make a faire shew outwardlie, when inwardlie they ment all devillishlie, And further he said in his sermons, if the wise men had retourned and brought Herode newes of Christ, they had suerlie lost there lyves, And so it fallethe owte in theis daies, That there ar in Countries, Cities, Towns and villedgs, bothe Herodes and Herodians, there partakers whiche wold if they could putt downe Christ and his gospell, the preachers and all the newes bringers thereof, to whome there dothe remayne Gods severe Judgement and Justice, as it did unto Herode, And that Gode wold punishe theime and theres to the third and fourthe generacion....

xix. ...he belevith that it is a common voyce and fame in Hull and thereabowtes of the premisses by him confessed.

Artycles additionales to the...[mutilated]...of Edmound Robertes against...Smith Vicar of Hull.

1. In primis ponit et articulatur that the said Melchior in tyme of his being Vicarr of Hull and in tyme of Mr. Aldered being Mayr of Hull and at the said Mayr table where the same Mr. Aldered being a man for his vocacione honestlye travaled in the scriptures did commend the woorkes of Saint Pawle to be excellent wherunto the said Vicarr extolling him self as the herers then supposed Awnswered verey arrogantlye and said that in comparisone of Pawl there were many Pawles in Englaund aswell lerned as ever Pawle was And had as great haboundaunce of the hoolye goost as ever Pawle had....

2. Item ponit that upon Sonday before fastene even[1] last in his sermond treating upon thoolye communyon [he] said that noone shoold be in the place where the communyon was ministred saving onelye thoos whiche did communicate And the residew eyther to be at the sermound or to be put furthe of the churche at tyme of communyon And so willed the same to be doone which doctryne is supposed not to be agreable with the quenes maiesties Iniunctions and publyke booke of common prayer....

3. ...that in his said sermound he declared that our Lord Christ ministred the hoolye communyon sytting, and the Germans standing or going And mislyked thoorder of receaving the same here knelinge

[1] Shrove Tuesday.

which doctrine also semethe to be against the said Iniunctions and booke of common prayer....

4. ...that [he] in tyme of his being vicar of Hull was desired and ernestlye required by the freindes of one Richerd Langton of Hull merchaundman and parishoner to the said vicarr [that] he woold coome to R.L. and visite him that he might have had his good counsell and exhortacione in certein matters towching his conscyence and the said vicarr neclecting his dewtye in that behalf refused and woold not coome nether yet did coome at him, Wherupon the said Langtone dyed withowt any suche counsell or exhortacione gyven by the vicarr which thing may be fered to be to the great danger of the sowle of Ric. Langton....

5. ...that the said vicarr sins the tyme of the articles of Informacione against him geven in this behalf hayth shewed him self verey stubburn and uncharytable to the moost woorshipfull of the towne of Hull whoome he suspected to have procured the said articles to be ministred against him, as Mr. Jobsone Mr. Thomas Dalton and others ones and dyvers tymes meting theim in the streete withowt any reverence not ones moving his capp or his hatt, nor speking any woord unto theim to the great offence of his parishoners seing suche uncharitable and stuburne demeanour in him who shoold be their pastor and Instructour....

6. ...that throughe his halte[1] and highe mynde and glorying in him self he hayth reported and said in his tyme of being vicarr there that Mr. Barnes admitted to preche by the lord Archbusshope of York his grace was not lerned saving that he has studyed the revelacions of Saint John and certein other common places of scriptur wherin he had soome knowledge And as for Mr. Lakin that he was but a clooker and a flatterer....

7. ...that he hayth spoyled taken down and letten down a great peece of the vicarr mansyon howse in Hull called the vicarage And haythe soold leed stoone and tymber therof to the valew of xxli. moore or lesser as shalbe proved.

[1] Probably for 'haughty'.

8. ...that upon all and singler the [premisses] there is common voyce name and fame w[ithin the] said town of Hull and other places there abowts.

9. Item ponit that the said Melchior Smyth being soore offended towardes Mr. Jobsone Mr. Dalton and others as towching certane articles exhibited against him to the lord Archbusshop of York his grace did say that their villanie and knaverye which caused the said articles to be exhibited shoold be known before all Counsailes in England or suche lyke woordes in effect not decent to be spoken by any charitable persone.

10. Item ponit that upon Sonday in the first weeke of Lent now instant the said Melchior did not onlye receave the blessed communyon muche unreverentlye as it was thought to many of his parishoners standing on his feet and not kneling, but also after he him self had receaved he caused his parishe clerk to breake the rest of the bread which then was to be ministred where yt is thought the minister him self ought to have broken the same.

11. Item ponit that the said Melchior Smyth at the tyme of his receaving of the said blessed communyon so unreverentlye as is aforesaid was not in perfyt charitye as he ought to have bene with the said Edmound Roberts and others his neighbours.

16 Martii Anno 1563.

The personall aunsweres of Melchior...clerke to the articles addiciona-...in by Edmound Robertes.

To the first article he aunswerithe that he belevithe he by the tyme articulate being once at the maiors table....Alrede then being Maior, a man in verey deide well...in scriptures there was talke towching the primityve churche and the churche in theis our daies where-...he belevithe that he said That the same w-...was preached the same spirit ruled and reyned and the same works were lyvelie expressed, (myracles onelie excepted) that were in the apostles daies And further he belevithe that he then said that there were some men in England in theis our daies which bothe could and also were willing to sett furthe good doctryne and orders as Paule haithe sett

222

furth and taught, for he belevith the verey same...that Paule sett furthe and taught, And otherwise he belevithe the article not to be true.

To the secound he belevithe that the Sondaie articulate he willed and exhorted all men to the often receyving of the holie Communyon And also affirmed that it was not ordeyned to be adored worshipped or gased upon, But onelie to be with a lyvelie faithe and thanks geving receyved And further that in many well ordered and reformed churches the byestanders and lookers on ar as unworthie and unthankfull people, reiected and putt owte of the dores, as men in some respects unmete to be present at the mynistracion of so hollie and devyne mysteries And otherwise....

To the iii th he belevithe that in his said sermon he said that Christ in dede did minister the Communyon sytting as they do presentlie in many other places, And whether it be receyved sytting standing or going, as they do in Germany or other places (so that good order be not broken) it is of no force, for the worthie receyving dothe not stand in any gesture or ceremonye as in his aunswer to one of his former articles he haithe declared And....

To the iiii th he belevithe that he was desired twyse onelie by ii severall men to go to Richard Langton whiche to do at either tyme he offered him self redye to go furthwith with either messinger, But eyther of the messingers then answered that Richard wold not have him to come presentlie But that he wold have one daie or other some good chere and then he wold send for this respondent, And then this respondent saide (yf he did send for him but for good chere) the matter was not so greate, And so the said Langton did never send for him so long as he lyved whiche he belevithe was abowte half a yeare after....

To the v th he belevithe that sence this suete b[egan] he haithe spoken and done other dueties to Mr. Job[son] and Mr. Dalton, but all was in vayne...to either of theime hys lowlynes and curtesye haith bene contemned, or at the leaste not accepted. Nevertheles, sence [he] perceyved there inward grudge, and there open and extreme mallyce shewed unto him. onelie for the Gospell and treuthe sake, he haithe staied his curtesie and reverence, Because that in respect of the Gospell he doughte[th] whether he maie either keipe compenye with theime or speike unto theime, unto they declare theime selfs to be new men. And otherwyse....

To the vith he belevith this article not to be true in any parte thereof.

To the viith he belevithe that there was on the...syde of the said vicaredg a porche and an...[entrie]...betwene the houses whiche at the commyng of this respondent to the said vicaredge, was lyke to fall and parte was fallen downe. And then this respondent after a vew first taken by the Maior and Aldermen of Hull, Emongs whome were Mr. Jobson and Mr. Tho. Dalton before namyd, by the advyse of the said Maior and Aldermen he this respondent did take downe the porche and entrie being so decaied, and solde certeyne leade of one onelie gutter, for the Somme of xiiis. iiiid. or there abowts and certeyne stones to the valor of xxvis. viiid. as he now remembrethe, For whiche pulling downe he this respondent to his greate charges and to his greate Indetting also yeate undischarged, haithe buylede and repaired twyse so muche as was pulled downe, as maie appere by the vewe thereof And....

To the viiith he belevith that there is a common voyce and fame in Hull and other places there abowts of so muche of the articles as he haithe confessed to be true, And otherwise....

To the ixth he belevithe That he haithe said that the articles promoted against him did conteyne nothing but Lyes grownded onelie upon mallice whiche maie be called vyllanye or knaverie, withowte naymyng either Mr. Jobsonne or Mr. Dalton, and withowte speakyng one worde of any counsell And otherwise....

To the xth he belevithe that he did delyver the sacramentall bread standing and going frome one to an other to all the Communycates as is commonlie used, whereat he belevithe no man was or could be offended And otherwyse....

To the xith he belevithe that he was in charitie at the tyme articulate with the said Edmound Robertes and all other his neighboures, And in this behalf referrith him self to the Judgement of God, to whome onelie belongithe to searche all mens harts, That his secret thought and harte is bothe searched and condemned by Edmound Robertes in so many places of the articles, yt is eysye to be knowne, frome whome they ar And what he is in thes his Informacions.

4. INFORMATION CONCERNING IMAGES, ETC., AYSGARTH

A.D. 1566/7 [Cause Papers, R. VII. G. 1297.]

This is the only surviving piece of its file, from a cause heard before two Ecclesiastical Commissioners. It is selected here because it has bearing upon several points noticed in these pages, particularly, the manner in which 'information' sent to the Commission was handled; the manner in which the work of the Commission supplemented the Visitations; the somewhat perfunctory way in which the first search for 'monuments of superstition' was sometimes carried out, especially in the remoter parishes; the manner in which the authorities persisted in repeated searches for 'monuments', guided perhaps by local gossip and often certainly by written information or petitions from someone well disposed to the existing order and government; the manner in which 'monuments' were treated when discovered.

Examinatio testium...coram Johanne Rokeby...Walt. Jones
et Will. Watson Aldermanno Ebor....xix die Martii 1566

The witnesses were examined on oath on Articles 'exhibited by Mr. Willm. Dunwiche necessary promoter [1] by the most reverend father in God Thomas by the grace of God Archbusshopp of York and other his associats the quenes majesties Commissioners in that behalfe assigned against Sir Ric. Bowes Curet of Askarth Edm. Jake Rog. Hawmond Chris. Hog Robt. Rogerson and Joh. Metcalfe of Askarth...'.

Adam Wraye of Thuresbie, yeoman, aged 63: '...To the first article examined he sayth that about the time articulate he was commaunded by the quenes majesties visitors to se all the bookes burnt which at that tyme did remayne in the church of Askarth And upon suche commaundement given to [him] by the Commissioners and for feare he shuld disobey there commaundement without tarieng or further delay at that tyme did go for a fier and made searche in every place of the churche for bookes And so many

[1] See footnote on p. 170.

bookes as [he] cold fynde at that present tyme did burne the same but what was the name of any of the books [he] cannot tell Et aliter nescit deponere saving that Sir Ric. Bowes and the churchwardens of Askarth was commaunded to take downe all such images as remayned in the churche and them to deface and breake.

Super tercio...dicit that he was present with Robt. Rogerson Chris. Hog and Rog. Baynes about two yeres sence when they did finde the images of Marie and John and certeyn little ymages in the Roode loft of the said churche but whether they were hide by any of the persons named in the first article or no he cannot tell.

Super quinto...he knoweth that some of the persons articulate were churchwardens of the parishe churche of Askarthe sence the yeres articulate but whither they received any Inventory of ther predecessors which were churchwardens before them any of the yeres articulate...he cannot tell.'

Robt. Thompson, schoolmaster of Wensley aged 31: '...super tercio...dicit that he teaching certeyn scholers in the churche articulate did se Mr. Robt. Heblethwaite in the churche; the said Mr. Heblethwaite loking in a chist did fynde one litle booke therein a pix a corporax with the case a cruet and laid them upon the Communion table and called this examinate, Chris. Hogg and others to him to se the same and desired this examinate and others then present to recorde the same And after that he had so riped[1] that chiste ymmediatly did go up into the Roode lofte and founde ther the ymages of Mary and John, this examinate Chris. Hog Robt. Rogerson and others then being presente at the fynding thereof But whether any of the premisses were hid by the persons articulate or no [he] cannot tell.'

Adam Kirkebye of Askarth, husbandman: '...super secundo... nescit deponere saving that he this examinate knoweth that two Images called Mary and John were hid in a lime kylne with in the churcheyard of Askarth and afterwards founde undefaced but by whose procurement they were so hid or if any of the persons named in this article did knowe of the same [he] cannot tell.'

[1] To rip, implying forcible and thorough search.

Super secundam posicionem addicionalem examinatus dicit eandem esse veram For [he] upon Sonday was a sevenight did se the same lyeing in the place articulate unburnt. Super terciam... dicit eandem esse veram For [he] did se the said Roger Kirkeby... being naturall sonne to this examinate cut thone of the armes of the imag called John And he did also se upon Sonday was a sevenight the imag of Mary remayning in a litle garthe of John Deanes and used as a chopping or hacking stock as is articulate.

Mr. Robt. Hebblethwayte, Mr. of Artes: '...Upon the third article examyned he saith that by vertue of a lettre sent unto my Lord of Chester frome the high Commissioners at London for ecclesiasticall causes for inquerye to be made of ymages and other supersticious monumentes throughout the hole dioces of Chester The said Busshopp did write to this examinat being his Commissary of Richmondshire parcell of his dioces to make inquery in that behalfe accordingly whiche he did and comyng to the churche of Askarthe upon thassencion eve next comyng shalbe thre or foure yeres And then and there did fynde in a chist within the queare of the churche one pix with the canapie which was wont to be hung over the same A crismatory and a litle box for oyle A corporax with a case for the same A super altare with certeyn other latten books whereof one was an ymnale but all the rest did not apperteyne to the old service And in a valte or a holow place in the rode lofte did fynde two great ymages holie undefaced of Mary and John And more of the premisses he did not fynde at his being there....'

5. Information and Answers, Parish Clerk, Holy Trinity, Kingston-upon-Hull

1 Dec. 1570 [Cause Papers, R. VII. G. 1487.]
Articles declar[atories of] the mysordered usages and wirkes of Willm. Steade, parishe clerke at the Trinitie Churche in Hull.

1. Firste he is a common and dalie drunckerd and was for that offence presented by the churche wardens and sworne men to tharchedeacon his official at his last visitacion and then and there enioyned and commaunded certayn punishments which as yet [he]

hathe not done neither dothe amende ne reforme his said faute but therin contynewethe to the greate offence of the godlie congregacion.

2. Item where as he was sworne before Mr. Parkinson late Archdeacon not onelie to execute his office in the churche trulie and faithfullie, but also to be obediente and diligente to the curate at all tymes and seasons, as to his office apperteynethe, yet not regardinge his said othe, not the daunger in breakinge the same, he neither dothe his office but for the moste parte is absente from the common praier, especiallie in hay time and harveste and that without licence of the preacher or curate, for he in that tyme plaithe the carter; and as for the preacher and curate, he regardethe them nothinge at all.

3. Item at sundry times thrughe his defaute at the communion there lackethe wyne And so aswell the mynister as the communicants are forced to staye till yt be fetched at the taverne, wherbie there arysethe great offence emonge the congregacion, and as for him self he will be no participante thereof, save onelie at Easter as all papists do for custom saike.

4. Item for the moste parte he absentethe him selfe from sermons and homilies, and if he somtyme tarye, he bestowethe the tyme in slepinge; and he will not come to the mynistracion of baptysme, neither at burialles but settethe a boy in his rowme, and at this the people be not a lytle offended.

5. Item he came not neither was present at the readinge of the firste or seconde lesson either at morninge or eveninge praier by the space of vii yeares last paste at the leaste, and upon the workdaies he usethe customablie to go from the Lessons as thoughe he despisethe the hearinge of them, or thinkethe them but fables.

6. Item when there is any Sermon (as commonlie and for the moste parte there is) every Sunday and holy day, he so consumethe the tyme with organes plainge and singinge, and furder in settinge forwarde the clocke, that ther can be no conveniente tyme for the worde to be preached, and where as the preacher and mynister have rebuked him for the same, he dothe not amende, but rather is worse and worse.

228

7. Moreover (as the godlie sorte do thinke) by his wicked behaviour and noughtie lif and his evill example, he is an utter enemye to the Gospell, a hinderer of Goddes worde to be taughte, a slaunderer and contemner of preachers and mynisters, as of late apperethe that the mynister or curate of the churche was forced thrugh his threatninge and manassinge of him, to crave thassistance of the mayor and other Justices and to taike the peace of him; for he is afraid to mynister with the wyne that he providethe, and so he hathe affirmed, and still dothe affirme.

8. This Stead (all thies notwithstandinge knowne to be trewe and unfayned) is of the papists not onelie well lyked but also maynteyned, but who they be, that is not certanelie known, but judged to be not of the sympleste in worldly estimacion.

9. Last of all, at burialles he makethe suche busynes with ringinge that the minister cannot be heard of the people, and upon All Saints day at night he suffred ringinge of a bell a longe tyme, and beinge in his house wold not rebuke the doers thereof. Yt is thought therefor that he did it of purpose rather, for all his delite is in ringinge singinge and organs plainge; for at every morninge and eveninge praer upon the holydaie he plaiethe foure severall tymes, and every tyme a longe space.

10. This forsaid clerke his lyvinge is worthe yearlie xx li. at the leaste, and as some say xl markes. Yt wolde helpe well to the maintenance of a good preacher of Gods word, whiche were very necessarie, and is muche to be whished etc.

per Symonem Pynder dei ministrum

[In Dean Hutton's hand] Lett him be cited to appeare 8 December.

2. The Answer of Willm. Steade to certane articles of Informacion exhibit againste [him] to the...Archbyshope of Yorke...and others the quens majesties Commissioners for causes ecclesiasticall within the dioces and province of Yorke or thre of them etc.

To the fyrste article of the Informacion answeringe that one of the churche wardens and one of the sworne men of Hull onlye of meare malyce and without the consente of the other churchewardons and sworne men of Hull dyd presente this respondente to be a dronkerde, and was enioyned to pay to the pore mens box iiis. iiiid. for the same offence which iiis. iiiid. he hathe bene and yet is redye to pay, when so ever it shall [be] demandyd of him, and otherwyse he belevethe this article not to be trewe And further he saythe that he neyther hathe bene nor yet is a common and dalye dronkerd neyther is ther any common reporte and fame that he is so, but is comon reputed and taken to be a quiet and sober man emongs his neyghbors at Hull.

2. To the second he sayth that he was sworne before Mr. Parkynson laite Archdeacon to do and exequute his offyce trewlye in the churche eyther by him selfe or a lawfull deputye and otherwyse he sayhte this article is not trewe, for he dothe say that he dothe and exequutethe his office diligentlye and trewly eyther by himselfe or his deputye and is never absente without speciall lycence of Mr. Maior of Hull.

3. To the thyrde he saith that upon a Sonday or holy day aboute ii yers synce Mr. Pynder curet at Hul dyd celebrate the holye communion in Trinitie churche at Hull at which tyme he receyved a numbre of persons to receyve and participate at the said communion, who had gyven no warnynge before as they oughte to have done, by reason wherof ther lacked wyne, but he saithe the faut was not in him but in the curet in so receyvinge suche a numbre not havinge gyven lawfull warnynge before, and as for him selfe he saythe that commonlye he receyvethe thre tymes in the yere but in dede he did not receyve this yere sence Easter but is redye to receyve at any tyme convenient herafter before Easter nexte.

[The 4th Article, and the 5th, he declared 'is not trewe'.]

6. To the vith he saythe that he never playthe of the organes in service tyme nor settethe forwarde the clocke, but the preacher hathe always twoe howers at the leaste to mayke his sermond in.

7. To the viith he saythe the same is not trewe, for emongeste his honeste neighburs he is reputyd and taken to be a favorer of Gods worde and not a hynderer nor a contemner of the same.

8. To the viiith he saythe he knoweth no papysts in the towne of Hull for yf he dyd he wolde presente them and therfore he saithe this article is not trewe.

9. To the ixth he saithe that accordinge to lawfull order prescribed in the metropoliticall articles or Injunctions he dothe rynge but one shourte peall before the buryall of any deade corpes and one shorte peall after the buryall, and dothe nether ringe nor knolle any bell in the tyme of buryall and commonlie of sondaies and holydays he dothe play fower tymes at the mornynge praer and fower tymes at the evenynge praer of the organs which playing dothe not contynewe longe, neyther is hurtfull or hinderance to dyvine servyce. And otherwyse he sathe this article is not trewe, sayvinge that ther was a bell ronge of all Hallowe day at nyght at vii of the clocke for Curfuw as the custume is ther usid and hathe bene a longe tyme, which bell was runge by one John Barber of Hull this examinat lyenge seke at his owne howse.

10. To the xth he saithe his clerkshipe is worthe xvili. yerlye and no more, furthe of which [he] dothe pay vili. yerlye to one that ryngethe a bell at v of the clocke in the mornynge and vii of the clocke at nyghte of holydays and at viii of the clocke at nyghte on workedays.

Note. The further history of this cause is at present unknown. There is no record at all in the entries of proceedings before the Ecclesiastical Commissioners as found in their Act Books. From the fact that Willm. Stead made answers to the Articles, it is to be presumed that the cause was heard at least in part *somewhere*; perhaps before the Archbishop's Court of Audience, since business was not seldom transferred between the Commission and the Archbishop's Courts, but the record has not been traced.

INDEX

Abrogate days, 14, 161, 162
Absence from Church, 5, 8, 38, 39, 40,
 43, 47, 74, 75, 76–8, 80, 82, 140, 169,
 172, 184, 186, 228
 fines for, 34, 65, 75–7, 184
Acaster, 85
Accidence, the English, 107
Accounts, Churchwardens', 9, 53, 183,
 185
Acklam (Acclam), 50
Acts of Parliament, 12, 61
Adel, 196
'Admonicion to the Parliament, an', 14
'Advertisements, the', 13
Adwick-le-Street, 181
Agnes Burton, see Burton Agnes
Ainderby Steeple, 25
Aislaby, 50
Alabaster tables of images, 27, 147
Aldborough (Awdbrough), 54, 94, 168
Aldbrough in Holderness, 182
Alderley (Alderleigh), 38, 186
Aldermen, see York
Alehouse, 5, 13, 23, 37, 55, 56, 65, 82, 92,
 159, 168, 169, 203, 204, 207
 in Vicarage, 3, 195, 196
Alewives, 8, 48
All Souls' Eve, ringing for dead on, 14,
 65, 73, 160, 174, 175, 219, 229, 231
Allerton, North, 123
Almon(d)bury, 60, 106, 181
Alne, 68, 110, 143
Altar, 26, 29, 30, 60, 62, 64, 178; and see
 Table
Altars, removal of, 4, 26, 62, 147, 164,
 184, 187
Altham (Altome), 157
Antiphoner, 27, 184
Apesthorpe, 44, 153
Apparel, lay, of clergy, 13, 28, 153, 154,
 168, 209
Appleton-le-Street, 113
Archbishop of York as Rector of Parish,
 53, 66, 182
Archdeacon, 15, 98, 126, 139, 227, 228, 230
 of Cleveland, Mr Colton, 110
 of Durham, 155
 Remyngton, 56, 58

Archdeaconries:
 Cleveland, 110, 111
 East Riding, 51–9 (227, 228, 230)
 Nottingham, xiii, 35, 128
 York, 61, 197
'Archer's Book', 149 and n. 4
Arksey, 24, 197
Armthorpe, 185
Arnall, 22, 199
Arnecliffe, 112
Arrest in Church, 93, 94
Articles of Faith, 3, 13, 62, 126, 129, 130,
 131, 133
 Visitation, xv, 2–15
Asburye, 39
Ashton-under-Lyne, 133, 158
Askham, 45
Askrig, 36, 152, 190
Assessments:
 for making bell, 53 (3)
 for buying Bible, 49
 for buying bread and wine, 49
 for Chapel, 49
 for Clerk's wages, 9, 46, 192
 for poor, 9, 53
 for repair of Church, 43–5, 47, 51, 53,
 54, 56, 58, 186, 188, 189, 193
Assher (Derby), 18
Aston, 23
Attendance at Church, 74–8, 95
Atwick (Attenwick), 51, 182
Auburn Chapel, 120
Audibility of services, 2, 6, 125–7
Audience, Court of, 15, 16, 167, 170,
 231 n.
Austerfield, 44
Aysgarth, 36, 144–6, 225–7
Ayton, 49, 143

Bagby, 108
Ballads, seditious, 15
'Ballet', 206
'Banner', 9, 13
Banner cloths, 31, 112, 176
Banner staves, 31
Banns of matrimony, 3, 5, 7, 8, 38, 71,
 72, 184
 Catechism prerequisite for, 130

232

INDEX

Needle, St Wilfrid's, 164
Nelson, 186
Ness Chapel, 114
Neston, 81
Nether Peover, 132
Newark, 107
New Malton, 113, 121, 125 n., 135
Newton, 110, 132, 138
Non-communicating, 5, 8, 13, 31, 38, 39, 41, 42, 46, 47, 57, 58, 59, 79–81, 111, 112, 166, 228
by clergy, 22, 26, 27, 210, 214
Non-residence, 17–20, 22, 23, 39, 43, 56, 58, 204, 207
Normanton, 88
North Cave, 116
North Clifton, 20
North Ferriby, 51
North Frodingham, 58, 182
North Leverton, 44
North Otterington, 124
North Wheatley, 18, 43
Northallerton, 143, 198; and see Allerton
Northerdon (Northenden), 38
Northumberland, Earl of, 166, 167
Norton, 105
Norton-Cuckney, 43
Norwell, 193
Nottingham, 174
St Nicholas' Church in, 199
Nunkeeling, 57, 117, 182
Nunnington, 113

'Office of the Judge', 16 and n.
Old Malton, 63, 70, 102
Priory, 125
Ollerton, 43, 123
Oram, see Ulrome
Orders, Letters of, 40, 210
Ordinary, 3, 7, 8, 11, 129, 134
Organ playing, 228–30
Ormesby, 49
Osmotherley, 123
Oswaldkirk (Oswouldchurche), 114, 140
Otley, 92
Ottringham, 51, 82, 117, 182
Over, Cheshire, 40
Overlooking offences, 10
Overseers of poor, 146
Overton, 110
Owthorne, 30, 52, 182

Oxford, 106, 108
St Mary's Hall at, 106
Oxton, 130

Paintings in Rood-loft, 31, 32–4
Pannal, 87
Papists, 2 (n. 2), 31, 37, 216, 229, 231
Paraphrases of Erasmus, 11, 29, 31, 33, 34, 64, 113, 184
Parish Clerk, 51, 52, 54, 189–94, 227–31
administration of Holy Communion by, 222
illiteracy of, 193
payment of, 9, 41, 46, 51, 59, 192, 193, 229
residence by, 191
Parson, 6, 7, 180–2
Parsonage houses, 197; and see Decay
Pateley Bridge, 103, 150
Patrington, 57, 118, 196
Paull (Pawle), 59, 182
Pax, 4, 15, 184, 185
Penance, 10, 67, 145, 159, 164, 190, 198
commuting of, 159, 202; and see Declaration
'Peniston', 95
Pennington, 133
Penrith (Pereth), 135
Perambulations, 37, 55, 63, 64, 155, 194
Peter Prison, see York
Pew, 65 n., 87–91, 95
right to hold, 87
social standing marked by, 87, 88
Pictures in churches, 30–4
'Piggins', 149 and n. 2
Piper, 39, 85, 94, 123, 169, 178
Pix, 4, 15, 29 n., 65, 67, 184, 226, 227
Plurality, benefices in, 3, 18–30, 39, 52, 56, 62, 116, 134, 168, 203
Poor, collection for, 29–32, 34, 184
distribution of 40th part to, 18, 20, 23, 24, 43, 48, 54, 58
exhortation for, 26, 134
Poor men's box, 4, 29 (4), 30–4, 64, 183, 193, 230
Portas (practas, portiforium), 13
Posy for ring, 205, 207
Poverty of benefice, 138, 139, 197
Poynton, 38
Prayer for the Queen, 141, 217
for magistrates, 217

240

INDEX

Surplice, 4, 6, 8, 13, 37, 38, 42, 46, 55, 59,
  65, 69, 153, 155–9, 183, 188, 193,
  194, 212, 217
Suspension of clergy, 30
Sutton-in-Cleveland, 111
Sutton-in-Holderness, 51, 182
Sutton-on-Derwent, 115
Sutton-on-Trent, 95
Swearer, 4, 7, 9, 44, 184, 191
Swettenham, 39
Swine, 34, 54, 117, 176, 182, 191
  St Martin's Chapel in, 117

Tabernacle, 29–31
Table (Communion), 4, 7, 63, 64, 126,
  183, 187, 202, 205, 226
  gilded and painted, 33
  cover for, 4, 7, 29, 64, 183, 202
Table of Ornaments, 113
Table of Ten Commandments, 7, 183
Tabler, 4, 7
Tables, 4, 5, 8, 13
Talking in Church, 65, 140, 184,
  211
Tanfield, 95
  West, 163 n.
Tattersall, 22
Taxall, 38
Teaching children, 190, 194, 216
Teaching neglected, 20 24, 30
Terrington (Tyrrington), 90, 91, 110
Thirkleby, 143
Thirnscogh (Thurnscoe), 25, 187
Thirsk, 77, 109, 146
Thormanby, 143
Thorner, 88
Thorngumbald, 56
Thornton (Dale), 121
Thornton-in-Lonsdale, 116
Thornton-le-Street, 143
Thorp-Arch, 138
Threatening against sinners, 62, 131
Thwing (Twhinge), 120, 185
Tickhill, 25, 165, 166, 197
Tilston, 73
Tindall's New Testament, 150
Tippling in service time, 91
Tithe, 180
Topcliffe, 65, 95, 143, 179
Treeton, 26
Tunstall-in-Holderness, 57
'Tuts', 95
Tuxford, 42

Ugglebarnby, 49, 124
Ulrome, 58, 117
Unknown tongue, prayer in, 185
Upleatham, 50
Usurers, 13, 184, 200, 201

Vagabonds (Popish priests), 6, 80, 185,
  198
Vestments, 4, 15, 31, 33, 123, 142, 147,
  148, 152, 177, 209
Vicar (Choral), of Ripon, 26
  of Southwell, 45, 46
  of York, 175
Vicarage, alehouse in, 3, 195, 196
  decay of, 7, 20, 22, 25, 34, 41, 221, 224
  too large, 25, 197

Wadworth, 60
Wafers for Holy Communion, 29, 66,
  79; *and see* Breads *and* Singing
  breads
Waghen, Waughen (Wawne), 33, 34, 54
Wakefield, 82, 83, 105, 173, 185, 186
Waldenewton, *see* Wold-Newton
Walesby, 43
Walking and talking in service time, 5,
  8, 82–4, 95, 184
Walkington, 118, 201
Walkringham, 41
Walsham, 25
Walton, 73, 138
Warberton, 133, 177
Warmingham, 40
Warning, of catechising, 129, 131, 133
  of Holy Communion, 129
Warrington, 94
Warsop, 18, 191
Warter (Wartre, Wauter), 119, 195
Warwick, 163 n.
Wath, 138, 188
Watton, 119
Waxam, 52
Weighton (Wyeton), 59
Welbury, 48
Welley, 18, 41
Welwick, 30, 58, 118
Wensley, 98
Wentworth, 188
West Drayton, 42
West Kirkby, 73
West Markham, 18, 41
West Retford, 42
Westerdale, 49, 124